In Search of
ANCIENT OREGON

In Search of
ANCIENT OREGON

A Geological
and
Natural History

ELLEN

MORRIS

BISHOP

TIMBER PRESS
Portland · Cambridge

All photographs are by the author.
Map and time line by Allan Cartography, Medford, Oregon.

Page 1, Painted Hills in the John Day Fossil Beds National
Monument; pages 2–3, glacial erratic, once part of Mount
Hood's eastern rampart, eroded and transported by
Pleistocene glaciers, now resting atop the extensive
moraines of Eliot Glacier; page 5, Anthony Lake and the
Elkhorn Mountains.

Published in 2003 by

Timber Press, Inc.   Timber Press
The Haseltine Building   2 Station Road
133 S.W. Second Ave., Suite 450   Swavesey
Portland, Oregon 97204, U.S.A.   Cambridge CB4 5QJ, U.K.

Designed by Susan Applegate.
Typeset in Carter and Cone Galliard, Frutiger, and Poetica Chancery.
Printed through Colorcraft Ltd., Hong Kong.

Library of Congress Cataloging-in-Publication Data

In search of ancient Oregon: a geological and natural history/Ellen
Morris Bishop.
    p. cm.
  Includes bibliographical references and index.
  ISBN 0-88192-590-X
  1. Geology—Oregon. 2. Geomorphology—Oregon.
  I. Bishop, Ellen Morris.

QE155.I5 2003
557.95—dc21   2003043449

To my mother,
Laura Ellen Hill,
an artist
to whom the world
was a place of wonder
and stones
the path to God.

Contents

Cambrian	Ordovician	Silurian	Devonian	Mississippian	Pennsylvanian	Permia

Paleozoic

505   438   408   360   323   286

Triassic		Jurassic	Cretaceous	Paleocene	Eocene	Oligocene	Miocene		Holocene / Pleistocene / Pliocene	Present

Mesozoic

Tertiary
Cenozoic
Quat.

248   208   144   Millions of Years   65   56   34   24   5 1.8

Prologue

Geologists inhabit a world of four dimensions. Like most people, we navigate the landscape's ups and downs and byways. But in addition, our journeys take us into the fourth dimension: time. Every rock has a history. The geologist's mission is to translate the mute stuff of stolid stones into a planetary biography. We are, in a sense, time travelers, deciphering past processes into a palpable vision of what the world once was. As pioneering Oregon geologist Thomas Condon noted, "In prying apart the stone layers of the rocks, the scientist is, in reality, opening the leaves of the past history of our world."

A little knowledge of Oregon's geology can bring long-vanished landscapes to life. Stand on a basalt in the Columbia River Gorge and imagine yourself as a witness to this place 15.5 million years ago, when seething lava oozed down a broad, oak-splashed, grass-covered Columbia River Valley. Shoot hoops at Portland's Mount Tabor Park and visualize yourself a million years ago on a volcano spouting red-hot cinders into the air. Climb to the top of Sacajawea Peak, highest summit in the Wallowa Mountains, and envision it 220 million years ago as a tropical coral reef awash in a sea where ichthyosaurs swim and parchment-winged pterosaurs glide overhead. Hike to Vulcan Lake in the Klamath Mountains' Kalmiopsis Wilderness and touch the Earth's

View into the canyon of the Imnaha River from Buckhorn Lookout, where Columbia River basalt flows constitute most of the landscape.

mantle. Any rock in Oregon (or anywhere else) will do, for each has experienced more than we can ever know.

Every rock, even the most humble, tells a long story. Hold an ordinary pebble of granodiorite in your hand and you can feel the weight of 140 million years, the pulse of a magma 10 miles below the surface, melted from ancient volcanic rocks of islands that were crushed beneath the continent's moving edge. Imagine the mass of an 8-mile-diameter, teardrop-shaped body of molten rock rising, shouldering aside the overlying crust, anointing surrounding rocks with steamy, acid fluids, leaving milky white quartz, adorned with flecks and veins of gold and silver in its wake. And think of this cold, bone white stone, the skeletal core of Cretaceous coastal mountains, a forgotten range uplifted 100 million years ago, with peaks so high they kept even tyrannosaurs at bay in Montana. Consider the vastness of time, 85 million years, that wore these mountains into a plain, and of these cool white rocks confined in consummate darkness far beneath the surface, suddenly split by the forceful and fast-rising, dark, and fluid basalt, torrid lavas that knifed through the subterranean whiteness, to erupt in 10-mile-long, 20-mile-long iridescent fountains, flooding the grassy landscape with basalt some 16 million years ago. And imagine, think of the power of faults that again lifted this massive body of hard white rock into towering plateaus and brooding mountains, and then remember the glacial ice scouring upland landscapes into chiseled peaks, a small matter of 25,000 years ago, excavating this rock, this very small and rounded stone that you picked from the edge of the Wallowa River and now hold in your hand.

Cast it back into the stream where time, abrasion, and chemistry will peel away its shape and mineral structure, transforming it into sand, and then to clay. And in another 100,000 years, in 1 million years, in 5 million years, or 500 million years, some of this same stone may tumble down this river or another, arriving at the sea, carried into the deep and most concealed ocean trenches, riding the plate down, down, miles beneath a continent, melting in the growing heat and pressure, resurrected into granite again, pressed into mountains, eroded and cast again into a stream 100 million years hence. Whose hand will hold it then?

There are a million such stories and a million other questions in Oregon's stones. To tell those stories, to ask the questions, is to bring the past to life, to know what preceded us, to understand the Earth and to consider its destiny as well as ours. This is what geology is truly all about.

The Aboriginal people of Australia call their landscape into being through songs and dreams, bringing every creature, every plant, every stone into being. By imagining a parallel universe where past, present, and future merge into one, Aborigines participate each day in creating the world, invoking its past and ensuring its ongoing creation. "Every landmark is wedded to a memory of its origins, and yet is always being born," says anthropologist Wade Davis, a scientist and author who has lived and traveled with Aboriginal tribes. "The land is encoded with everything that has ever been, everything that will ever be . . . . To walk the land is to engage in a constant act of affirmation, and endless dance of creation."

In a less spiritual and more science-savvy way, geologists, too, call ancient landscapes and ecosystems into being. Our visions spring from data: chemical composition that reveals a rock's source and parentage like geologic DNA; isotopes that provide an age; clays from ancient soils that in their structure and constitution bear the stamp of temperature and rainfall, of grassland savanna or tropical rain forest; impressions of leaves, and wood, and fragmented fossil bones, that bespeak the diversity and function of ancient ecosystems. In a way, geologists are doing no less than the Aborigines. We call the ancient world into existence when we gather a stone.

Sometimes our visions change. New data and new techniques will inevitably refine, sometimes radically change, our understanding of how the ancient world worked. In the nineteenth century, to suppose that continents moved was unthinkable. Today, it is unthinkable that continents might remain stationary. The difference lies partly in technology, which allows science to gather and interpret increasingly precise data, and tackle problems that were unanswerable before. It also lies partly in creative thought and, hence, in the development of new hypotheses by individual scientists. Combine both, and a question answered by new technology may ricochet into a new comprehension of the ancient world. Apply better trace-element analysis to determine the composition of the fine sediments deposited at the Cretaceous–Tertiary boundary, the geologic moment when dinosaurs disappeared, and discover that it is laden with iridium. Consider where that iridium may have come from and hypothesize collision with an enormous meteor, leading to new questions, and discoveries.

Rocks are more than touchstones of the history of the Earth and its past life. They are proof that climates change, ecosystems unravel, volcanoes erupt with dev-astating consequences, and that once a species becomes extinct, it never returns. There are no more dinosaurs. The woolly mammoth is gone; so is *Merychippus,* a horse ancestor.

With *In Search of Ancient Oregon* I try, in some small measure, to envision the past and consider the implications for the future. For, with or without an Aboriginal song, we are traveling through time just as surely as we travel to the store, scramble to the summit of Sacajawea Peak, or amble down the trail to the bottom of Hells Canyon. And what better companions to guide us than the spirits of ancient stones.

CHAPTER I

In the Beginning

Once upon a time, when dinosaurs roamed Montana and pterosaurs ruled the skies, there was no Oregon. In those days, more than 100 million years ago, Pacific waves broke on Idaho shores. McCall, 50 miles east of the border with Oregon, would have been a seaport, and Boise a coastal town. The Pacific Northwest was yet to be born. The oldest rocks of Oregon lay far off-shore, gathering as coral-fringed islands in a shallow tropical sea.

Oregon's most ancient rocks are almost 400 million years old. They developed in a Devonian world where armored fish patrolled the waters and amphibians pioneered the land. If we had flown past the Devonian Earth in a spacecraft we might not have recognized our blue planet as home. The Earth's continents clustered in the Southern Hemisphere. North America embraced Europe. Gondwana—the southern continent that included Antarctica, India, South America, and Africa—straddled the South Pole. There was no Atlantic Ocean, and the ancestral Pacific, an ocean known as Panthalassa, stretched two-thirds of the way around the globe.

Oregon's most ancient bedrock occupies the Blue Mountains and the Klamath Mountains. It once was ocean bottom, shallow-water coral reefs, and a variety of volcanic islands far from North America's abbrevi-

Rocks as old as the Devonian are found in the Greenhorn Mountains between Baker City and John Day. They are part of the Baker terrane, an exhumed subduction zone of the Paleozoic and Triassic Blue Mountain island arc.

ated coastline. There was no Oregon until plate tectonics cleaved North America from Europe and northern Africa, and moved the continent westward to collide with these reefs and islands, and the disheveled seafloor that held them.

The fragmented islands, coral reefs, and volcanoes now sequestered in Oregon's remote mountains once resembled the modern cluttered seas of Indonesia. They were added to the main landmass from 150 million to 90 million years ago by collisions with an opportunistic continent that gathered orphaned landscapes from an island-dimpled sea and claimed them for its own. North America's western coast, Oregon included, is a collage of exotic geology swept onto the prow of a westward-moving continent like pond scum on the bow of a giant canoe.

It has taken us a long time to understand Oregon's beginnings. Until the dawn of plate tectonics and the revelation that seafloors move and continents collide, geologists who mapped the Blue Mountains and Klamaths labored mightily to conjure order out of seeming chaos. They employed masterful strategies to explain the puzzling patchwork of Oregon's oldest landscapes: why, in the hills north of Burns, shallow-water Devonian limestones lay placidly adjacent to Permian deepwater cherts, or how, in the Klamaths, mangled gabbros intruded into orderly beds of shale. They invented vast and complicated folds to justify a disheveled stratigraphy. Before plate tectonics, there was no mechanism to account for the rumpled, random order of things.

Oregon geologists have mapped the Blue Mountains and Klamaths with painstaking accuracy. Today, some of their pre-1970 explanations for how rocks were folded and faulted into place seem oddly contrived, but they were the only logical explanations then. One memorable example of someone who valiantly tried to comprehend plate tectonic-induced chaos using conventional folds and faults was a capable petroleum geologist named Harold Buddenhagen. In the early 1960s, a decade before plate tectonics would become fashionable, Buddenhagen mapped the contorted geology along Grindstone Creek and in the vicinity of Suplee, open landscape in the navel of the Blue Moun-

tains. His detailed work shows each stone in its proper place, each slanting outcrop dipping into the Earth at precisely the proper angle.

But in Buddenhagen's world, sediments accumulated in tidy, stratigraphic layers and were deformed in a systematic manner at a later time. He could not envision subduction zones mashing neatly stacked sediments into wads of tight folds, or imagine chunks of Devonian limestone slapped carelessly next to Pennsylvanian sandstones 100 million years younger, and the whole jumbled mess slipping into a trench only to be metamorphosed and regurgitated 200 million years later. He interpreted the welter of rock ages and orientations as best he could. His map depicts the locations of each rock with excruciating accuracy. But Buddenhagen's interpretations of contorted plunging folds and concealed faults that moved layers of rock for tens of miles were imaginative leaps of faith in pre–plate tectonics geology. Within a decade, explanations that had made complete sense in a world without plate tectonics, subduction, and accretion would seem as absurd as modern explanations of colliding islands and landmasses would have seemed in the early 1960s.

Despite its accuracy and the encouragement of his peers, Buddenhagen never published his exquisitely detailed and accurate map of the area around Grindstone Creek. Instead, he simply filed a copy with the Oregon Department of Geology and Mineral Industries, where it sits today in the agency's library. In 1966, when he completed his work, the light of plate tectonics was dawning. Buddenhagen knew that conventional mechanisms were insufficient to explain the jumbled formations he had mapped so well. But 1960s' science was illiterate in the language of this new order. Words and map symbols for subduction zone, mélange, and exotic terrane did not exist in geologic lexicons.

Harold Buddenhagen's suspicion was correct. Today, we know this landscape as the Grindstone terrane, a geologic collage assembled by submarine landslides that occurred more than 200 million years ago on the brink of a subduction zone. The Grindstone's more modern biography was unraveled in the 1980s by two paleontologists and a stratigrapher—Merland Nestel, Charles

Blome, and Emile Pessagno—all conversant in the new dialect of moving plates and the chaos of subduction zones.

The notion of plate tectonics, that continents shift—separating, rotating, and reconnecting like participants in a slow-motion square dance—has intrigued people for centuries. In 1838, the Scottish philosopher Thomas Dick first proposed that the continents had moved. Dick noticed how neatly Africa and South America seemed to fit together and in a book titled *Celestial Scenery, or, the Wonders of the Planetary System Displayed,* he wrote that is was "not altogether improbable that these continents were originally conjoined, and that, at some former physical revolution or catastrophe, they may have been rent asunder by some tremendous power . . . ." Unfortunately, Dick lacked proof beyond what seems obvious from continental outlines on any world map. And proof, or an understanding of how things work, is essential to science. Without understanding the mechanism, the how of things, science (like the rest of us) simply does not change.

In 1915, a German meteorologist, Alfred Wegener, again proposed that the continents had moved. His evidence was more compelling. He cited the similarity of rock formations in Africa and South America, and Europe and North America, as stronger justification than mere geographic outline. But Wegener lacked a mechanism, and like Thomas Dick's suggestion, his ideas languished as well. Not until technology allowed us to map the seafloor, read the subtle magnetic fields of ocean bottoms, and measure deep earthquakes along continental margins did the mechanism become obvious. The seafloor spreads apart at the mid-oceanic ridge, pushing continents before it or diving back into the mantle in subduction zones, abandoning scraps of seafloor and errant islands at the continental edge like mud scraped off shoes on a front-porch doormat.

In the early 1900s, a remarkable Oregon geologist named Thomas Condon, a contemporary of Wegener, may have recognized intuitively that the oldest rocks of Oregon are immigrants, rocks that originated somewhere else, non-native scraps of crust that had become naturalized citizens by virtue of long residence. In his

landmark 1902 book, *The Two Islands,* Condon wrote, "The geological history of the Pacific Coast consists chiefly in the description of the slow elevation of successive belts of the bed of the ocean into dry land, and the progressive additions of these to the western border of North America."

Condon was ahead of his time. He, like most other scientists of his day, had no inkling of plate tectonics, of moving seafloor and colliding continents. To suggest that the oldest rocks of Oregon had been added to the continent was not only heresy, it was simply a hypothesis without a provable mechanism. And therefore, it was unsound science. So in 1902, Condon's explanation for these exotic rocks was simply that they rose from the seafloor and in the process were heated and deformed. But in his language, "the progressive additions of these to the western border of North America," there is the specter of a deeper and insightful understanding of what we now recognize as truth.

Indeed, the title of Condon's work, *The Two Islands,* referred to the two widely separated locations of Oregon's oldest rocks: the Klamath Mountains tucked into the remote southwestern corner of the state and the Blue Mountains of northeastern Oregon. Both areas began their lives as volcanic archipelagoes. Both harbor geologic formations about 400 million years in age. Rocks in the Klamaths, if you count the tangled landscapes of the Siskiyou Mountains, and the Marble Mountains and Trinity Alps across the border in northern California, sequester rocks of Silurian and possibly Cambrian age: seafloor perhaps more than 500 million years old. At least one of these Silurian gabbro intrusions, note Rodney Metcalf and Wendy Barrow of the University of Nevada, Las Vegas, include older, Precambrian zircon—a mineral that suggests the gabbro was melted from rocks of an ancient and unknown Precambrian continental fragment.

There is a specific geologic name for a group of rocks that formed in one place and were tacked onto another by plate tectonics. These immigrant landscapes are called terranes, or sometimes, if the rocks have traveled great distances, exotic terranes, a play on the more familiar word terrain. Terranes are fragments of ancient

The open landscape of the Grindstone terrane exposes Oregon's oldest rocks, Devonian limestones (in the foreground) about 400 million years in age, surrounded by younger chert and shale.

landscapes that have been moved about like plate tectonic chess pieces. Their rocks formed at one location; today they are somewhere else. A terrane is not the landscape before our eyes, but one that requires a deeper vision; it is a geologic landscape. The original mountains, lakes, and rivers are long gone. But their record in the rocks remains. The Aleutian Islands will one day collide with mainland Alaska and Russia and, like a bug on the continental windshield, become a new North American geologic terrane. The Hawaiian Islands are well on their way to becoming a terrane as their extinct volcanoes are carried toward Russia on the back of the Pacific plate. One day, 100 million years in the future, when Hawaii is scraped off the Pacific plate and added to Russia, its rocks will be deformed. Its flora and fauna will be fossils. It will be part of Asia, but its rocks will be recognizable as a former seamount by their chemical composition and mineralogy. The fossils will indicate that the Hawaiian volcanoes once erupted in a tropical climate. And so the history, age, and origin of the Hawaiian terrane will be deduced by future geologists.

In the moving panoply of plates, oceans have opened and closed, continents have separated and melded together in different configurations, just as Thomas Dick speculated nearly two centuries ago. Antarctica has flirted with the tropics, the Amazon with the poles. But even from our sophisticated perspective, we are a bit unsure of the world's precise configuration in the Devonian, 400 million years ago when the rocks of Oregon began.

CHAPTER 2

Paleozoic

Oregon's oldest rocks

Oregon's oldest rocks are found as exotic terranes in disparate corners of the state: the Blue Mountains in the northeast and the Klamath Mountains in the southwest. They are, essentially, Thomas Condon's two islands. These terranes are Paleozoic and Mesozoic in age, between about 400 million and 100 million years old. There are even older rocks in the Klamath Mountains of California. These ancient rocks of the Blue Mountains and the Klamaths have similar geologic histories. Both include fragments of volcanic islands and subduction zones, bits of seafloor and coral reefs, bulky bodies of intrusive granites, and scraps of the mantle. Both collided with North America during the Cretaceous period more than 100 million years ago, a time when dinosaurs roamed Montana. Their geologic biographies are sufficiently similar that many geologists believe the rocks of the Klamaths and Blue Mountains developed in adjacent chains—or even the same chain—of ancient islands. But the dates of many significant geologic events in the Klamaths differ from those of similar events recorded in the rocks of the Blue Mountains. And there is little evidence that places the rocks side by side. So the terranes of the Klamaths and Blue Mountains were likely separate island systems generated by similar mechanisms, but not part of the same ancient archipelago.

Oregon's oldest known rock is a Devonian limestone that rises above sagebrush and bunchgrass near Suplee.

In the Blue Mountains, exotic terranes are exposed from Hells Canyon west to Mitchell. They crown the Wallowa, Elkhorn, Strawberry, Aldrich, and Greenhorn ranges. Rocks that were coral reefs and forested volcanic islands, deep ocean floor and shallow sea bottom, far to the west of North America, now lie scattered throughout the high plateau country between Burns and Post, Seneca and Suplee.

Three hundred miles to the southwest of the Blue Mountains, similar exotic terranes occupy most of the Klamath Mountains' landscape. The Rogue River canyon, the Kalmiopsis Wilderness, the Illinois River drainage, and Mount Ashland are all composed of exotic terranes. The geology is more intricate in the Klamaths. These rocks represent multiple generations of islands and microcontinents that merged offshore and were added to North America as a single and geologically complex block. At least a dozen separate terranes have been recognized throughout Oregon's Klamaths.

All these ancient and exotic terranes of the Blue Mountains and the Klamaths developed as part of long-lived systems of volcanic islands that erupted above a subduction zone—the place where the seafloor dives back into the Earth's mantle. These systems, including the modern Aleutians, Marianas, and Tonga, are called island arcs. The concept of an island arc is simple. We know what an island is; the arc refers to a curving line or series of islands. Think of the Aleutians: an arcuate chain of volcanoes rising from the seabed. Importantly, these island arcs are generated above a subduction zone, the place where the seafloor descends back into the mantle.

Volcanoes that arise above a subduction zone are largely a result of the disturbance of the mantle by the down-going oceanic crust. The crust, composed of seafloor basalts and sediments, carries small amounts of seawater into the mantle. There, 20–30 miles beneath the surface, the water acts as a flux, helping melt portions of the mantle to produce basaltic or andesitic magma. These magmas may include small amounts of the melted residue of the down-going ocean crust and sediments, the ultimate in geologic recycling. The melted rock rises, then erupts into a line of volcanoes. Depending on the amount of mantle that is melted and the amount of oceanic crust mixed in, these volcanoes erupt andesite or basalt. They erupt explosively and produce ash as well, building peaks of both lava and ash; they are composite volcanoes, or stratovolcanoes.

The process of plate tectonics—subduction, magma generation, and volcanic eruption above the subduction zone—is fundamental to the dynamics of a living planet. Plate tectonics crafts these curving chains of island volcanoes worldwide. They are especially obvious around the Pacific as the Ring of Fire. Island arc volcanoes form much of Japan. They are the Marianas, the Solomon Islands, the Philippines. And they are cousins, many generations removed, of the Blue Mountain island arc. Some volcanic arcs erupt on continents that lie above a subduction zone: the Cascades, the Andes, and the temperamental volcanoes of Mexico and Costa Rica. Some volcanic arc systems are very long-lived. The Cascades arc system has erupted discontinuously for about 45 million years. Its modern volcanoes, including Mount Hood and Mount Rainier, represent only the most recent phase of Cascade activity that began nearly a million years ago.

The ancient arcs of island volcanoes represented in Oregon's exotic terranes are even more long-lived than their modern Cascade kin. The arc system represented by the Blue Mountains erupted periodically over a span of 150 million years. And the multiple, ancient systems of the Klamaths appear to have been active at least that long.

Cambrian to Devonian
Island arc systems in the vast global sea

To understand Oregon's earliest history, we must venture briefly into the Trinity Alps of northern California, where the oldest rocks of the Klamaths reside. In this rugged landscape, deformed, iron-rich igneous rocks (basalts, gabbros, and peridotite) known as the Trinity Complex form knobby peaks and narrow ridges, glaciated summits and grass-lined valley floors. The rocks here range in age from 472 million to about 560 million years. They are at least as old as the Cambrian, and their pedigree may extend into the Precambrian.

In their heyday, the rocks of the Trinity Alps looked a lot like the modern mid-Atlantic ridge. They were part of a long line of squat, submarine volcanoes, a mid-oceanic ridge. They represent a once-active part of the ocean bottom, where basalts erupted from a linear chain of volcanoes, creating an ever-moving conveyer belt of ocean floor. These relict fragments of mid-oceanic ridge were once part of a spreading system in the ancestral Pacific that pushed North America eastward, closing the early Atlantic Ocean (known as the Iapetus and Rheic Oceans) and creating Pangaea, the single supercontinent. Like modern mid-oceanic ridges, this older one probably supported life, though there is scant fossil record of it, especially in the Trinity terrane.

Between Mount Shasta and Scotts Valley, west of Interstate 5, a rough topography reveals somewhat younger terranes. These rocks are mostly 340–500 million years in age. Known as the Yreka terrane, the rocks include Devonian limestones with interbedded volcanic ash and deep-sea cherts, limestones, and sandstones, all severely deformed. These rocks seem to represent a subduction zone: the geologic crushing and blending zone where ocean floor burrows its way into the mantle, scraping off fragments of sediments, islands, and ocean ridges on its way down. The rocks beneath the Yreka terrane are Cambrian in age, more than 500 million years old. They may represent the same very early seafloor exposed in the Trinity Alps, according to interpretations by Bradley Hacker at Stanford University and Simon Peacock at Arizona State.

The Devonian rocks of the Yreka terrane must have been fairly close to a continent. The sandstones of the Yreka terrane contain tiny grains of zircon, a mineral that generally comes from continental granites. The zircons in these sandstones are more than 2 billion years old. Hence, they were eroded from very old granites on a nearby landmass. But exactly which landmass, or what happened to it, is impossible to say. Plates have moved a long distance since then, and then there is a chance that the entire continental fragment may have been eroded away or subducted.

Life of the Precambrian and Early Paleozoic
The seas before Oregon's birth

Life was very different from today's in the Precambrian sea. There were no fish, no crabs, no clams. Instead, 560 million years ago, when the rocks of the Trinity Alps were erupted, the ocean bottom hosted an assortment of soft-bodied life. The indistinct fossils are controversial. Some paleontologists think they are more likely microbial colonies rather than soft-bodied, animate creatures.

Know as the Ediacaran fauna, for the Ediacara Hills in Australia where the fossils were first found, these animals include forms interpreted as the fernlike ancestors of modern sea pens, and broad, segmented worms and tubular, spongelike animals. Some, like *Cloudina,* a cone-shaped bottom-dweller, sported the first skeletal materials known on the planet. And while there is no fossil record of any life associated with the Trinity terrane, there is a record that tells us whatever life might have been found then, it was fairly simple in form and function.

Only 10 million years after the Ediacaran animals appeared, life would make a major gamble. The ruins of this biological casino are found at an elevation close to 8,000 feet in the Canadian Rockies of British Columbia. Known as the Burgess Shale, it contains what paleontologist Stephen Jay Gould has called the most important animal fossils: a series of early invertebrate marine organisms, diverse and often chimerical, that is at least in part ancestral to all of today's life, including humans.

The Burgess Shale, 550 million years in age, likely originated close in space as well as time to the rocks of the Yreka and Trinity terranes. We cannot know for certain, for it is hard to extrapolate plate tectonic motions more than 500 million years old. But close or not, a similar fauna may have inhabited the submarine landscape of the Trinity Alps. There is no record of life in these early Klamath rocks largely because most of the oldest are igneous (few lava flows preserve fossils, especially those of soft-bodied animals) and partly because the animals were so soft that their remains are only rarely preserved, in locations where conditions were favorable.

The animals found in the Burgess Shale represent, to modern eyes, a bizarre and highly experimental fauna. Most had soft bodies, and some were the direct ancestors of today's sponges, jellyfish, and sea urchins. There was *Anomalocaris,* a 2-foot-long, sleek, swimming, predaceous slug with tiny arms that grasped its prey. And *Opabinia,* a puzzling, five-eyed invertebrate that sported a long nozzle with a claw at the end as its primary feeding appendage (feeding on what?) and a body lined with one of the Burgess fauna's prized inventions: gills. Strangest of all was *Hallucigenia,* an inch-long, worm-shaped animal with pikelike legs, shoulder spikes, a trunklike appendage on one end, and a knobby head on the other. *Hallucigenia* was, as Gould succinctly notes, "really weird."

Hallucigenia, Opabinia, and *Anomalocaris,* among more than 65,000 Burgess Shale fossils, represent the Cambrian explosion, one of nature's grandest and boldest experiments with life. In this biological wager, many apparently well adapted designs disappeared. Only a few forms would prosper and proliferate. There is no apparent reason for which of the Burgess forms thrived and which perished. It seems to have been, says Gould, a lottery. This monumental winnowing of life ultimately shaped the destiny of all subsequent beings, including us. Although there is no record of Burgess Shale-type fossils in Oregon, the Burgess fauna would largely determine all animals that appeared subsequently, including the 400 million years of Oregon's geologic history.

Devonian to Carboniferous
Early history of the Blue Mountains

Oregon's geologic record begins in the Devonian, about 400 million years ago and 160 million years after the Burgess Shale's ecosystem evolved into other things.

By then, corals were abundant and armored fish dominated the seas.

Multiple island arcs developed across and around the global ocean during the late Devonian about 350 million years ago, say Charles Rubin and Megan Miller of Cal Tech. Remnants of some are found in exotic terranes that extend from the northern Sierra Nevada and Californian Klamaths to tiny exposures in the Blue Mountains into British Columbia and Alaska.

The middle to late Paleozoic record is scant in both the Blue Mountains and the Klamaths. Devonian rocks are found only in the Californian portion of the Klamaths, so the honor of oldest rock in Oregon is reserved for the Blue Mountains. There are only a few exposures: gray, weather-smoothed rocks on grassy knolls in open landscape. But a few are enough. The Blue Mountains' Devonian limestones rank as the oldest rocks in Oregon.

In Grindstone Creek's watershed, the landscape rolls gently between junipers and sagebrush. South a few miles along the dusty single-lane roads that thread between stock ponds and thinly layered outcrops, there is a limestone monolith. It rises 60 feet above the surrounding shales, an ancient whale breaching from a sagebrush sea. Its tawny gray surface is dimpled with lichens. Wind has scoured its surface; water has washed it clean. A few tiny whorls pimple its hide.

On closer inspection, bathed in acid and scrutinized by microscope, some of these whorls prove to be fossils: corals, bryozoans, and tiny, mysterious, toothlike objects known as conodonts. Less than ¼ inch in length, serrated on one side and with a smooth cusp on the other, conodonts are tiny, phosphorus-rich teeth. They are virtually the only remains of a euconodont, a lamprey-shaped marine invertebrate with large eyes and multiple rows of teeth. Although millions of the teeth have been preserved, only two fossils are known of the soft-bodied euconodont. One was found in Scotland in 1983; the second was recognized in South Africa 2 years later.

Once the euconodont died and sank to the sea bottom, its soft body decayed and disintegrated rapidly. But many sedimentary rocks are littered with the teeth. Because euconodonts evolved rapidly and the shape of their teeth changed every few million years over a very long expanse of geologic time (they lived from 540 million to 250 million years ago), their teeth (simply called conodonts) provide valid ages for much of the sedimentary record. Conodonts are like fossil bread crumbs that guide us through the wilderness of Paleozoic time.

The conodonts retrieved from the limestone near Suplee are middle Devonian, a type known as *Polygnathus*, about 380 million years old. Along with a few fossil brachiopods and three types of corals (*Grypophyllum*, *Heliolites*, and *Thamnopora*), they bestow the honor of oldest rock in Oregon to this lonely outcrop near the geographic center of the state. Two other scraps of Devonian rocks have been found in Oregon. Both are stashed in the Blue Mountains: one on Vinegar Hill near the tiny town of Greenhorn, the other in the northernmost portion of Harney County.

The limestone near Suplee is part of the Grindstone terrane. These sediments were deposited in shallow waters and warm seas. This limestone represents a fragment of a larger reef crafted beneath the waves 380 million years ago and uplifted sometime later. About 350 million years ago, this limestone broke from its moorings during earthquakes or storms and plummeted down submarine slopes, coming to rest in the soft ooze. At least that is the best geologic guess for the reason that the oldest rock in Oregon, this 380-million-year-old Devonian limestone, sits as an isolated block amid younger, 350-million-year-old shales of Carboniferous age, part of the seafloor that fringed the Blue Mountain island arc, part of the apron of rock and sediment between the volcanoes and the subduction zone.

The scant geologic record here fast-forwards some 30 million years to the Carboniferous, 350 million years ago. The wispy shale and sandstone outcrops along Coffee Creek, about 5 miles from the Devonian limestone, record life during the Carboniferous, a time when plants flourished, reptiles evolved, and amphibians grew ever larger. Glaciers scoured polar regions. But wherever the lime-laden shales of the Coffee Creek Formation were deposited, it was warm, if not tropical. These rocks include the horn coral *Campophyllum* and warm-water sponges, animals for whom warmth is essential and chilly water spells doom.

In another 30 million years, at least some of this sea bottom would emerge from the water to become an island. At Spotted Ridge, 20 miles from the whale-gray limestone, khaki-colored rocks of the Spotted Ridge Formation preserve leaves from a ferny forest. These rocks are Pennsylvanian in age, altogether about 320 million years old, and about 30 million years younger than Coffee Creek's corals.

The plant fossils at Spotted Ridge include horsetail rushes as well as a type of early sedge known as *Phyllotheca*. There were forests, too, including the earliest relatives of conifers (*Cordaites*) and scraps of the diamond-patterned bark of a *Lepidodendron* tree: a soft, fernlike, but straight-trunked forest giant more than 6 feet in diameter that reached heights of 90–100 feet at other North American sites. These straight, soft-stemmed plants were treelike in stature but fernlike in function. They towered above the brushy ferns, mosses, and horsetails at their base.

Similar forests grew worldwide. The Carboniferous, often subdivided into the Mississippian and Pennsylvanian periods, left a global legacy of carbon-rich plant deposits. The most productive coal beds of Pennsylvania, West Virginia, Europe, and Asia are the legacy of

The presence of coral in the Devonian limestone indicates that it formed in warm seas. This coral, from the collection of the University of California, Berkeley, was found near Suplee by Thomas Condon's students about 1920.

Top: An early relative of rushes and sedges, *Phyllotheca* grew in Carboniferous wetlands.

Above: Fossils of horsetail rush, *Equisetum*, from the Spotted Ridge Formation are about 320 million years old. They are virtually the same as modern horsetail rushes that grow in Oregon today.

the lush forests of that time. But there is no Carboniferous coal in Oregon. All we have to show are a few leaf impressions from this long-lost island and its shoals.

Permian

Volcanoes build the first island arcs

By the end of the Pennsylvanian period, 286 million years ago, the stage was set for volcanoes. As the major landmasses merged into a single continent of Pangaea, plates shifted at the edges of the world ocean, Panthalassa. Subduction began, and with it, far from North American shores, volcanoes erupted and the construction of new island arcs began.

We are unsure of the exact spatial or genetic relationships between the Permian island arc of the Blue Mountains and the volcanoes of similar age now exposed in the Californian Klamaths' Trinity terrane. How close these two systems were and whether they shared the same subduction zone are unclear. However, there is considerable evidence that the two volcanic systems were part of the same large-scale island arc system. The chemical compositions and ages of the rocks are similar. They share similar fossils, including large Tethyan (or Asiatic) foraminifera known as fusulinids that are found in the McCloud Limestone south of Mount Shasta and in the limestones at Dog Creek near John Day.

In fact, many geologists argue that the Permian and later volcanoes now strewn from the northern Sierra Nevada through the Klamaths, Blue Mountains, British Columbia, and Alaska were all part of the same volcanic chain. There is considerable merit in the idea. But one could also argue that the two terranes are not related. Island arcs anywhere have generally similar chemistry, especially after the original compositions have been modified by later alteration. The chemistry of rocks from Tonga in the southwestern Pacific Ocean is generally similar to rocks from the Aleutians, but they are hardly part of the same island arc system. And there are differences between fossil faunas of the Klamaths and Blue Mountains. Brachiopods that are abundant in Blue Mountain rocks are absent from the Klamaths, and vice versa. Although this problem can be attributed to local differences in habitat, the presence of deep waters and strong currents between volcanic islands, and the uncertainties of fossil preservation and discovery, it remains a sticking point for those who lump the Klamaths and Blue Mountains into the same system, and for those who envision a single chain of long-lived volcanoes strewn along North America's western coast.

The Trinity Arc
Eruptions form the eastern Klamath Mountains

To find the Permian rocks of the Klamath Mountains, we must head for California again. South of Mount Shasta, stretching in a narrow, 5-mile-wide band from McCloud Reservoir to Shasta Lake, are the ragged remains of coral reefs and volcanoes that once might have rivaled Shasta in size. This band of greenstone, limestone, sandstone, and tuff is known as the Nosoni and Bully Hill Formations. They are younger than the nearby Yreka terrane and were probably deposited above the remains of the Trinity and Yreka arc.

Early in the Permian, about 280 million years ago, the old igneous rocks of the Trinity and Yreka terranes had become a sea bottom in shallow tropical water. Coral reefs flourished. They were similar in extent to today's Great Barrier Reef off Australia, but much farther offshore. More than thirty-three genera of gastropods, ranging from conchs to snails, lived here. The coral reef was diverse: twenty-eight different varieties of corals built colonies. There were brachiopods, and there were probably fish, likely including primitive sharks, though no fish fossils have been found.

By the middle Permian, about 270 million years ago, subduction started somewhere adjacent to the old arc, and volcanoes began to erupt on this carbonate platform. Stratovolcanoes, like the modern Cascades and the volcanoes of the Blue Mountain island arc, they produced ash, mudflows, and lava. And like the Permian volcanoes found in the Blue Mountains, their eruptions were richer in silica than the rocks of modern arcs. But whether they were part of the same chain of volcanoes, or were different arcs above different subduction zones, remains an unanswered question.

The Blue Mountain Island Arc

In its most rugged and remote recesses, Hells Canyon sequesters a scrap of seafloor that has been dated by geologist Nick Walker as 309 million years old. The barren rocks at the mouth of Cougar Creek are dimpled with minerals and are dark green with age. They represent seafloor basalts and gabbros that provided the foundation for the next generation of Oregon's geology: the volcanoes of the Blue Mountain island arc.

About 270 million years ago, a series of volcanoes began to erupt above a subduction zone somewhere far to the west of the shore of the giant landmass, Pangaea. The ocean that encircled these volcanic islands differed from the modern Pacific; we call it Panthalassa. It extended, unbroken except for volcanic islands, from pole to pole and two-thirds of the way around the globe. A somewhat smaller and more sheltered marine body extended east to west around perhaps a third of the globe; it is called the Tethys Sea. During much of the time that the islands of the Blue Mountain and Klamath arcs erupted, from about 300 million to 180 million years ago, the Tethys Sea provided a warm-water pathway for island-hopping marine animals, from coral polyps to brachiopods. Today, the last remnants of the Tethys Sea exist as the Mediterranean. Relict Tethyan seafloor caps the Alps and the Himalaya, and provides the rich oil deposits of the Middle East. Fossils of animals that lived in this sea are referred to as Tethyan.

On the Permian globe, there was no Atlantic Ocean. The seven continents were fused into one: Pangaea. With its huge landmass, Pangaea was a continent of arid deserts and a southern polar ice cap. But far from the landmass, in the sea where the volcanoes that would be Oregon erupted, rain was abundant and the waters were warm.

The Wallowa Terrane

First volcanoes of the Blue Mountain island arc

To find the Permian in the Blue Mountains, to venture back 270 million years, you need only drive to Oxbow Dam, a concrete and earthen structure that blocks the Snake River about 80 miles east of Baker City. At Oxbow, the razor-straight course of the river makes a spectacular detour, a single tight meander—an oxbow in the parlance of geomorphology.

The Permian rocks of Hells Canyon represent the first generation of a long-lived family of volcanic islands. These are part of the Wallowa terrane, a group of rocks that represent volcanoes, streams, shallow bays, and coral reefs. The rocky relicts of this ancient island landscape are found today in Hells Canyon and the Wallowa Mountains, westernmost Idaho, and southeastern Washington. Similar formations occupy British Columbia's Vancouver Island.

About ½ mile north of Oxbow Dam, pistachio green rocks flecked with blocky white crystals peer from outcrops along the narrow paved road that leads north to Homestead. Once, 270 million years ago, these rocks oozed as sticky, molten lavas from a volcano that resembled the South Sea island volcanoes of the Marianas. The altered green rocks once were dacites and andesites, the trademark rock of island arc volcanoes. Even after 270 million years of change, their chemical fingerprints—trace elements like europium or lantha-num—are similar to fresh andesites of the Aleutians or the South Sea island chains. These altered rocks are called greenstones.

Hot springs bubbled on the seafloor adjacent to these Permian volcanoes. Some deposited copper, gold, and silver in pyrite-laden massive sulfide deposits. These ores form when metals accumulate around a hot spring vent, similar to the black smokers of modern mid-oceanic ridges. The minerals are deposited in veins and in rock cavities when hot, oxygen-poor volcanic waters encounter cold, oxygen-rich seawater. The Irondyke Mine, about 2 miles north of Oxbow Dam, is one example of such a massive sulfide deposit. From 1910 to 1934, about 35,000 ounces (2,200 pounds) of gold, 256,000 ounces (8 tons) of silver, and 7,200 tons of copper were reportedly produced from this mine. The mine closed in 1935 but reopened in 1979 as gold prices rose. Another 20,000 ounces (1,250 pounds) of gold, 40,000 ounces (2¼ tons) of silver, and 1,900 tons of copper were mined during the ensuing 8 years before the mine closed again. Farther north in the canyon, the

---

Below left: Greenstone outcrop in Hells Canyon. Greenstone is an altered volcanic rock.

Below: A slice of greenstone viewed through a polarizing microscope.

Right: Permian greenstones in Hells Canyon above the Snake River near Oxbow Dam were part of volcanic islands.

Red Ledge Mine extracted copper and gold from similar rocks.

Only a few remnants of life around these Permian volcanic islands have been preserved. The limestones near Oxbow at the southern portal to Hells Canyon contain abundant walnut-sized brachiopods (*Megousia*). These animals, characterized by ornately patterned shells, lived in temperate waters. Their presence in Permian rocks of the Wallowa terrane indicate that the waters surrounding the volcanic islands were not tropical and that the islands were as much as 30° or 35° north of the equator—at the latitude of southern Florida or northern Mexico. The Blue Mountain arc, located in warm, tropical waters 350 million years ago, had moved north during the next 50 million years.

This finding is echoed by another set of the Wallowa terrane's fossils. The relics of a submarine catastrophe lie on steep slopes above Eagle Creek in the southern Wallowa Mountains. Volcanic ash and debris, hurled onto the ocean floor by violent eruptions, entombed an entire community of sea life in a volcanic deposit: clams, sea urchins (crinoids), and spiny brachiopods.

Allan Kays of the University of Oregon found these fossils while exploring for Wallowa terrane greenstones (metamorphosed basalts). His discovery was the sort of serendipity that comes to the alert scientist. No one was looking for fossils that day. In fact, the find at first seemed preposterous to the students and professionals who accompanied Kays. The clams and brachiopods

Below: Volcanic greenstones of the Blue Mountain island arc line the canyon of the Wallowa River. Like similar greenstones in Hells Canyon, they are part of the Wallowa terrane.

Right: Ancient sedimentary sandstones in Hells Canyon are the remnants of beaches and seafloor that ringed the Permian volcanoes of the Blue Mountain island arc.

seemed out of place in a greenstone, a volcanic rock. But closer scrutiny revealed that the rock was originally a mudflow: a lumpy, lukewarm accumulation of ash and volcanic debris rather than a torrid lava flow.

University of Oregon paleontologist Bill Orr's student Cindy Shroba ultimately identified many species of marine organisms buried by this volcanic eruption 260 million years ago. Like the fossils of *Megousia* found near Oxbow, the well-preserved animals in these rocks, including the tongue-twistingly named brachio-

pod *Waagenoconcha*, were not truly tropical. They lived in cooler waters where equatorial corals never venture. The types of corals and mollusks preserved indicate that in the Permian, 260 million years ago, the ancient volcanic islands of the Wallowa terrane were 1,000 miles north of the equator.

The idea that the Wallowa terrane originated somewhat north of the equator is corroborated by paleomagnetic studies. Tiny crystals of iron oxide in volcanic rocks act as miniature magnets, oriented north–south and dipping into the Earth at an angle that steepens toward the poles. Geologists can measure the orientation of these tiny particles and thereby determine the latitude at which a volcanic rock originally cooled and solidified. The Permian volcano's magnetic signature places the Blue Mountain island arc at about the latitude of Belize or El Salvador some 250 million years ago.

The Subduction Zone of the Blue Mountains

Island arcs like those of the Wallowa terrane cannot live alone. They receive energy and their supply of lava, ash, and gas from the seafloor that slips constantly downward into the mantle. This conveyer belt of rock and sediment is called a subduction zone. As the seafloor slides beneath the adjacent crust, it scrapes some of its sedimentary baggage off before it descends, stuffing scraps of seamounts and coral reefs into the oceanic trench wall. But it also carries a variety of rocks down with it. The most common passengers on this subducting plate include cherts, the silky-fine sediments of the deep-sea floor, as well as fragments of reefs and seamounts.

Today, we can walk around on the subduction zone that slid beneath the Wallowa terrane's volcanoes. It has been exhumed by plate tectonics, exposed at the summits of the Greenhorn and Elkhorn Mountains. It extends west to Mitchell, north almost to Pendleton, and south to Seneca. The older Grindstone terrane rides on its far-western exposures. This landscape of rocks digested in a subduction zone and then heaved back to the surface is called the Baker terrane, after Baker City

Left: The Baker terrane stretches across much of northeastern Oregon, from the western foothills of the Wallowa Mountains to Mitchell, including this view from the Greenhorn Mountains to the Strawberry Range, 45 miles to the south.

Above: Fusulinids help date the Paleozoic rocks of the Blue Mountain island arc.

limestones that bear Permian fossils. The tiny animals preserved in the rocks are the size and shape and color of barley grains. They are foraminifera called fusulinids, and they lived from about 500 million to 220 million years ago, from the Ordovician to the Triassic.

Fusulinids, like conodonts, have a very precise stratigraphy and geographic distribution. The fusulinids in the Greenhorn Mountains and at Dog Creek in the Strawberry Range are *Pseudofusulinella, Pseudoschwagerina,* and *Schwagerina,* Permian varieties that are also found abundantly in limestones of China. These Permian fusulinids inhabit other limestones in the Baker terrane, notably in the southern flanks of Vinegar Hill along Badger Creek, and along the summit of the Elkhorns. The same fusulinids also appear in the Permian McCloud Limestone in the Californian Klamaths. Animals the size of a barley grain tenuously tether these two giant island systems together.

How did the fusulinids and other animals navigate the Tethys Sea, spreading from Asia to the Klamaths and the Blue Mountains? Paleontologists have several ideas. The most logical and attractive is that the fusulinids rafted on ocean currents. This does not work quite as well for larger animals that also share the Asian link, but the larvae of corals and mollusks may have launched themselves into the currents for a free ride. Or they may have ridden one geologic system that moved long distances, colonizing islands en route; this is called the ark model. Or, if the island systems were close together, the animals may have dispersed early into suitable habitats. The similarity of the fauna across the Tethys Sea argues against long-term isolation and for the presence of multiple and complex island systems. The broad Permian sea was not a lonely ocean.

on the terrane's eastern edge. Like the Wallowa terrane, composed of ancient volcanoes, this subduction zone fragment is part of the Blue Mountain island arc.

The Baker terrane is a strange landscape, a knobby and chaotic world. For in the process of subduction, the rocks dragged beneath the seafloor are jumbled, stretched, and steeped in hot waters and silica-enriched fluids. Under intense pressures, some transform from a dark gray, salt-and-pepper gabbro to a rock of greenish stripes called mylonite. Sediments metamorphose into a fine-grained, blue rock with layers squeezed as thin as book pages that forms only in subduction zones: a blueschist. Most are scrambled and changed in some way.

While the volcanoes whose flanks now rest in Hells Canyon and the Wallowas erupted, the subduction zone offshore (Baker terrane) consumed seafloor, Permian reefs, and limy sea bottom. But how old were these chunks of rock? And where did they come from? For many rocks, it is difficult to ascertain their precise origin. But for many limestone fragments, fossils can help tell the tale.

About 90 miles west of Hells Canyon and just east of John Day, along the banks of Dog Creek, there are

Beneath the Volcanoes

The Canyon Mountain complex

If you are curious about what, exactly, lies deep beneath a volcano, you need only look at the ridgetops above John Day, above Dog Creek, on Canyon Mountain. Canyon Mountain forms the westernmost summit of the Strawberry Range. But 280 million years ago in the Permian, it was a seething magma chamber beneath the Blue Mountain island arc. Its summit is composed of gabbro, the compositional equivalent of basalt that has cooled more slowly underground. But there the similarity to the average large magma chamber, or batholith, ends. This is not just any magma chamber; it is or was a volcano sitting directly atop the upper mantle. And at the base of Canyon Mountain there is a slice of mantle peridotite to prove it. The magma chamber of the Canyon Mountain Complex also includes a variety of layered igneous rocks, which develop in larger mag-

ma chambers where pulses of fresh magma periodically replenish the supply of iron, calcium, and magnesium. This diverse package of rocks is called the Canyon Mountain Complex.

While gabbro and greenstone occupy the summit of Canyon Mountain, the mountain's rocks become progressively richer in iron and magnesium on the way down. There is a zone of layered peridotites about 2,000 feet below the ridgetops. Below these are even denser peridotites, rocks that represent the Earth's upper mantle. This lower, peridotite zone of Canyon Mountain harbors deposits of chrome. During World Wars I and

Above: Gabbro, a dark, iron-rich plutonic rock, is commonly layered in the Canyon Mountain Complex.

Left: Chromite ore from the Canyon Mountain Complex.

II, chrome mines operated here, extracting several million dollars' worth of dark, shiny black chrome ore (chromite) from the base of Canyon Mountain.

Analyses indicate that the rocks in the upper parts of the Canyon Mountain Complex are related to an island arc system. This comes as no big surprise. Permian arc rocks are abundant in the Blue Mountains, though most are farther east. The westerly location of the Canyon Mountain Complex, along with its association with mélanges related to subduction zones, suggest that it represents a special kind of island arc eruptive center that developed at the front of the main volcanoes, or the forearc. Alternatively, it may be part of a Wallowa volcano isolated from its brethren by faulting and changes in the direction of subduction.

The Wallowa terrane's Permian volcanoes erupted for more than 30 million years, crafting multiple islands, of which we have only a meager sample. Their eruptions quieted about 270 million years ago as subduction beneath them slowed. Subduction, and the next generations of island arc volcanoes, would resume about 25 million years later.

But first the Earth would have to endure the greatest extinction event in its history, when more than 90 percent of the species living disappeared forever. This was the cruel and invisible boundary between the ancient life of the Paleozoic and the dawning age of dinosaurs, the Mesozoic. It is known, simply, as the Permian extinction.

The Permian Extinction

By the end of the Paleozoic, 248 million years ago, the Blue Mountain island arc—the rocks that today constitute parts of Hells Canyon, the Wallowas, Elkhorns, Strawberry Range, and the upper reaches of the Crooked River drainage—was a chain of silica-rich volcanic islands far from any continental landmass. It lay north of the equator at about 20° north latitude. The islands that would become the eastern Klamath Mountains were not far away. During a 60-million-year life span, these two island chains had ridden the back of a rotating,

drifting oceanic plate from the nearly equatorial latitudes to 28–30° north and then turned south again.

Coral reefs and warm carbonate banks similar to those of the modern Solomon Islands or Mariana Islands grew offshore. Brachiopods lived in near-shore sands. There is no record of plants or animals that lived on the islands, but the fauna was probably limited to vagabonds and hitchhikers: light-bodied animals that could survive long trips across the sea.

The world was poised to change. The extinction of life at the end of the Permian eradicated more than 50 percent of animal families and 96 percent of all species. Brachiopods, crinoids, and trilobites virtually disappeared. Fusulinids expired. More than 80 percent of amphibian families died out. Two major families of corals disappeared completely. And perhaps as many as 98 percent of all four-footed animals, or tetrapods, vanished.

The obituaries are long, distinguished, and numerous. Paleontologists estimate that only 4 percent of all existing species crossed the Permian threshold into the Triassic period. So enormous was the loss, so great the new opportunities for evolution and change, that this rolling event ended one major era of Earth history, the Paleozoic, "old life," and ushered in a new one, the Mesozoic, when dinosaurs ruled and mammals waited in the wings.

Unlike the Cretaceous–Tertiary extinction that wiped out dinosaurs in one, fell, meteoric swoop 65 million years ago, many geologists think that the beginning of the Permian extinctions was long in the making and gradual at their start, though the final coup de grâce may have been sudden. As the Earth's landmasses gradually merged into the supercontinent of Pangaea, worldwide climate and sea level changed. Once-balmy continental interiors became hot and arid; margins buckled into higher mountains that created a rain curtain of increasingly moist seacoasts and hot, dry continental interiors. Computer models suggest that at the end of the Permian, average seasonal temperatures may have swung by more than 90°F (32°C).

Pangaea, once constructed, stretched from pole to pole. Although the Tethys Sea still took a large, pointed bite out of the equatorial regions, the bulky unified continental landmass inhibited the global circulation of warm, climate-moderating tropical water. In today's Atlantic Ocean, the Gulf Stream warms the northern latitudes of Europe. In the Permian Panthalassa, there was nowhere for a Permian Gulf Stream, had there been one, to go, save perhaps across an already temperate Tethys. So it is little wonder that, in places, Permian climates verged on the uninhabitable.

The Paleozoic forest, consisting of ferny trees and giant club moss, was poorly adapted to this new regime. Gradually, over the last 5–10 million years of the Permian, trees better adapted to the drier climate moved in as old forests died out. Conifers and ginkgoes replaced the Paleozoic trees in what became uplifted, more arid habitat. Cycads invaded lower elevations as the climate became warmer and drier. This decline, says paleontologist Michael Benton of England's Bristol University, took place piecemeal, in fits and starts. But whatever the rate, the overall effect was to eliminate more than half the plant species.

Another sinister effect on life was the worldwide lowering of sea level. As much as 70 percent of continental shelf areas were left high and dry by the end of the Permian. The slow fall of the seas and exposure of the shelves may have been accelerated about 250 million years ago by the growth of glaciers in what is now eastern Australia and in Siberia. Continental shelves are biofriendly seafloor regions of generally shallow, calm, warm, nutrient-rich water. They are prime habitat for all manner of fish, corals, and foraminifera. But at their edges, they fall off rapidly to the deeper seafloor—the slope and the abyssal plain. Dry them up, and there is no place for these animals to go except steeper substrate and inhospitable waters—a habitat they cannot endure.

And it is likely that climate change, driven by changes in atmospheric composition, also played a role in the Permian extinction. As continental shelves dried out, large amounts of easily weathered lignite coal, sequestered in Carboniferous and early Permian deposits formerly covered by cold seawater, were exposed to an oxygen-rich atmosphere. The result, according to British geochemists Tony Hallam and Paul Wignall, was release of carbon dioxide gas. Whether exposure of coal deposits to the atmosphere was the only cause, it is certain that atmospheric composition shifted drastically at

the end of the Permian. The isotopes of both carbon and oxygen from limestones and other late Permian sediments tell the same story: carbon dioxide increased; oxygen decreased. This fluctuation in atmospheric composition contributed to the extreme climatic variations of the late Permian. Hallam and Wignall have estimated that the level of atmospheric oxygen fell from about 30 percent of atmospheric gas (slightly more than the modern atmosphere's 28 percent) to only 15 percent. This change is roughly the difference in ease of breathing you might experience in going from sea level to the summit of Mount Everest. Oxygen in the sea may have decreased to less than 20 percent of its early Permian levels.

In addition, says Douglas Erwin of the Smithsonian Institution, a lower sea level may have resulted in increased atmospheric methane, another critical greenhouse gas. On cold, deep sea bottoms off the continental shelves, the methane that is released when organic material decays becomes trapped in icelike solids known as hydrates. Gas is held in these compounds largely by the confining pressure of the overlying water. Remove some of that burden by lowering the sea level, and the gas is no longer contained. Methane will rise through the water and escape into the atmosphere. Cold climates in the early Permian would have locked considerable methane into hydrates on the seafloor, Erwin notes. The rapidly warming climate and low sea level of the late Permian would have released many tons of methane into the atmosphere annually, exacerbating the global warming generated by carbon dioxide. Convincing evidence of sudden methane release has been documented by University of Oregon graduate student Evelyn Krull.

These climate changes were geologically sudden, though they actually occurred over hundreds of thousands of years. But they were persistent and they were global. There was no way for either animals or plants to escape. Few, evidently, could adjust. Many died. The agent of extinction, says Michael Benton in *The Book of Life* (Gould 1993), was "a slow suffocation of life while the land fell silent and the sea stagnated."

Large-scale volcanic eruptions may have contributed to climate change and atmospheric degradation. The

Siberian Traps—flood basalts larger in extent and similar in composition to Oregon's Columbia River basalts —spewed carbon dioxide, sulfur dioxide, and other gases into the atmosphere 249 million years ago, just before the Permian curtain fell. Giant volcanic calderas in the north of Pangaea, in what is now China, coughed up gas-rich clouds of choking, climate-cooling ash that circled the globe. The resulting ash layer is widespread in the last Permian sediments of Asia.

There is mounting evidence that the final Permian coup de grâce was sudden, and delivered by a huge meteor according to work by Kunio Kaiho of Tohoku University, Japan, and other researchers. There is no known crater, but chemical evidence points at a likely collision with a huge bolide—perhaps six times as large as the one that caused the extinction of the dinosaurs. Kaiho has found evidence of the sudden release of massive amounts of sulfur from the Earth's mantle, precisely at the Permian–Triassic boundary. The release of this gas might have consumed 20–40 percent of atmospheric oxygen. The acid rain from the sulfur dioxide-laden atmosphere would have raised the acidity of the world's oceans far beyond what most marine life could tolerate. Kaiho determined that sediments deposited at the Permian's end have very high concentrations of sulfur along with nickel, an element that is concentrated in

meteorites. Other sediments contain trapped helium and other noble gases that likely have an extraterrestrial origin, according to Luann Becker of the University of Washington. Impact by an enormous meteor or asteroid would have extinguished most terrestrial life. Combined with other likely environmental effects, it is hardly a surprise that 95 percent of all species were exterminated at the end of the Permian.

At the end of the Permian, the Earth's landmasses consisted of a giant continent whose interior was a hot and inhospitable desert. The ocean was fringed with island arcs denuded of trees, with mud-wrinkled platforms and dead coral reefs shrinking into sand dunes where once there was an indigo sea. On land, the most abundant four-footed animals in South Africa, China, western Russia, and India seem to have been lonely groups of large herbivores, the burrowing, barrel-chested reptile *Lystrosaurus,* an animal better adapted to the acidic, low-oxygen atmosphere of the new Triassic world. Ocean waters were anoxic. The atmosphere contained less oxygen than today and perhaps ten times the present level of carbon dioxide, along with substantial methane released from gas hydrates as sea level fell. Only four other animal taxa survived across the globe. All in all, the Earth's environment was hostile to life. The Mesozoic would have to be a brave new world indeed.

CHAPTER 3

Triassic

The Blue Mountain island arc builds tropical islands

Time's curtain rose slowly on the Triassic 248 million years ago. The transition from the Permian to the Triassic was a time-consuming journey from one geologic era, the Paleozoic, the time of ancient life, to the Mesozoic, when dinosaurs would rule. In the span of a few million years the planet's lifestyle changed dramatically. What had been a deliberately paced world of brachiopods, trilobites, ponderous reptiles, and oversized insects became a livelier realm of faster animals, milder climates, and far more diverse ecosystems. But such pervasive changes do not occur overnight. A lingering malaise of hot climates and low biological diversity would persist for at least 10 million years into the Triassic. Coral reefs would not recover for almost 20 million years.

During this transitional time, global temperatures remained elevated. Atmospheric carbon dioxide levels were higher in the early Triassic than today. In contrast to the Permian's low sea levels, Triassic seas rose, inundating coastal swamps and estuaries. Pangaea, the supercontinent, held together through most of the Triassic, maintaining inhospitable deserts in its vast interior. Landmasses would not begin to disperse toward today's

The Snake River, here viewed looking north toward Hells Canyon Dam, exposes rocks that once formed volcanic islands as well as the ancient coral reefs that thrived offshore.

configuration until the very end of the Triassic and the beginning of the Jurassic, another 40 million years in the future.

Early Triassic

New species speed recovery from extinctions

The rocks of Oregon's Triassic, deposited from 248 million to 208 million years ago, represent a second generation of island arc volcanoes and their allied subduction zones. These volcanoes erupted atop the eroded remnants of older Devonian and Permian arcs. They brought a new kind of volcanism. The rocks of the Triassic volcanoes are generally darker and richer in iron than their forebears. Their chemical compositions are similar to rocks of modern oceanic arcs like the Marianas or Aleutians. And while we are unsure of their exact relationship with the Pangaean supercontinent, models of how and where these new volcanoes erupted suggest they were relatively close to its western shore.

So few species were left at the end of the Permian that the early Triassic was a time of worldwide evolutionary opportunity. There were niches to fill, fresh landscapes to pioneer, and plenty of places for animals and plants to establish new orders.

Oregon's terranes played a role in several evolutionary success stories. Ichthyosaurs ranked among the best new adaptations. In the early Triassic, reptiles found a new home in the slowly rising sea. Dolphin-shaped marine reptiles known as ichthyosaurs ("fish-lizards" in Latin) took advantage of the new habitat on broader continental shelves. Their fossils are found in Triassic, Jurassic, and Cretaceous Oregon rocks. Ichthyosaurs are dinosaur relatives that would swim the Mesozoic seas for almost 180 million years, from the time before dinosaurs appeared until their doomsday 65 million years ago.

Dinosaurs did not appear until the middle Triassic, about 240 million years ago. They are not a paleontological force in Oregon's past. Their fossils are unknown (as yet) in the Mesozoic rocks that formed Oregon's first landscape. (Although dinosaur fossils have been found in rocks along Oregon's southern coast, these rocks have been faulted north from California in the last 10 million years.) The reason for Oregon's lack of native dinosaurs seems logical: In the Triassic and throughout most of the Mesozoic, the exotic terranes that would create Oregon's first land were isolated islands. They lay some distance off the Idaho shore. Marine reptiles like ichthyosaurs could—and did—visit these hideaways. Flying reptiles (pterosaurs) could—and did—make the journey. But the Blue Mountain island arc was simply out of range for Triassic and Jurassic dinosaurs. If dinosaurs emigrated over the daunting Idaho mountains after the Blue Mountain and Klamath terranes merged with North America in the middle Cretaceous, their remains have not yet been found.

Several other significant orders of reptiles first appeared in the middle Triassic, including turtles and crocodiles. And then there were the cynodonts. Survivors from the Permian, these dog-sized, mammal-like reptiles of South Africa developed a throat and nasal system with a bony palate that, for the first time in 4 billion years, allowed a land-dwelling animal to eat and breathe at the same time. They developed a mouth full of specialized teeth: canines, incisors, and molars. Their skulls, with tiny conduits for the blood vessels and nerves that would support whiskers, suggest that by the middle Triassic the cynodonts had developed hair. They were warm-blooded; they were on their way to becoming mammals. The journey would take another 100 million years.

Unlike the rapidly radiating animal kingdom, Triassic vegetation would change little from that of the Permian. Pangaea would remain intact through most of the Triassic. Coastal regions supported forests while climates in the vast continental interior remained largely arid. The atmospheric composition returned to a more normal balance gradually as polar regions warmed, sea levels rose, and carbon dioxide levels fell.

In Oregon, Triassic rocks are found in both the Klamaths and the Blue Mountains, but they are not distributed equally. Triassic rocks are rare among the welter of Klamath terranes. In the Californian Klamaths, a jumbled band of Triassic and Jurassic rocks known as the Rattlesnake Creek terrane swings past Weaverville and the Marble Mountains in a 10- to 15-mile-wide swath of poorly organized geology. In Oregon, similar but more reclusive rocks south of Grants Pass are called the Applegate terrane. They appear on Buckhorn Ridge and Bolan Mountain, Little Grayback Peak, Grants Pass Peak, Oregon Caves, and Roberts Mountain. In the Klamaths, exposures of Triassic rocks are comparatively rare. The island arc systems were quiet during most of the Triassic, erupting only late in the period, about 210 million years ago. If other Triassic formations were buried in the Klamaths by faulting or were erased by erosion, no trace of them remains today.

In contrast, the Triassic is boldly present in every Blue Mountain terrane, leaving a record of volcanic eruption, subduction, and faulting. Triassic rocks appear as coral reefs and mauve sandstones in the Wallowas, jet black basalts laced with green veins and peppered with white feldspars in Hells Canyon, olive-tinted pillow lavas in the Greenhorn Mountains, crumpled phyllite (a thinly layered metamorphic rock) in the Burnt River Canyon, stately shale and sandstone in the Aldrich Mountains, and contorted blueschist near Mitchell. The reason for this richness of Triassic stones lies in the vigor and fecundity of the rejuvenated Blue Mountain island arc that grew upon the extinct Permian system.

Middle Triassic

Rebirth of the Blue Mountain island arc

The Blue Mountain arc was reincarnated about 235 million years ago. Evidence from fossils and paleomagnetic data suggest that when the volcanic system awoke, its foundation lay about 20° north of the equator, roughly adjacent to where it would eventually dock with North America. The island chain, notes Tracy Vallier, extended east–west. The subduction zone lay to the south of the line of volcanoes, hauling chunks of more tropical sediments and fauna northward to the base of the arc, then downward, to jumble them with the rocks of the upper mantle in a plate tectonic blender. Triassic plate tectonics moved rapidly, building a chain that might have rivaled the modern Aleutians in scope. Most of this arc has long since disappeared, subducted beneath North America or moved elsewhere by faulting. But we still have the remnants of at least two volcanoes, the surrounding sediments, and the ambitious subduction zone.

It is hard to recognize these Triassic volcanoes today. Rather than towering peaks, they are exposed in canyons as greenstones and altered basalts, andesites, and sedimentary rocks, smashed and faulted by the force of collision, and exhumed by the Snake River between Asotin, Washington, and Homestead, Oregon. Tracy Vallier, a geologist who devoted much of his career to mapping and unraveling Hells Canyon's daunting geology, considers these formations to be the remnants of two Mount Hood-sized volcanoes. In the late 1960s, Vallier named them the Wild Sheep Creek and Doyle Creek Formations. In the Wallowa Mountains, similar rocks are known as the Clover Creek Greenstone. The remnants of Triassic volcanoes and seafloor continue into the Seven Devils Mountains of Idaho and make brief curtain calls in the canyon of the Tucannon River of southeastern Washington.

It is these dark greenstones that give the inner gorge of Hells Canyon its ragged, foreboding terrain. Unlike the overlying and much younger basalts, these volcanic rocks have been so crumpled and altered, folded and tilted, that they have largely lost their original layering. Instead of a rhythmic layered landscape, they weather unpredictably along faults and cracks called joints, surfaces that plunge precipitously toward the Snake River. Riverbank trails are notched into these rocks, one side indented into a cliff face, the other an eye-closing, breath-holding brink.

The volcanic greenstones of this arc are part of the Wallowa terrane—the mashed remnants of the Triassic island arc. These metamorphosed rocks represent lavas that erupted 225–235 million years ago on the shambles of the old Permian arc. Once they were light-colored rhyolites, somber gray andesites, and umber basalts. Most, like arc volcanics today, were andesites. Aside from a slightly elevated content of the trace element titanium, these ancient Triassic volcanic rocks were virtually the same as modern lavas from the Aleutians, Tonga, or the Kermadec Islands.

Above: The rugged terrain of Hells Canyon
is carved from the remnants of Triassic
as well as Permian volcanic islands.

Left: Rocky Mountain bighorn sheep forage
among the sedimentary rocks of the Wild Sheep
Creek Formation along the Snake River.

Right: Idaho's Seven Devils Mountains,
on the east side of Hells Canyon,
are composed of remnants of the Triassic
volcanoes. Geologists include these rocks
in the Wallowa terrane.

The magma chambers that fed the Triassic volcanoes are exposed in the Wallowa terrane as well. At Deep Creek, just south of where Chief Joseph's band of Nez Perce made their historic crossing of the Snake River on May 31, 1877, ragged cliffs reveal dark gray rocks of the Deep Creek pluton. Dated at 231 million years in age by Nick Walker, the coarse-grained rocks of Deep Creek and nearby Wolf Creek coincide with major eruptions of the Wallowa arc. Their composition is similar to that of lavas erupted from the volcanoes (now andesites and greenstones in the lower walls of Hells Canyon). Downstream, where the Imnaha River meets the Snake, another magma chamber known as the Imnaha pluton is exposed. Dated at about 225 million years in age, it is also contemporary with the last activity in the Blue Mountain island arc. Other island arc magma chambers are distributed through Hells Canyon and the adjacent landscapes of the Wallowa terrane.

A system of Pacific islands holds much more than just volcanic rocks and magma chambers. The islands nurture atolls and offshore reefs, beaches of volcanic sand, calm bays, and deepwater shoals. The Triassic Blue Mountain arc was no different. But today, thanks to faulting and plate tectonic collisions, we have to hunt harder for the parts.

The beaches are interbedded with lava flows where sizzling andesites and basalts overran the shoreline, steaming and exploding their way into the sea. The sedimentary sandstones that once were tropical beaches now are exposed along Doyle Creek and elsewhere in the central portions of Hells Canyon. The sandstones and shales are red now, baked by the heat of basalt lava and oxidized by the steam of boiling and evaporating water. The lavas are pillowed. Instead of stately columns, they appear in ball-shaped forms where fluid rock met the cold ocean and curled like a woolly worm to ward off the sea's fatal chill. Tuffs and shards of exploding rock, lava frozen instantly to glass, are preserved here, too. In the Wallowa Mountains, the Clover Creek Greenstone tells a similar, though calmer tale: perhaps the flank of a different volcano, or a different shore of the same island.

As volcanic activity diminished, coral reefs grew. By 225 million years ago, there were abundant coral reefs offshore. Today, we find them as orphaned limestones, outposts of a former world, at Summit Point in the southeastern Wallowas, and Sacajawea Peak (9,839 feet), the highest peak in the Wallowa Mountains. In Hells Canyon, the Martin Bridge Formation, a steely gray band of limestone exposed in canyon walls and rims about 15 miles north of Homestead, contains limy sediments of similar age.

There were storms in those days. We can still see their wreckage in the slopes of Hells Canyon. The limestones of Spring Creek, about 10 miles north of Homestead and Oxbow along the Hells Canyon trail, are composed of broken shells, fragmented corals, and spiraled scraps of snails. These animals lived on the Triassic beach, the sort of community we might visit in tide pools along the Oregon coast. But the fury of a powerful storm 225 million years ago swept shells, sponges, sea urchins, and snails from the beach and left them in a tumbled heap miles offshore. They are what geologists call a storm lag deposit. The remains of these creatures, now marooned 2,000 feet above the Snake River near Spring Creek, include clams with ornate spiny shells. These are typical of warm, though not tropical, climates. Importantly, they are a mixture of American and Japanese (or Tethyan) species, suggesting that by late Triassic, 220 million years ago, the Blue Mountain arc lay not far from North America. In 15 million years it had moved many miles north to about 20° north latitude.

The coral reef at Summit Point is another eloquent representative of this Triassic sea. On the southeastern side of the Wallowas, about 30 miles from the town of Halfway, narrow gravel roads lead to a limestone ridge

at 6,700 feet in elevation. It overlooks the forests from the Wallowas to the Snake River, and the grass-covered hills south toward Huntington. A Forest Service fire lookout straddles the highest knob.

Few fire spotters realize that their lookout tower sits above a coral reef. This isolated limestone sports nine different species of reef-forming corals, four species of sponges, and untold numbers of mollusks, according to work by paleontologists George Stanley and Michael Whalen. The presence of a reef here, especially one with plenty of delicate sponges, emphasizes that Triassic waters around the Blue Mountain arc were warm and generally calm. Triassic coral colonies, worldwide, grew in bays and inlets rather than in high-energy, wave-churned environments.

Not surprisingly, there is little similarity between the fossil species and paleoecosystem of this low-energy environment and the fossils at Spring Creek, where storms and high-energy waves were more frequent. Although the rocks are the same geologic age—late Triassic—they may be as much as several million years different in age, and tens to hundreds of miles apart when they were deposited. Seas and seasons change with such time and distance, so the variation between these two limestones is hardly surprising.

The lacy outlines of fossil brachiopods in dark limestones of the Wallowa Mountains reveal the detailed structure of the animals' shells. They lived in muddy bottoms and were partly supported in the soft substrate by wings that projected from their large shells.

There is one other fascinating detail about the Summit Point reef. The many species of corals present are almost identical to fossil coral communities in the Austrian and German Alps. But, importantly, that does not mean that the Wallowas and the rocks of the European Alps were ever even remotely connected. They were not, and to assume some solid, physical connection is simply wrong.

During the Permian and Triassic, unlike the modern world, both localities were connected by water. They shared the same sea: the Tethys. East–west circulation aided the migration and distribution of species, much like the Gulf Stream today helps distribute species between North America and Europe. Coral polyps, like earlier fossil species, hitched a ride on currents, hopped from Tethyan island to Tethyan island, and spread across vast areas of the globe.

Not far from Summit Point, U.S. Forest Service Road 77 dips into the canyon of Eagle Creek. The canyon here is stacked with fragile, thinly layered shales and thicker, sturdier limestone. One of the most famous visitors to the Wallowa Mountains is buried in these rocks: an ichthyosaur named *Shastasaurus*.

Ichthyosaurs, including *Shastasaurus,* were dolphin-like marine reptiles. They were powerful and fast swimmers, well adapted for a life lived completely at sea. Paleontologists Bill Orr and Kurt Katsura note that based on analysis of body shape, "ichthyosaurs fall easily into the sustained-high-speed-cruiser class." Some species reached impressive size: 50 feet or more in length. They hunted by sight; their eyes were huge, the largest in proportion to body size of any animal known. The eyes of an adult, 8-foot-long *Shastasaurus* were about 3 inches in diameter. These animals were cousins of the dinosaurs, creatures of the Mesozoic with worldwide distribution. But unlike other reptiles, they gave birth to live young. Fossil remains of female ichthyosaurs with young still in their womb have been found at several localities worldwide. The most spectacular are from the Solenhofen Limestone in Germany where one fossil is a female in the process of giving birth. Paleontologists also have found what amounts to fossilized ichthyosaur dinners: tentacles and beaks of squidlike belemnites and ammonites as well as ichthyosaur upchuck: the remains of a shellfish dinner that evidently did not agree with the animal and was redeposited on the shallow seafloor.

The *Shastasaurus* discovered along Eagle Creek by University of Oregon geology student Kurt Katsura in 1981 probably was about 6 feet long. On the basis of the jaw and fourteen vertebrae recovered from the rocks, Bill Orr determined the genus and species. It is similar to other late Triassic ichthyosaurs found in northern California and Nevada. It remains Oregon's closest (though still distant) link to the dinosaurs.

Fossil vertebrae and jaw of a Triassic ichthyosaur, *Shastasaurus,* were found in these clay-rich limestones of the Martin Bridge Formation along Eagle Creek in the southeastern Wallowa Mountains. Fossils of *Hallobia,* small brachiopods that lived in muddy bay and ocean bottoms, are abundant here.

animals that lived in tidal zones, including some sea urchins and bryozoans, disappeared as sea level dropped.

Late Triassic to Jurassic
Plates shift

Nothing lives forever, and even volcanoes have to die. For 10 million years, during the late Triassic, from 235 million to 225 million years ago, the volcanoes of the Blue Mountain island arc erupted, building a chain of islands that rose from the sea bottom and towered more than 1,000 feet above the waves. They spewed lavas and mudflows, sequestering beaches and bays. They might have lived forever, but North America had other plans. It was time for a fledgling continent to break free of Europe and head out on its own.

In the late Triassic period, the Atlantic Ocean began to open. North America separated from Europe and northern Africa. The first vestiges of this split appeared as multiple steep-sided, flat-floored rift valleys. They may have been similar in size and shape to Kenya's Great Rift Valley and the Afar Desert in Ethiopia. Like the modern African rift, North America's first attempts at rifting stalled. Today, some of these failed Triassic basins—the Connecticut River Valley and the Newark Basin—are left for us to explore. Dinosaurs left their footprints here, in the red spring muds of a barren desert playa in the midst of a desiccated continental interior that would soon become the shoreline of a new ocean: the North Atlantic. Pushed by the irresistible force of a new, spreading seafloor, North America inched westward, easing from its berth against Africa's great paunch, moving steadily into the waters of Panthalassa at about the rate a fingernail grows.

In Panthalassa and the Tethys Sea off the new continent's western shore, plates shifted to accommodate this motion. The scene might be likened to breakup on an ice-covered Arctic sea. Larger ice flows nudge smaller ones, making them rotate, fracture, and move. In plate tectonics the motion of the larger plate (North America) slowly shouldered the smaller ones aside and likely shifted subduction zones and volcanic activity as well. A series of extinctions about 225 million years ago may be linked to this change in plate motions. Conodonts (and presumably the euconodont animal) vanished. Many

Subduction Zones
The Baker terrane

As the Atlantic Ocean began to open and the continent was shunted westward, eruptions halted in some island arc systems to the west of North America. The Blue Mountain arc's subduction zone stopped in its tracks. Today, we can find the exhumed remnants of this subduction zone along ridge crests and canyons from Baker City to Mitchell: in the Elkhorn Mountains, the Greenhorns, the Aldrich Mountains, the Strawberry Range, and protruding from low, dusky hills a mile south of downtown Hereford and at the summit of Mine Ridge south of Unity. The landscape of this Triassic subduction zone is called the Baker terrane after Baker City, where it begins. It is a vital a part of the Blue Mountain arc, and its rocks tell us a lot about the seafloor and surrounding terranes.

Where this ancient subduction zone is exposed, geologic chaos reigns. There is no sensible stratigraphy. Barn-sized chunks of island arc greenstones, Permian in age, lie adjacent to football-sized clasts of Triassic deep-sea sediments. Speckled green gabbros rest uneasily next to Devonian limestone. Rocks, huge and diminutive, poke out as angular fragments from a green, but barren, landscape. It is a tossed salad made of stones. Geologists call this kind of jumbled, stochastic landscape a mélange, French for mixture.

The rocks in the Greenhorn Mountain mélange rest in a matrix of serpentinite, a shiny green and white rock that is a cousin of jade. Serpentinite is a trademark stone of subduction zones, created when water released from the down-going slab of seafloor combines with normally dry, water-free mantle rocks. The result is called serpentinite for its luminous green, scaly appearance. The surface of these rocks is highly polished by the pressure and the constant, slow movement in subduction zones. Like the mantle rocks it is made from, serpentinite is high in magnesium but destitute of elements like potassium and sodium that nurture plants. In the Blue Mountains and in the Klamaths, zones of serpentinite (or its parent rock, peridotite) are often barren, rock-strewn slopes, bereft of trees, supporting only a meager cover of grass and a few hardy shrubs.

We might not understand that the Baker terrane's chaos was once a subduction zone except for some thinly foliated, blue-gray rocks on a ridge north of Mitchell. They are called blueschist. They carry a delicate, blue-violet mineral, glaucophane, which forms only in the unique high-pressure, low-temperature environment of a subduction zone. The rock's subtle blue color, best seen on a rainy day, reflects the presence of this mineral. Its age, 225 million years, coincides with the final eruptions of the volcanoes buried in Hells Canyon. It also matches the first opening of the North Atlantic Ocean and the death of the Baker terrane's subduction zone. Blueschist of identical age also occurs in the Klamaths' Rattlesnake Creek terrane, suggesting that the Triassic subduction zones of the Klamath and Blue Mountain arcs were contemporaries, and possibly part of the same system.

And there are tiny fossils that have helped unscramble the Baker terrane's chaos: radiolarians. These minute animals are no larger than the head of a pin. They live by the billions in ocean water, building tiny ornate shells from silica that they extract from seawater. When they die, the silica-rich shell, or test, sinks slowly to the sea bottom. Billions of these tiny shells collect on the seafloor. Partly dissolved into a gel, the radiolarian tests combine with other silica-rich minerals to form a very hard, fine-grained rock called chert.

Fortunately for us, not all radiolarian shells dissolve completely in the process of making chert. Some retain their integrity and structure. Because radiolarians, like conodonts, evolved rapidly, the forms and shapes of their shells provide a reliable guide to the period when they lived and were deposited.

Radiolarian-bearing chert is a common component of mélanges. By identifying the radiolarians and the time period they represent, micropaleontologists can date the chert clasts in mélanges. These dates, combined with dates from other fossils, especially conodonts and fusulinids, have helped demonstrate just how mixed

Top: Serpentinite is a shiny, slippery green to black rock that is abundant in subduction zone mélanges like the Baker terrane.

Above: Blueschist and limestone near Mitchell certify that the Baker terrane includes portions of the subduction zone that carried seafloor beneath the Blue Mountain island arc. These rocks are 225 million years old, the same age as similar rocks in the Klamath Mountains.

Cherts in the Baker terrane represent portions of the deep-sea floor that probably entered the subduction zone and were mixed with other rocks to create a mélange. The chert is composed of silica dissolved from the skeletons of millions of microscopic animals called radiolarians.

mélanges really are. For example, in the Greenhorn Mountains, the mélange along Vinegar Hill includes limestones of Devonian age (corals and conodonts), Pennsylvanian age (conodonts), and Permian age (fusulinids), and late Triassic chert (radiolarians.) In the Elkhorn Mountains, chert blocks range in age from Permian to late Triassic, dated by the tiny, silica-rich radiolarians dissolved from their bedrock prisons by the slow work of paleontologists' acids.

Burial of the Wallowa Volcanoes

The Izee terrane

In the late Triassic, as North America began to move, mantle currents shifted. Subduction zones and seafloor plates changed direction. As a result, faulting and deformation compressed some parts of the arc and extended or pulled apart others. The arc's supply of magma disappeared, and with it, volcanic eruptions ceased. The once active volcanoes cooled, eroded, and slowly succumbed to Pacific waves.

The volcanic obituary is inscribed in the rocks of the high Wallowa Mountains: in the banded red sandstones along Hurwal Divide, the soft gray limestones and coral reefs of Sacajawea Peak and Summit Point, and the dark fissile shales along Eagle Creek. Some of the story can be unraveled in limestones perched along Spring Creek in Hells Canyon. Farther away, the thick Triassic and Jurassic sediments of the Aldrich Mountains, west of John Day, tell more of the tale. Rain, wind, and time wore the extinct volcanoes away, covering their remnants and the surrounding seafloor with a sedimentary shroud.

Throughout the late Triassic and into the early Jurassic, from 225 million to 180 million years ago, the volcanoes of the Wallowa terrane continued to erode and subside. Sediment from their decaying peaks filled the basin of the forearc. It washed into the trench. It settled like dust in a grandmother's attic, shrouding the relics of the arc's former life. These late Triassic and early Jurassic sedimentary rocks are known as the Izee terrane.

The sediments of the Izee terrane appear in the Aldrich Mountains and the high plateau where the John Day and Crooked Rivers rise near Izee and Post. They are most readily accessible as the striped and slanted outcrops where U.S. Route 395 twists south from Canyon City toward Seneca. They poke from road cuts and peer from quarries. Soft and easily covered by vegetation, they form few outcrops in the backcountry.

The oldest rocks of the Izee terrane include conglomerates—rounded gravels carried to the sea by energetic streams. This evidence of fast-flowing rivers suggests that after the Wallowa terrane volcanoes stopped erupting, the islands remained rugged for millions of years. Eventually, the mountains wore down. The rivers were less energetic, so the Izee sediments, carried into deltas and offshore deep-sea fans from the eroded landscapes, are fine-grained sandstones or shales.

Ammonites are the largest and most telling fossils in the Izee terrane's fine, gummy seafloor sediments. With shells coiled like an oversized watch spring, ammonites were the precursors of the chambered nautilus. They looked, essentially, like a squid living in a miniature French horn. They could levitate their cumbersome shells above the gooey sea bottom and swim, using a jet of water for power, and short, slender tentacles to steer. In the Izee terrane, ammonites varied from the size of a quarter to a dinner plate. Late in the Cretaceous, ammonites would get even larger, with some the Klamath specimens (*Anisoceras*) growing to more than 3 feet in diameter.

This was a sea that harbored crocodiles as well as giant shellfish. The shattered, scattered remains of a 6-foot-long crocodilian—*Teleosaurus,* the only Jurassic crocodile in North America—were found on the Weberg Ranch near Suplee by pioneering geologist Earl Packard in 1902. Packard failed to publish his find, though he shipped the bones to the Smithsonian Institution for identification. They were rediscovered in 1978 as French paleontologist Eric Buffetaut was researching the history of crocodiles. The fragments of the Izee terrane crocodile include only teeth, a partial snout, and several vertebrae. But they are enough to identify this animal as a very lonely relative of European crocodiles that lived in marine bays and shallow-bottomed seas of France, Italy, and Switzerland. A more complete skull was found subsequently by paleontologist Dave Taylor. Although there was abundant habitat for crocodiles in North America, no middle Jurassic crocodile remains have been found in Wyoming, Montana, or the Dakotas, where Jurassic dinosaurs like *Allosaurus* stalked along the shallow inland Sundance Sea.

By 150 million years ago in the late Jurassic, North America moved closer to the volcanic islands that became the Wallowas. We begin to find evidence of a continental presence in Blue Mountain rocks. Along the Snake River in the northern part of Hells Canyon, sediments of the late Jurassic Coon Hollow Formation, a contemporary of the Izee terrane, include tiny granite pebbles that came from a nearby continental source. These subtle bits of rock are like finding North America's fingerprints. We know the continent was nearby.

In addition to telling us that North America and the islands were close together, and in fact, in the process of colliding during the late Jurassic, the Coon Hollow Formation provides a glimpse of what the late Jurassic landscape of the Blue Mountains might have been like. The sandstones, gravels, and shales of the formation were deposited in streams and lakes on the small islands that overlooked the Izee terrane's shallow seafloor.

Top: Interbedded sandstones and shales are typical of Izee terrane sedimentary rocks. Composed of eroded bits of quiescent volcanic islands, Izee terrane rocks extend from John Day south toward Paulina and are more than 2 miles thick.

Above: Ammonites are common in Izee terrane rocks as well as in some Cretaceous rocks near Mitchell and Ashland.

These rocks preserve remnants of forests and wetlands as well as shorelines and the mollusks that inhabited the beaches of the arc's terrane 150 million years ago. Ginkgo trees and conifers grew in the upland forests. Cattails, horsetail rushes, cycads, and ferns grew along bays, inlets, and lowland lakes. The climate was temperate. There were streams that deposited conglomerates, and small volcanoes that occasionally coughed up rhyolite. These small eruptions may have been the venting burps of the Jurassic granitic magma chambers we find today in the Wallowas, though there is scant evidence either to support or deny this idea.

The Izee terrane rocks also have counterparts farther to the east between Huntington and Baker City, and in the Wallowa Mountains. The shroud of sediment covered most of the Wallowa terrane where it is known as the Hurwal Formation: reddish shales and fine sandstones that crown many Wallowa Mountain peaks. North of Huntington, these rocks form knobs of white limestone and deep maroon shales along Interstate 84. Occasional beds of gypsum suggest that in the early Jurassic, these were warm-water tidal flats where seawater evaporated, leaving deposits of calcium sulfate behind. These rocks, known as the Weatherby and Jett Formations, are included in a new Blue Mountain volcanic terrane yet to come: the Olds Ferry island arc.

Left: Fall Creek tumbles over late Triassic limestones and shales of the Martin Bridge and Hurwal Formations in the Wallowas near Joseph. The finely bedded sedimentary rocks in the Wallowa Mountains, like those of the Izee terrane, are the burial shroud of Wallowa terrane volcanoes.

Above: Marine gastropods are found in the youngest Izee terrane rocks.

Right: Coon Hollow, sequestered in the northern end of Hells Canyon, contains the fossils of a Jurassic deciduous forest that grew on volcanic islands close to North America. The sedimentary rocks contain tiny granite pebbles that originated on the continent.

Birth and Death of the Last Blue Mountain Islands

The Olds Ferry terrane

There is a last generation of islands tucked beneath the eastern skirt of the Blue Mountains. After the volcanoes of the Wallowa terrane quieted, the plate on which they rode continued to move northward. As the Wallowa terrane's volcanoes ceased activity, the Blue Mountain island arc's third generation of volcanoes began to erupt about 225 million years ago. These rocks, known as the Olds Ferry terrane, are exposed where the most daunting portion of the Oregon Trail meets the Snake River at Huntington.

What caused the Wallowa terrane volcanoes to stop and a new group of volcanoes to erupt? Probably a change in subduction zones and shift in the direction of subduction, says Tracy Vallier. The chemical composition of the new lavas is subtly different than that of the Wallowa terrane. The new volcanoes had shallower magma chambers and erupted above a subduction zone that dove less precipitously into the mantle.

Today, between the older Wallowa and Baker terranes and the new volcanoes, there is a highly deformed group of rocks known as the Burnt River Schist. Along the Burnt River upstream from Durkee, the rocks have been compressed into a thinly layered rock called phyllite. Knobs of limestone poke from the more fragile phyllite. They were once part of continuous limy beds, but some monstrous tectonic force folded and disarticulated them. The Burnt River Schist consists of Triassic sediments and volcanic rocks that were likely caught in a plate tectonic vise as the subduction direction changed.

The new volcanoes erupted on top of the Baker and Wallowa terranes. They would persist for 35 million years—much longer than the Wallowa terrane volcanoes—but their exposures are less glorious, and the rocks relatively unsung. To find the Olds Ferry terrane, go south from Baker City toward Ontario along Interstate 84, or take the more leisurely, bifurcated path of old U.S. Route 30, past towering knobs of bleached white limestone and tilted beds of magenta sediments to Huntington, then turn north along the Snake River road. Along this route, and up the Snake, the youngest terrane of the Blue Mountain arc is well exposed.

The rocks along the river are the last whisper of Blue Mountain arc activity. Most of its lavas were iron-rich andesites and even darker basalts, similar to the lavas of the modern Tonga Islands. They are distinct from the andesites of the middle Triassic arc and the dacites of the Permian. Like its predecessors, the Olds Ferry arc sported volcanic breccias, mudflows, and a variety of sediments. And like its predecessors, it, too, would be extinguished. In the Jurassic, impending collision with North America would quiet its eruptions forever.

The Blue Mountain arc, including three generations of volcanoes, subduction zones, and sedimentary shrouds, is one of the longest-lived island arc complexes known. The earliest traces of lavas are rhyolites in the Grindstone terrane, at least 320 million years old. The youngest volcanic rocks, greenstones of the Olds Ferry terrane near Huntington, are Jurassic, about 190 million years old. This arc system persisted for at least 120 million years through changes in the direction and angle of subduction, and changes in the location and configuration of spreading mid-oceanic ridges. In contrast, the modern High Cascades have erupted for less than 1 million years, and the entire Cascade system has operated less than 40 million years. Humans seldom

Top right: Vertical beds of limestone and dolomite (a magnesium-rich variety of limestone) exposed along the Burnt River west of Durkee yield Triassic conodonts. These rocks are part of the Burnt River Schist, highly deformed seafloor sediments and volcanic rocks that may have been squeezed as plate motion changed in the late Triassic and early Jurassic.

Right: Contorted, folded, and squeezed, the Burnt River Schist represents rocks caught in a geologic wringer as the location and direction of subduction switched in the late Triassic.

Far right: Folded sedimentary rocks near Huntington attest to deformation and collision in the Olds Ferry terrane.

think in this timescale, especially when we consider the future. (In fact, the English language has a paucity of words that even express the concept of future.) But it is intriguing to consider whether the Cascades, an arc built on a continental margin, might eventually rival the Blue Mountain island arc in longevity. It is even more tantalizing to grasp the idea that the planet and its landscapes, animals, and plants not only have a history that spans hundreds of million of years, but a future that should last at least that long.

CHAPTER 4

Jurassic

Age of intrusions

The continental distribution we see today was conceived in the Triassic, as mantle convection and plate movements changed. But our familiar global geography was born in the Jurassic. During this time, between 208 million and 144 million years ago, the Atlantic widened from a narrow channel to a mature ocean with a vigorous, spreading mid-oceanic ridge. North America disengaged from Europe and Africa. South America moved away from Africa's belly. Although the continents were still far from their present positions, the Jurassic globe was one that we might, for the first time, recognize as our own.

During the Triassic, the Blue Mountain island arc flourished. During much of the Jurassic, its volcanoes quieted and eroded, creating thick stacks of sedimentary rocks while far beneath the surface, granite-like magmas formed. The geologic action happened in the Klamaths. Most of the Klamath terranes we see today were produced and assembled during the Jurassic period. The tale of how the Klamaths were woven into a single, amalgamated block is a complex history of eruption, expansion, and collision pieced together by many geologists, including Calvin Barnes of Texas Tech Uni-

Anthony Lake and the northern half of the Elkhorn Mountains have been carved from the Bald Mountain batholith. Composed of granitic rocks about the same age and composition as the Wallowa batholith, the Bald Mountain batholith is slightly smaller and less complex.

versity, Mary Donato, William Irwin, and Bob Coleman of the U.S. Geological Survey, and Gary Ernst of Stanford University.

Jurassic Volcanoes Erupt in the Klamath Island Arc

On the Klamath arc's eroded base of moribund Triassic volcanoes, vigorous new activity began in the early Jurassic. This activity coincided with the Olds Ferry volcanoes of the Blue Mountains and may represent an extension of the same system.

From about 212 million to 192 million years ago, a line of volcanoes erupted atop the older Devonian and Ordovician rocks on the eastern Klamath terrane (west of Mount Shasta) as well as above the Triassic Rattlesnake (California) and Applegate (Oregon) terranes. It is unclear whether these areas were part of the same Jurassic landmass or separate island systems that joined at a later time. But we do know that the Jurassic eruptions coincided with a change in North America's motion to a more northerly direction. The change in plate motion generated magmas and spawned widespread eruptions. After 192 million years ago, the volcanoes quieted. The Klamaths would maintain this volcanic tranquility for the next 20 million years.

Another, bigger, more powerful arc system appeared 170 million years ago. Its remnants are well exposed in the Oregon Klamaths, especially in the Kalmiopsis Wilderness and along the Chetco and Illinois Rivers. Known as the Rogue arc (or, in California, the Hayfork arc), the volcanic rocks surround the community of Wolf Creek and wall the dark canyon of the Rogue River. Raine Falls and Grave Creek Falls plunge over Rogue arc greenstones. The Wildcat and Tyee rapids are cut into the dark volcanic rocks and amphibolites that formed the floor of the arc. The magma chambers that once fed volcanic flows are ensconced farther west along the upper reaches of the Chetco and Illinois Rivers.

Like most volcanic rocks of the Klamaths, the Rogue arc contains gold, copper, and other ore deposits. Most of these are volcanic massive sulfides, formed in places where submarine or at least low-elevation hot springs concentrated gold and other metals, and deposited either through bacterial action or as a result of increased oxygenation of the hot water as it rose to the surface and boiled. Others deposits, like the Benton Mine 20 miles southwest of Glendale, are located where Jurassic granitic intrusions remobilized and concentrated the sulfides. Operating mainly from 1934 to 1942, the Benton Mine used a cyanide process to produce gold worth more than $500,000 from 10,000 lineal feet of shafts and tunnels as deep as 1,000 feet underground.

Granites Invade the Klamath Mountains

The Jurassic's powerful volcanoes and voluminous magma began to weld the Klamaths into a single unit. Between 165 million and 170 million years ago, faulting consolidated the Klamath terranes. We have a name for this 3-million- to 5-million-year episode of intense tectonic activity: the Siskiyou orogeny. But we do not know what the driving force was. Some geologists have suggested that the Klamath block was sideswiped by a passing microcontinent, specifically the Insular Superterrane that is now lodged in Canada. Whatever the cause of the Siskiyou event, faulting and convergence were so intense, says Calvin Barnes of Texas Tech University, that some sedimentary rocks were buried deeply enough to melt, giving rise to the granitic rocks we see today in the Grayback and Ashland plutons.

It takes a long time to melt enough sediment to make a 100-cubic-mile granitic batholith. Almost 10 million years would pass before the sediments and greenstones buried by faulting combined with mantle melts to generate—and cool into—the salt-and-pepper granitic rocks of the Ashland pluton and other plutons. The granitic batholiths of the Klamaths are between 165 million and 140 million years old, late Jurassic and early Cretaceous in age. In Oregon they form four linear belts of elongate plutons, each distinctly different in age. The Ashland pluton lies in the oldest belt; its age range is 141–164 million years, but most rocks are about 161 million years old. The Grayback batholith, located to the east of Oregon Caves National Monument, is slightly older, 156–160 million years, with most dates of 160 million. Smaller plutons to the west are somewhat younger, including the Grants Pass pluton (139 million years), Gold Hill pluton (150 million years), and Jacksonville pluton (154 million years)

Multiple ages are not unusual in large granitic intrusions. These granitic batholiths—from the Greek *bathos,* deep, and *lithos,* rock—like their cousins in northeastern Oregon and the Sierra Nevada, have a complex history. They are usually not a single intrusion. Rather, multiple episodes of melting or invasion of magma from the mantle produce a series of intrusions over several million years (sometimes tens of millions). For example, the Ashland pluton is exposed over about 150 square miles in Oregon and California. It is minimal in size to be considered a true batholith and includes two separate intrusions. The larger Wooley Creek batholith, in the Californian Klamaths, is composed of at least seven separate intrusions over more than 5 million years.

These melts are generated and rise from depths of 5–25 miles in the crust, then cool slowly 1–5 miles below the surface. How do batholiths rise into place? Geologists envision these huge bodies of viscous, molten rock either shouldering aside adjacent rocks, like the last person getting onto a crowded elevator, or simply melting and assimilating the rocks above them and rising by, in part, incorporating the surrounding geology into their fluid mass. There is ample field and geochemical evidence for both mechanisms. Emplacement methods and time vary from pluton to pluton.

Gold and other precious metals usually dissolve into molecules or occur as compounds of arsenic, selenium, or other transition metals in the hot fluids that circulate through magma chambers. As the granitic body cools, these fluids, along with quartz, are usually the last things to solidify. They invade cracks and crevices in the enveloping, now solid granite. More often, the fluids pursue joints in the surrounding country rock—cracks in the adjacent shale or greenstone that the granite pluton intruded. As these final fluids solidify, quartz crystallizes first, then gold or gold arsenides and selenides, other metals or metallic compounds, and sulfides like pyrite (fool's gold). Hence, miners look for quartz veins, the prime habitat of the mother lode.

The Klamath gold rush began in 1850 when a group of miners traveling north from the California gold fields found placer gold in Josephine Creek near the Illinois River. By 1851, rich placer deposits had been discovered near the present site of Jacksonville. Lode gold deposits generally came into production in the 1880s and 1890s.

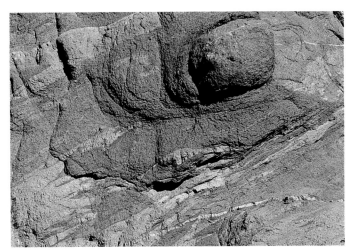

Granitic rocks of Mount Ashland show clear evidence that Klamath magmas digested surrounding sedimentary rocks. Dark clots are sedimentary xenoliths, foreign inclusions in igneous rock, that were included in the magmas.

Some of the Klamaths' most prolific lode gold deposits found in granitic plutons include the Ashland Mine in the Ashland pluton, which produced about $1.5 million in gold from 1890 to 1947, with 11,000 lineal feet of shafts that followed a twisting vein of quartz and gold ore for more than a mile underground.

The Josephine Ophiolite and the Galice Basin

Following the thrust faulting and convergence that generated many of the Klamaths' granites, there was one last flurry of extension and eruptions. About 160 million years ago (the same time that many of the granitic batholiths were generated) a small oceanic basin opened in the northwestern part of the Klamath microplate. This small, spreading seafloor lasted only a few million years before its eruptions ceased. The basin filled with silts and sands eroded from the surrounding terrain. Then about 155 million years ago, as compression telescoped the Klamath block, the entire seafloor and its sediments were thrust over older Klamath rocks of the Rogue arc.

Today, we recognize the sediments as the late Jurassic Galice Formation: fragile, metamorphosed shales, almost 10 miles in thickness, appearing along the lower Rogue River in Curry County. The Galice also includes some of the basalts, tuffs, and volcanic breccias erupted from the small and fleeting mid-oceanic ridge of the Josephine Basin.

The basal part of this seafloor now sits atop the Kalmiopsis Wilderness. Known as the Josephine ophiolite, it forms the rough, reddish brown rocks at Vulcan Lake, Red Mountain, Chetco Peak, and Josephine Mountain and the solid gray stone of Johnson Butte, north of Vulcan Lake. It is responsible for the shiny, barren serpentine along the western flanks of the Illinois River. The ocher rocks at Vulcan Lake, and throughout the southwestern Kalmiopsis Wilderness, are an iron- and magnesium-rich rock called peridotite. (The reddish brown is the result of the oxidation of the rock's iron and is strictly a surface color. Break a chunk of peridotite open, and its true color—very dark green—becomes evident.) This type of igneous rock is extremely dense. It is rarely seen on the planet's surface because it comes from the upper mantle, 5–10 miles beneath the ocean floor. These odd, tawny peridotites of the Kalmiopsis Wilderness are among the world's best examples of the rocks that form the mantle. The remnants of the seafloor—dark, intrusive gabbro and the overlying pillow basalts—are distributed along the northern and eastern fringes of the large peridotite body.

This scrap of Jurassic seafloor is an example of an ophiolite, a geologic term for a coherent chunk of seafloor that is thrust onto land, where geologists can examine it. This seafloor includes in bottom-to-top, layer-cake order: dense, iron- and magnesium-rich rocks of

Above: Layered peridotites of the Josephine ophiolite in the Kalmiopsis Wilderness once were part of the upper mantle. They were uplifted by faulting as a small oceanic basin in the middle of the Klamath microplate.

Right: Olivine-rich peridotites (dunite) of the Josephine ophiolite host deposits of chrome.

Far right: Vegetation grows sparsely on peridotites and similar rocks in the Kalmiopsis Wilderness near Vulcan Lake.

the upper mantle (peridotite); dark gray, granite-like rocks (gabbro) that represent magma chambers below the spreading ridges; and the pillow basalts that constitute most of the seafloor, including the mid-oceanic ridge itself. Wherever there is an ophiolite, it usually marks the site of a former sea that closed as two plates collided. In the Himalaya, ophiolites mark the boundary between India and Asia. In the Alps and on Cyprus, they are the remnants of the Tethys Sea, thrust into mountains as Africa moved closer to the underbelly of Europe. In England, the 450-million-year-old Lizard ophiolite was once the bottom of ancient seas (the Rheic and the Iapetus Oceans) that separated Europe and the Americas long before the modern Atlantic. In Indonesia, ophiolites mark the collisions of multiple plates, creating most or part of large islands like New Guinea. In

the Blue Mountains, the rocks of the Canyon Mountain Complex are a sort of ophiolite, though they represent island arc basement and not true ocean floor.

Ophiolites are important economically. Their peridotites contain deposits of chrome and nickel. Their seafloor basalts hold deposits of copper. On Cyprus, Java, and even Cuba, important chrome mines are associated with ophiolitic rocks. From our home-grown Josephine peridotite, mines yielded chrome worth more than $3 million between 1917 and 1960. Nickel mines at Riddle and elsewhere still extract ore from altered peridotite of the Josephine ophiolite and other peridotite bodies. In the southwestern corner of the Klamaths, the Turner-Albright deposit contains copper, gold, silver, cobalt, and zinc sequestered in basaltic rocks that once formed the floor of the Josephine Sea

above the Josephine ophiolite. The Turner-Albright ores are massive sulfide deposits, metals and sulfides concentrated by submarine hot springs similar to the black smokers of modern mid-oceanic ridges.

Gold Beach Terrane

Exotic among exotic terranes

Along the coast in Curry County, Oregon, there is a slice of California. It consists of dark, jumbled shales, buff, contorted sandstones, rosy, folded chert, and scraps of greenstones. Nothing is at peace here. This mélange of metamorphosed sedimentary rocks is known as the Otter Point Formation. Fossils prove it to be Jurassic in age. Faults suggest that much of the Otter Point Formation moved northward from California. Its rocks are part of the Gold Beach terrane, a hodge-podge of mélanges that were assembled in a forearc set-ting. The terrane is similar to rocks of the Franciscan Formation, which crops out in the coastal ranges of northern California from Eureka to San Francisco.

The Otter Point Formation has brought Oregon its only true dinosaur: a fragment of a hadrosaur, or duck-billed dinosaur. It has also provided the remnants of an ichthyosaur: a beak and teeth of *Ichthyosaurus californicus*, discovered in the mid-1960s by geologist Norman Peterson.

It is probable that the Otter Point Formation, and the entire Gold Beach terrane, was not part of the original Klamath block but was faulted northward after the Klamaths docked with North America. As such, these rocks qualify as an exotic terrane, but they are not truly part of the Klamath block. Other Jurassic and Cretaceous terranes along Oregon's southern coast, including the Sixes River and Yolla Bolly terranes, also are mélanges of uncertain heritage, and although clearly linked to accreted rocks of California, they seem to be late additions to the Klamath block.

Left: Sea stacks along the southern Oregon coast are composed of rocks from exotic terranes.

Above: Silica-rich chert forms thin bedding and tight folds at Rainbow Rock north of Brookings. This chert is part of the Otter Point Formation.

Right: Jurassic sediments of the Otter Point Formation on the Oregon coast were crumpled by submarine landslides while they were still soft, then further mashed by faulting and subduction.

Klamath Mountains Assemble and Rotate

The final piece of the Klamath terranes fell into place near the very end of the Jurassic, from 152 million to 148 million years ago. Once again, the oncoming North American plate changed its direction of motion. We know that by this time, the Blue Mountain island arc and probably the Klamath block were close to North America. Sediment washed from the continent appears in the late Jurassic Coon Hollow Formation of the Blue Mountain arc. Klamath sediments incorporated mineral grains from continental granites.

During the Triassic and Jurassic, while Klamath arc volcanoes erupted and subduction zones moved, the Klamaths were not exactly stationary. They rotated. Just as a leaf on a pond can be turned by the force of the current, the rocks of the Klamaths responded to mantle forces by rotating in a generally clockwise direction from the Permian through the late Jurassic and very early Cretaceous. Altogether, the Klamath terranes rotated more than 100° clockwise in the Triassic, and at least another 70° in the Jurassic, so the terrane as a whole rotated through nearly half a complete turn during the 100-million-year time span of the Triassic and Jurassic. And although they rotated, the Klamaths remained at generally the same latitude, moving neither north nor south of where they were in the Devonian until they docked with North America 300 million years later. At least, that is what their paleomagnetic data suggest. In contrast, the Blue Mountain island arc rotated 110° counterclockwise in the Permian and Triassic, and about 60° clockwise during the Jurassic. The errant Blue Mountain arc originated about 35° north of the equator, then moved south to about 20° north of the equator by the late Triassic, according to Tracy Vallier of the U.S. Geological Survey.

When the motion of North America changed at the end of the Jurassic, it probably applied some tectonic pressure to the Klamath block, thrusting the seafloor Josephine ophiolite over the rocks of the Rogue arc. In the Californian Klamaths, entire batholiths were shoved over adjacent sedimentary rocks. Thrust faults buried some terranes so deeply that their rocks melted. The Jacksonville, Gold Hill, and Grants Pass plutons are the solidified remains of that melt. One granitic body, the Grants Pass pluton, includes tiny zircons that are Precambrian in age, indicating that at least some sediments that melted and that were incorporated into the granite originally eroded from a continental source.

There is no firm date for the accretion of the Klamath block to North America. Paleomagnetic evidence suggests that it occurred about 135 million years ago. At that time, the Klamath block ceased to rotate independently and took up the motions of North America instead. Some researchers consider an even earlier date for accretion 150 million years ago, at the time the last major thrusts shoved the Josephine ophiolite over the Rogue arc.

The Klamaths' history of rotation and movement is very different from the Blue Mountains. While the Klamaths rotated only clockwise, the Blue Mountains spun slowly first one way, then the other. And while the Klamaths maintained the same latitude, moving not far north or south of its global position in the Permian, the Blue Mountain island arc evidently had gypsy blood, moving through at least 20° of latitude. The dates of their accretion to North America differ as well. While the Klamaths were in place about 135 million years ago, the Blue Mountains did not arrive until about 30 million years later.

Blue Mountain Granitic Intrusions
The storm before the collision

When we think of tropical islands colliding with North America, we tend to overdramatize. We envision the islands as an onrushing tsunami-like wall of rock, crushing and overwhelming everything in their path. In truth, nothing that lived on islands or the continent would have noticed the islands' stealthy approach, anymore than residents of San Francisco today notice that Los Angeles is closing on them at a centimeter or two each year and in about 12 million years will be an adjacent suburb. (This, of course, does not take the rate of urban sprawl into account, a rate that much exceeds that of plate tectonics.) The process of plate movement and accretion is agonizingly slow in human terms, and largely carried on in private.

The first stage of collision—melting Blue Mountain island arc crust—probably began about 150 million years ago in the middle Jurassic. The ages of the granitic rocks now scattered across the Blue Mountains range from 165 million to 115 million years but may be slightly younger, 145 million to 115 million, according to research by Nick Walker.

Like their contemporary and slightly older counterparts in the Klamaths, the granitic plutons of the Blue Mountains were largely generated by heat and compressive forces during collision with North America. And like the Klamath plutons, they include melted volcanic rocks and sediments of the arc. Unlike the Klamaths, however, the intrusions of the Blue Mountains do not represent separate belts of magma intruded during a sequence of deformations. Instead, the Blue Mountains' intrusions were generated during a protracted collision with the continent.

In the Blue Mountains there are two major plutons and many smaller ones. The largest is the 240-square-mile Wallowa batholith, which occupies the central high country of the Wallowa Mountains and Eagle Cap Wilderness. The second is the 175-square-mile Bald Mountain batholith, exposed in the northern half of the Elkhorn Mountains west of Baker City. Both are Jurassic in age, and both have complex histories: major

Top right: Granitic batholiths in both the Blue Mountains and the Klamaths display a complex history of intrusion and cooling. Near Moccasin Lake in the Wallowas, dark inclusions suggest that the granitic rocks assimilated nearby sedimentary rocks. The crisscrossing, light-colored dikes were one of the last phases of the batholith's activity.

Right: Oxidation and other alteration of iron-rich minerals often creates a colorful surface of pink, yellow, and magenta on weathered granitic rocks like this outcrop in the Lake Basin, Wallowa Mountains.

intrusions that constitute most of each batholith, followed by a welter of smaller intrusions in their last few million years of life. These two large batholiths of granitic rock have been mapped by Bill Taubeneck of Oregon State University.

In the Wallowa Mountains, several small, iron-rich intrusions preceded the four major sequential granitic intrusions that make up most of the Wallowa batholith, according to Taubeneck's work. The earliest intrusions are exposed in the northwestern part of the Wallowas, including Hobo and Chimney Lakes. Steamboat Lake lies in the second body to intrude. Eagle Cap and much of the Lake Basin as well as Aneroid Lake are part of the third major intrusion. And Traverse Lake, at the head of West Eagle Creek, is in the fourth and youngest major intrusive unit. At least twenty-two smaller intrusions followed. Other granitic bodies intruded into rocks along the border of the batholith; these are known as satellite intrusions and include the famous Cornucopia stock. This body of granitic rock not only has a unique aluminum-rich composition (it includes the aluminum-rich mineral cordierite, and the rock is called a cordierite trondhjemite), it also generated the largest gold deposit of the Blue Mountains. The Cornucopia Mine extracted lode gold worth more than $15 million from 1880 to its closure in 1941. The mine extends to a depth of about 3,000 feet underground and includes 36 miles of tunnels.

In the Elkhorn Mountains, the Bald Mountain batholith is equally complex. It includes nine separate intrusive bodies that vary in size and composition. The largest and one of the oldest is the granodiorite of Anthony Lake. This rock encompasses almost half the batholith, including the scenic and accessible area around the Anthony Lakes ski area. In general, the Bald Mountain batholith's intrusion into surrounding rocks of the Baker terrane was so forceful that it mashed, cooked, and recrystallized these rocks into forms that resemble ancient Precambrian gneiss.

Granitic boulders and glacial polish occupy Lake Basin, north of the Matterhorn, 9,832 feet high, in the Wallowa Mountains.

Most of the mines in the Elkhorn Mountains glean gold and other precious metals from the deformed greenstones and fine-grained sedimentary rocks adjacent to granitic intrusions. There, hot, highly acid fluids forced outward from the granitic plutons migrated through joints in the country rock. Some probably dissolved additional minerals from greenstones or sediments as they moved. As these fluids cooled far from their mother granite, they dropped gold and silver as well as sulfide minerals. These vein and lode deposits are the mainstay of many mines that were active in the Greenhorn Mountains and the Bourne district north of Sumpter. Among these, the North Pole–Columbia Mine, 11 miles northwest of Sumpter, was among the richest, producing almost $8 million in gold over its operation, 1894–1930.

Left: Rising above the Lake Basin in the Wallowa Mountains, 9,595-foot-high Eagle Cap, with Sunrise Lake in the foreground, is composed of 140-million-year-old granitic rocks of the Wallowa batholith.

Above: The heat and pressure of intrusion recrystallized and deformed the sedimentary rocks around both the Wallowa and Bald Mountain batholiths. Sacajawea Peak (9,839 feet), highest summit in the Wallowa Mountains, is mostly a sugary-textured, compressed, and metamorphosed limestone— a rock known as marble.

Other profitable Jurassic intrusions in the Blue Mountains are found at Pedro Mountain and Dixie Butte, and in the headwater canyon of the North Fork of the John Day River. Equivalent intrusions are found in the Seven Devils Mountains across the Snake River in Idaho. The storm of granitic magmas foretold the coming Cretaceous collision with North America.

North America Meets the Blue Mountain Island Arc

The record of the collision is written more clearly in Idaho's stones than Oregon's. The Permian and Triassic rocks near Riggins in westernmost Idaho were so severely crumpled, deformed, and metamorphosed that early geologists thought they were Precambrian. They have lost all semblance of the original greenstones, sandstones, and shales. Instead, they are slates and schists, thinly foliated and highly contorted. They are considered part of the Blue Mountain island arc's Wallowa terrane, severely deformed by collision in the late Jurassic and early Cretaceous, from about 130 million to 90 million years ago.

This metamorphic age dates the final accretion and suturing of the Blue Mountain arc to the continent. Using gravity data and isotopes, we can track the suture line across the modern Idaho landscape. The line that joins North America together with the Blue Mountain arc runs through New Meadows and Cambridge, Idaho. Riggins and Grangeville are part of the arc. McCall and Moscow are on the continent. Geologists Larry Snee and Karen Lund have dated the metamorphism of these Idaho rocks. Their data suggest that accretion of the Blue Mountain arc to North America— a long and time-consuming process—occurred between 118 million and 93 million years ago. By roughly 100 million years ago, the middle Cretaceous when tyrannosaurs roamed Montana and thin-winged pterosaurs ruled the skies, the Blue Mountain island arc had come home.

CHAPTER 5

Cretaceous

Mountains, rivers, and wave-swept beaches

However gingerly an island arc docks against a continent, it is not a gentle process. Rocks fold, melt, and metamorphose. Mountains rise. A new landscape emerges like Leviathan from the sea, sheds itself of water, and begins a new life.

The first lands of Oregon, the Klamaths, were in place by the early Cretaceous, about 144 million years ago. The Blue Mountains completed the first coastline by the middle Cretaceous, about 100 million years ago. The primeval, palm-fringed shoreline ran from Mitchell southwest to Medford, curving into flat-bottomed bays and broad beaches with a shallow sea offshore. Dayville and Grants Pass might have been seaports.

Fossil evidence and the presence of coarse sands and conglomerates suggest that the seas on this new coastline were often rough. Waves, unhindered now by offshore islands, pounded the new beaches with glee. The mollusks that lived along this cobbled shoreline 100 million years ago were adapted to turbulent water. *Trigonia* and *Inoceramus* grew thick shells with valves that locked together tightly. They were engineered to weather storms, floods, and anything else the new coast could conceive.

The conglomerate of Goose Rock, near the John Day River, represents the rounded gravels carried by an ancient streamthat emptied into the ocean near Mitchell about 80 million years ago.

Above: The zone of deformed rocks that mark the suture between North America and the Blue Mountain island arc follows the Salmon River near Riggins, Idaho.

Left: Rocks of the Blue Mountain island arc were squeezed and folded during the collision with north America. These outcrops near Riggins, Idaho, display contorted quartz veins that crosscut highly metamorphosed sediments.

The lowland areas extended inland perhaps 30 miles. But then the landscape leapt into mountains. Where the modern Elkhorns and Wallowas stand, and where in southern Oregon we find the Cascades, the skyline would have been a crenulated mass of newly uplifted peaks. Over time, Cretaceous sea level would rise, the climate warm, and shorelines migrate inland with the rising water. A hundred million years ago, when Oregon's land first emerged from the ocean, sea level stood about 300 feet higher than today. By the late Cretaceous, 80 million years ago, sea level would be almost 1,000 feet higher than the modern ocean, creating a large and shallow inland sea, the Sundance Sea, east of the Rocky Mountains, and driving Oregon's coast inland.

As Oregon's accreted terranes rose from the sea, the force of arc-continent collision uplifted the Bitterroot Range of Idaho and made an upthrust shambles of the accreted terranes themselves. No geologist was there to measure and record the resulting mountains. Today, whatever heights they reached are only empty sky.

The Postaccretion Landscape

Mountain ranges cannot come and go without leaving some trace of their presence. Their peaks may disappear, but geologists can trace their remains. We know where they went: downriver as rounded clasts, rolling stones, and muddy, angry waters of seasonal floods. A general rule is that the steeper the mountains and the more catastrophic the torrent, the larger the clasts in riverine sediments. We can gauge the peaks by measuring the girth of their sedimentary progeny.

To envision the first peaks of the Blue Mountains, one need only examine Goose Rock. Today, Goose Rock forms sturdy cliffs along the John Day River along Oregon Highway 19 about 20 miles northwest of Dayville. At the first, 50-mile-per-hour glance, Goose Rock looks like a drape of polka-dotted fabric. Closer scrutiny reveals that it is composed of rounded stones, some the size of fists, some of marbles, some of basketballs. In the Cretaceous, Goose Rock was a riverbed. Now it is only a stack of bedded gravels, cemented and pressed together into a rock called conglomerate.

Most of the rounded pebbles and cobbles included in the conglomerate of Goose Rock are greenstones and chert, gabbros, and granite. All were once rocks of the uplifted arc. The cobbles have been smoothed by the nimble fingers of running water. Their presence in the 80-million-year-old conglomerate tells us that only 10 million or 20 million years after accretion, the ancient arc's terranes had been thrust and crumpled into mountains. The rounded shapes of Goose Rock's clasts suggest they were transported at least 30 miles in the river's ceaseless tumbler. The newly uplifted ranges probably lie about where the Wallowa Mountains rise today, as well as where the modern Snake River carves a 5,000-foot-deep gorge through Hells Canyon.

Similar Cretaceous gravels occur near Ashland and Medford. Like the conglomerates of the Blue Mountains, these southern Oregon conglomerates and sandstones suggest fast streams and sizable peaks near the Cretaceous coast. Known as the Hornbrook Formation, these coarse-grained rocks represent a cobbled beach. The sandy bottom beyond the breakers supported clams. In muddier environments, marine animals thrived, including a tuba-sized and -shaped semispiraled ammonite, *Anisoceras*, which grew to more than 3 feet in diameter. Plant fossils suggest shoreline forests and include fragments of charcoal—possible remnants of ancient forest fires.

The conglomerate of Goose Rock, near the John Day River, represents the rounded gravels carried by an ancient stream that emptied into the ocean near Mitchell about 80 million years ago.

Top: Sandstone and conglomerate of the Hornbrook Formation east of Ashland represent Cretaceous cobbled beaches and coarse offshore sediments.

Above: Fossils in the Hornbrook Formation include carbonized wood fragments, suggesting ancient coastal forest fires.

At Goose Rock and in the Cretaceous Gable Creek conglomerate near Mitchell, an unfamiliar clast occasionally appears, light-colored and hard, with a sugary sort of texture. These clasts are quartzite: metamorphosed sandstone. Quartzite is a Precambrian rock. It does not belong to the ancient arc; it comes from the continent, from Idaho. The closest source of the quartzite found at Goose Rock and Mitchell is Precambrian rock near Elk City in north-central Idaho, the heart of the Bitterroots. And so the river, perhaps the ancestral John Day, rose in central Idaho, flowed fast and strong through steep canyons in rugged Blue Mountains, across a broad and swampy lowland plain, emptying into the sea, likely near Mitchell.

Offshore, this powerful river built a delta and a deep-sea fan. In flood, it carried gravels to the sea. Today, these sediments can be found in outcrops near downtown Mitchell. They are known as the Gable Creek conglomerate, and they rival Goose Rock for clast size and composition. But unlike Goose Rock, these are not river sediments; they are marine, the remnants of cobbled terraces and deltas that lay offshore, the sediments brought down the Goose Rock River and laid to rest at sea. Finer sediments—shales and sandstones—appear in road cuts a few miles west of Mitchell. Known as the Hudspeth Formation, they were faulted, folded, and deformed by subsequent collisions and rotation. They seem to perform acrobatics along the highway, appearing as fragile vertical beds, sharp chevron folds, and tilted layer cakes of strata. They have yielded a wealth of ammonite fossils along with remnants of a pterosaur and an ichthyosaur, and an abundance of fibrous plant debris.

The Cretaceous Hudspeth sediments extend far to the north and west beneath the cover of much younger Cenozoic volcanic rocks. At Paulina, near Oregon's geographic center, an exploratory Texaco drill hole found a thick section of middle Cretaceous, Hudspeth-like sediments buried beneath the younger volcanic rocks that form the modern landscape. These rocks bear freshwater foraminifera and represent a lake or estuary rather than the deep ocean. Beneath them are volcanic rocks of the ancient island arc systems, perhaps part of a long-buried connection between the Klamath and Blue Mountain terranes, or perhaps just the extensive subsurface reach of the ancient Blue Mountain island arc.

Geologists who hunt for hydrocarbons have repeatedly drilled through the volcanic cover and into this ancient estuary and delta, hoping to find oil. But to date, they have found none. The reasons are twofold. First, to make oil, you have to have organic material, a lot of it. Life, especially the gooey kind of mollusks, fish, and microscopic animals that easily convert to fluid oil, seems to have been largely absent from Oregon's rugged Cretaceous coastline. Second, you not only need the right stuff but the right temperature. The volcanoes that erupted on this landscape from about 50 million to 30 million years ago simply made things too hot for oil to develop or may have volatized any hydrocarbons present within the sediments. Exploratory wells drilled into the Cretaceous rocks have yielded only meager showings of natural gas.

Top: Gable Creek conglomerate, the remnants of a cobble-strewn Cretaceous beach, forms cliffs and spires near Mitchell.

Above: White cobbles of quartzite, transported from central Idaho to central Oregon by a powerful Cretaceous river, are present in the Gable Creek conglomerate.

Left: Road cuts west of Mitchell expose the sandstone and shale of the Cretaceous Hudspeth Formation. These rocks were part of an extensive marine delta and fan about 100 million years ago.

Below: Cretaceous sedimentary rocks exposed along U.S. Route 26 about 10 miles west of Mitchell were deposited in a delta or deep-sea fan when the coastline lay slightly east of today's town. These formations have yielded fragments of a Cretaceous ichthyosaur, pterosaur, and fish as well as ammonites and gastropods.

Right: The fine-grained Cretaceous rocks near Mitchell were deformed during and after their deposition.

Life in Oregon's Cretaceous

The mountains above the ancestral Blue Mountain river probably supported trees similar to those found in Coon Hollow about 40 million years earlier: pines, ginkgoes, cycads, and upland ferns. Similar forests grew to the south, near where Medford is now. Grass was still in the future. Flowering plants were a new development and perhaps the most significant change in the flora in the entire Mesozoic. They included plants familiar to us today—trees like oak, maple, and alder that would later become common as well as deciduous shrubs and common wildflowers. But there are few records of flowering plants in Oregon's scant Cretaceous record. Although flowers bloomed east of the high coastal ranges (Bitterroots and early Blue Mountains), they had only barely spread to the Pacific coast. The beaches near Mitchell sported palm trees—the genus *Attalea,* according to Bill Orr. Their seeds were found in the Cretaceous sediments north of town. Similar palms flourished in Florida, Georgia, and South Carolina. They apparently were rare on Oregon's emerging coastline.

The plants that grew in the Cretaceous mountain foothills, and along bays and beaches by the slowly rising sea, were a mostly ferny flora. Today, along Lightning Creek in the Greenhorn Mountains, the petrified remnants of a massive, thick-trunked tree fern (*Tempskya*) sometimes leak out of gravels between the old rocks of the Blue Mountain island arc and the younger volcanic rocks that overlie them. This fern grew to a height of 50 feet. Its spindly branches sprouted from a massive trunk that often exceeded 10 feet in diameter. *Tempskya* is rare in North America, and it lived only during the Cretaceous. Its petrified trunk is prized by rock hounds for its dimpled patterns and deep golden yellow color.

More importantly, *Tempskya* was (and is) venerated because it grew along the lowland channels of the ancestral John Day River. These channels carried the dunnage of uplifted mountains. And in the Cretaceous, the dunnage often included rock from newly unroofed granitic plutons, and the gold that had gathered in veins atop these intrusions. Placer miners along Lightning Creek were assured of gold whenever they unearthed Cretaceous gravels and the trunks of *Tempskya,* which grew along the ancient gold-bearing stream.

Which animals prowled the peaks, swam the rivers, or hunted along the *Tempskya*-shaded stream banks is a mystery. Few of them died in places conducive to preservation, or perhaps few were present. This seems doubly odd. The Cretaceous climate was mild, the newly emerged land offered opportunity for expansion, and on the other side of the high, rugged mountains, dinosaurs ruled.

The Cretaceous was the time of *Tyrannosaurus rex,* duck-billed hadrosaurs, and multihorned *Triceratops.* Yet despite the dominance of dinosaurs east of the Rocky Mountains, evidently there were no dinosaurs in Oregon—at least none that have been found, save a fragment of a duck-billed dinosaur exhumed in the southern Klamaths. But this duck-billed dinosaur was apparently a migrant, one of the first Californians to move north. This early immigrant, however, had geologic justification for its immigration: it originally lived in California and only moved to Oregon later in the

Cenozoic when the bedrock that held its bones was faulted many miles northward.

Why there were no dinosaurs in Oregon is a mystery. Perhaps it was the daunting heights of mountains that kept them at bay. Perhaps their lives were too busy or their numbers too few to support migration. Whatever the reason, none has been found, yet. We do have the tattered remnants of their cousins. A few fossil scraps of a Jurassic ichthyosaur have been found in coastal Curry County. And there is a Cretaceous ichthyosaur, a saucer-eyed, dolphin-shaped marine reptile similar to the Triassic ichthyosaur *Shastasaurus.* The Cretaceous animal died or was washed into a mud-bottomed bay near Mitchell about 95 million years ago. Its scant remains—two vertebrae according to University of Oregon paleontologist Bill Orr—were found in the late 1920s.

Although many Cretaceous dinosaurs (including *Tyrannosaurus rex, Diplodocus,* and *Triceratops*) and crocodile-like reptiles (*Sarcosuchus imperator,* a 40-foot-long African crocodile that preyed on dinosaurs) reached enormous size, the ichthyosaur found near Mitchell probably avoided the Cretaceous rush to bodybuilding. Unlike the Triassic *Shastasaurus,* which lived in island-dotted seas, the Cretaceous descendent braved an open Pacific Ocean bereft of sheltering islands and warm waters. Things had changed.

The other dinosaur relative native to Oregon is a pterosaur, a flying birdlike reptile that resembled a cross between a crow and a bat on steroids. Again, it is the Cretaceous sediments near Mitchell that yielded the remains of a single pterosaur: a delicate bone from the arm, and a neck vertebra. This single specimen, discovered in the late 1920s by paleontologist Earl Packard (the same scientist who found the only Jurassic crocodile in North America sunning itself in limy sediments near Suplee), is the only member of the order yet found in Oregon.

Pterosaurs sported featherless wings, a long bill or snout that often sprouted needlelike teeth, and taloned feet that grasped prey with authority. Despite their ungainly appearance, pterosaurs were fascinating experiments in both aeronautics and thermodynamics—the first experimental birds. These flying reptiles originated

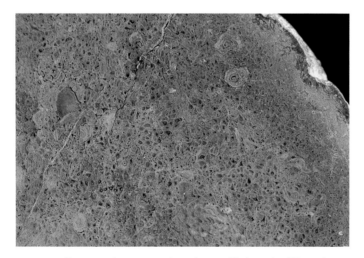

Close-up of a cross section of a petrified trunk of *Tempskya* collected near Greenhorn shows the fernlike structure of the stem and vascular system.

in the Triassic, like most dinosaurs. By the Cretaceous, pterosaurs may have become warm-blooded, according to University of California, Berkeley, evolutionary biologist Kevin Paden. Their parchment-thin wings consisted of a membrane stretched over a grotesque set of fingers and were extended only by the hyperelongated fourth finger. They had no feathers. Instead, fine hairs, less thick than the modern bat's silky coat, kept pterosaurs warm in the temperate skies above North America. Pterosaurs developed an enormous diversity in size, exceeding that of modern birds. The smallest had wingspans of less than a foot. Some, like *Quetzalcoatlus northropi,* which lived (where else?) in west Texas, grew to huge size with a wingspan of almost 40 feet and a body weight estimated at 280 pounds. Studies of their wings and flight dynamics by Sankar Chatterjee at Texas Tech University indicate that small, crow-sized pterosaurs (like the one found near Mitchell) were capable of extended flapping flight. The giant Cretaceous pterodactyls such as *Quetzalcoatlus* were excellent soarers. The gliding air speed for *Quetzalcoatlus* may have been as fast as 45 feet per second, or 30 miles per hour. Small pterosaurs, like the one whose rare remains were found near Mitchell, could easily take off from the ground, just as a crow might today. But larger pterosaurs such as the west Texas *Quetzalcoatlus* were limited in their takeoff capabilities. They could manage a running takeoff with a moderate headwind and thermal updraft. Generally, a soaring leap from a high cliff would have been far easier than a ground takeoff.

The Cretaceous climate warmed somewhat from about 120 million to 90 million years ago. Ice caps melted. Sea level rose. In the newly accreted land of Oregon, stubby palm trees grew along the Mitchell shoreline. As the sea rose, the beach moved inland. By the late Cretaceous, 90 million years ago, the Oregon shoreline probably skimmed the base of a coastal mountain range. Prairie City and perhaps Klamath Falls would likely have lain along the late Cretaceous beach. By 60 million years ago, in the early morning of a new age, this trend would reverse. For a while in the Paleocene, the seas would shrink, the planet would cool. But first, life on Earth would experience its greatest known cataclysm.

Impact
The last day

The Cretaceous ended dramatically 65 million years ago. In a breathtakingly short time, perhaps a week, perhaps a month, more than 70 percent of all species died. Dinosaurs disappeared. Ammonites vanished. Pterosaurs were gone. Any animal bigger than a breadbox was wiped from the face of the planet. The end of the Cretaceous came not with a whimper, but a bang: meteorites.

In fact, the Earth likely encountered a swarm or series of errant asteroids. At least three impact craters around the globe, including the Boltysh Crater in the Ukraine and the Silverpit Crater in the North Sea just east of the English coastline, are dated at 65 million years. Given the uncertainty range of geologic dates, multiple meteors may have hit our planet simultaneously, or the impacts may have occurred over several hundred thousand years, delivering a number of small but environmentally destructive events before a final, sudden catastrophe. We may never know the full extent of the Cretaceous impacts. Some craters, possibly huge, may have been subducted. Others may have been thrust beneath mountains. But we do have evidence of one impact with devastating consequences—the collision that created the 65-million-year-old crater at Chicxulub on the northern tip of Mexico's Yucatán Peninsula.

This was no ordinary falling star. It was a 6- to 10-mile-diameter chunk of carbon-laced rock (carbonaceous chondrite) that struck the Earth with the energy equivalent to 100 million times the eruptive fury of Mount St. Helens, a billion times the energy released by the atomic bomb dropped on Hiroshima. The evidence for this impact is now irrefutable. At Hell Creek in east-central Montana near Fort Peck Reservoir; Gubbio, Italy; Raton, New Mexico; Zumaya, Spain; and more than 100 other places around the globe where rocks of the proper age are exposed, there is a thin layer of clay. It rests like a cushion between times, marking the contact between the rocks of the Cretaceous and the new era that would follow, the Tertiary. This thin and seemingly insignificant bed of clay is known simply as the K-T boundary layer. And it is a telling witness to unimaginable tragedy. (The name Cretaceous comes for the Latin *creta,* chalk. To avoid confusion with other time periods beginning with the letter C, geologic shorthand reverts to the German *Kreide* for chalk. Hence, K refers to Cretaceous, a time when chalk deposits, including the White Cliffs of Dover, were abundant. The T stands for Tertiary, the three major time periods within the Cenozoic era: the Eocene, Oligocene, and Miocene.)

As much as a foot thick, the K-T boundary layer contains the debris of sudden impact. It is a global charnel house in which the ashes of billions of creatures may lie. It also contains the telling fingerprint of the vaporized meteorite: the element iridium. This heavy element is virtually nonexistent in the Earth's crust. Iridium is a trace element that is far more abundant in the mantle, and in meteorites.

What has, since the 1980s, become a clear and compelling understanding of impact and global catastrophe began in 1980 with the insightful detective work of geophysicist Walter Alvarez and his Nobel Prize-winning father, chemist Luis Alvarez. It has since been expanded by many scientists, and doggedly doubted by a few. What we know is the following: The K-T boundary layer contains iridium-rich dust sprinkled around the globe like cosmic holy water. There is a 65-million-year-old crater, Chicxulub, buried in the Yucatán Peninsula like a festering, 150-mile-wide thorn in Mexico's thumb. There are deposits from a tsunami wave 300 feet tall strewn across Texas, Louisiana, and the Caribbean, and charcoal from global fires ignited by the searing 2,500°F (1,400°C) shock wave. The K-T extinction of 70 percent of species globally seems as sudden as the snuffing of a candle. Almost 80 percent of the plants growing at Hell Creek, Montana, at the instant the boundary clay was deposited never reappear—anywhere.

For the survivors of the initial blast and rain of fire, the end likely was agonizing. The impact would have created thick clouds of dust, blocking light from most of Earth's surface. How long this meteoritic night lasted, and how extensive the damage to plants, is a matter of debate. Some researchers have suggested months if not years of darkness. More recently, based on new estimates of the total amount of dust produced, Kevin Pope has suggested that the overall darkness was two to three orders of magnitude *less* than needed to shut down photosynthesis, and no worse that a cloudy winter day in Portland. What did the real damage to plants, Pope suggests, was the huge quantity of sulfur and other damaging aerosols created by impact, and the dense soot from global wildfires.

Whatever blocked the sunlight, it is evident that global temperatures plummeted to below freezing. In the perpetually dim and acidic atmosphere, green plants left standing after the blast and fires withered and died. The animals that depended on them soon followed. Carnivores' prey disappeared. Scavengers would have had a gloomy heyday, a feast before the famine when millions of rotting carcasses were too far gone for sustenance. The Cretaceous extinction is often portrayed in television productions as a mercifully abrupt though wrenchingly painful event—dinosaurs blown to bits by supersonic blasts rushing outward from the impact site, drowned by tidal waves, or broiled alive by the searing heat that followed. This was undoubtedly true for animals that lived within a few thousand miles of Chicxulub. For life on the other side of the globe, and for marine animals, the end was slower.

The meteor's impact terminated most marine life in surface waters. The scalding rain of molten rock heated the sea surface to lethal temperatures. For those animals that survived the impact, death was slower and perhaps more agonizing. The impact site was rich in carbonate and in sulfur. Vaporized into the atmosphere, these elements began to form acids. Rainfall turned acidic, says University of Oregon geologist Greg Retallack—so acidic, with a pH of about 5.5, that both aquatic and terrestrial plants withered around the globe. Soils were leached of nutrients, and the top few hundred feet of the seas and oceans may have become too acid to support life. Animals that could remain in the depths survived in cold water. Fish and shellfish such as ammonites that lived close to the surface cooked. Ichthyosaurs and other marine reptiles that required air to breathe perished in a boiling, acidic sea.

Cretaceous end-time conditions were likely exacerbated by a second and much lesser cataclysm: volcanic eruption. There is, in western India, a landscape called the Deccan Traps, reminiscent of eastern Oregon's basalt-rimmed canyons. It covers more than 380,000 square miles. There is good reason for the resemblance. These basalt flows, like Oregon's Columbia River basalts, belong to the tribe of continental flood basalts: dark lavas that inundate the landscape quickly in quiet but voluminous eruptions. The lavas of Oregon are quite young, dating to about 16 million years ago, but the basalts of India are much older. They erupted from 67 million to 62.5 million years ago. They may have been erupting at the time of the K-T meteorite, and some geologists have suggested that their major outpourings were triggered by impact. The remains of dinosaurs are found in sediments interbedded with the older Deccan basalt flows but vanish above the K-T boundary layer within the Deccan basalts.

These massive basalt flows did not instigate the K-T extinction. Yet the eruption of so much lava produced huge volumes of ash, further choking off sunlight and spewing huge amounts of gas into an already toxic atmosphere. Their eruption may have been the last straw for some dwindling species, especially for the flora and fauna that lived far from ground zero at Chicxulub.

As true for all geologic history, the conditions at the end of the Cretaceous are a matter of conjecture, of educated guesses. No one was there to record it. Few dinosaurs kept diaries save for those recorded in their bones. So the yarn we weave today is little more than a boldly stated working hypothesis. It is supported by evidence; the case has gone to trial. In science, all cases are constantly on trial. A century ago the idea of a huge meteor eradicating the dinosaurs would have seemed preposterous. In the 1960s it seemed absurd. Even as late as the 1990s, many geologists resisted the idea of impact because it seemed that a one-time catastrophe did not fit with geology's time-tested principle of uniformitarianism.

Developed by James Hutton in the late 1700s and reinforced by Charles Lyell a half century later, uniformitarianism considers time and geologic process as a clock, a predictable, steady progression. Rain falls. Mountains erode. Rivers run. What happens today has happened in the past and vice versa, with comfortable predictability. The tenet of Hutton and Lyell, that the present is the key to the past, is still the foundational principle of geology. Volcanoes erupt today; volcanoes erupted in similar style a million, 2 million, 100 million, and a billion years ago.

But we have learned that in the lives of planets as well as people, there are events that transcend the everyday drip of time, the grain of sand that drops each second through a cosmic hourglass. Sometimes a force beyond our comprehension seems to turn the hourglass over and start the cosmic clock all over again. In fact, such large events are the yeomen agents of change. They are part of the planet's operating system, though not very predictable. Cataclysms are just one more facet of the way the world works. Thus paradoxically, they fit the idea of uniformitarianism perfectly.

We have no record of the K-T cataclysm in Oregon. Here, 2,500 miles from the site of impact, there is no known geologic memento from the last day of the Cretaceous: no tsunami deposit, no graveyard of shattered bones, no iridium-rich K-T boundary layer of soot-saturated clay. We can only assume that as the rest of the world seethed, withered, and died, much of Oregon's flora and fauna perished as well. Ichthyosaurs, pterosaurs, and *Tempskya* disappeared forever.

All that was left for a new beginning were animals that lived in the deep ocean, seeds of plants stored safely below the scorched, ash-mantled surface, and animals that hid from the meteoritic fury in burrows underground. On the first morning of the Cenozoic, the age of modern life, tiny mouselike mammals would emerge from their burrows, witness the devastation around them, and get on with their lives. Theirs was the kingdom to come.

CHAPTER 6

Paleocene

Mammals take center stage

Those of us who live in the Pacific Northwest know resurrection firsthand. In 1980, Mount St. Helens blasted its landscape into oblivion. We wrung our hands. We mourned. We anticipated a forever-desolate moonlike terrain mantled by taupe-gray ash, devoid of forests and their fauna. We were wrong. If we have learned nothing else from the experience, it is that terrestrial ecosystems are incredibly resilient and resourceful. Seeds sprout. Insects hatch. Squirrels emerge from burrows. Life goes on. We are a planet full of survivors.

In the centuries immediately following the Cretaceous–Tertiary devastation, planetary processes wavered. But the Earth is resilient. After an 8-million-year slowdown, subduction continued. Volcanoes erupted. The Earth breathed. And life moved on.

This period of ecological and geologic recovery is known as the Paleocene, from 65 million to 56 million years ago—nearly 9 million years of survival and biological experiment, 9 million years of learning to get along without dinosaurs. Around the globe during the next 9 million years, the neonatal Atlantic Ocean widened. North America inched westward while a new subduction zone developed off the West Coast. As Africa moved north, pushing into Europe, the Tethys Sea narrowed into the recognizable precursor of the Mediterranean, and the first traces of the modern Alps rose.

The rolling topography along the East Fork of Bridge Creek exposes a variety of Paleocene and early Eocene outcrops.

Tethyan ocean floor was shoved upward toward where Leonardo da Vinci would recognize seashells on mountaintops 50 million years later. Europe and Asia joined at the Urals. North and South America remained apart. In the Paleocene, for the first time in 4 billion years, the globe's configuration became one that we might feel comfortable with.

The Warming Climate

Throughout most of the Paleocene and even more so in the longer Eocene epoch that would follow, the global climate warmed. Although it would never approach the torrid conditions of the late Permian, the Eocene climate was mild, apparently around the globe. Greenland sported broad-leaved jungles instead of ice caps. Antarctica and Australia, joined together over the region of the South Pole, were covered with an Antarctic landscape featuring a deciduous forest of alder and oak. Between the tropics of Cancer and Capricorn, dense forests proliferated.

Part of the reason for the worldwide balmy climate was an enhanced east–west, equatorial oceanic circulation. Pacific waters could flow through the gap between North and South America (where Costa Rica, Nicaragua, and Panama are today) into the Atlantic, propagating the steamy equatorial warmth northward, mingling their memory of corals and limy bottoms with the Atlantic's cool and shallow brine. The warmth washed through the expanding sea, touching Labrador and Sweden, turning south to Brazil and Patagonia, Cape Horn, and Antarctica. Circling north, Atlantic water poured through the narrow Tethyan-Mediterranean Sea, warming again in sun-basked shallowness. From there it sluiced back into the Pacific Basin, already warm, and moved north again toward the pole, carrying mellow Mediterranean heat. In a Paleocene and Eocene world that would also be warmed somewhat by the carbon dioxide of exultant volcanoes, this oceanic heat engine ensured that life revived, thriving in a natural greenhouse.

Oregon's Paleocene World

Evidence of the Paleocene is rare in Oregon, lodged in only two locations. Near Roseburg, pillow basalts are remnants of offshore eruptions that began about 62 million years ago. They mark the inception of the Siletz River Volcanics—a mid-oceanic ridge that continued erupting for almost 15 million years, well into the Eocene, and would become Oregon's youngest accreted terrane. And in northeastern Oregon, there are the remains of a streamside forest.

At Denning Spring, south of Pendleton, thinly bedded, 60-million-year-old rocks were once the swampy, coastal floodplain of a show-moving stream. Tuff-laden shales and fine sandstones, along with dacite of unknown but possibly Paleocene age, are found nearby along the East Fork of Birch Creek. The shales and fine-grained sandstones represent an estuary or river delta. At its wettest, this Paleocene Oregon landscape resembled a Mississippi bayou. Perhaps there were alligators. Perhaps not. Evidence from elsewhere suggests there were, but for now, all we have of are the remnants of a riparian forest preserved in stone.

Sixty million years ago, the Denning Spring riparian area, according to paleontologist Ian Gordon, sported at least thirty-two different types of wetland-loving plants. Paleontologists refer to these samples as the Denning Spring flora. Six kinds of ferns covered the low ground. Horsetail rush (*Equisetum*), a plant that still persists, little changed in 400 million years, fringed shallow ponds and sluggish streams. Early versions of hydrangea, citrus trees, birch, and bald cypress shaded the ground along with alder, water elm, moonseed, and palm.

This eclectic plant community is something of an ecological puzzlement. The specimens include trees like alder and birch that produce serrated leaves. The serrated or cleft leaf is usually a sign of a temperate climate. Modern Oregon's deciduous trees, including maples, oaks, alders, and cottonwoods, sport leaves with jagged or incised edges. Trees adapted to more tropi-

Above: Paleocene sandstones and shales along the East Fork of Bridge Creek, 30 miles southeast of Pendleton, may represent the remains of a 60-million-year-old floodplain or river delta. The micas in these rocks indicate that they were deposited by a river that traversed eastern Idaho (Chapter 7).

Right: The lower beds of shales and fine sandstones of the Herren formation, found near Arbuckle Mountain about 40 miles southwest of Pendleton, may be as old as Paleocene according to Edwin Shorey. Like the rocks near Denning Spring and along the East Fork of Bridge Creek about 28 miles to the northeast, they likely represent a delta or broad floodplain.

cal, rainy habitats develop thick-skinned, smooth-edged leaves—think avocado, magnolia, cinnamon, and fig. At Denning Spring the more tropical trees included *Euodia*, a member of the citrus family, and broad, thick-leaved moonseed. Hence, the leaves that were shed 60 million years ago at Denning Spring represent both tropical and temperate environments. Perhaps the climate and geography resembled southeastern Arkansas, where today bald cypresses rise like cathedral pillars from a soggy Mississippi floodplain, oaks hold nearby ridges, and sweetbay magnolias blossom above water-lily-lined ponds.

The Fossils at Denning Spring and the East Fork of Birch Creek provide a glimpse of Oregon's Paleocene plants, but there is simply no record of Oregon's Paleocene animals. We can only assume that life here resembled life elsewhere at that time. Worldwide, mammals began to carve out ecological niches through trial, error, and opportunism. The hungry dinosaurs were gone. At the beginning of the Paleocene there were few mammals bigger than the proverbial breadbox. Over the next 8 million years, many species—many genera—would emerge, change, and then disappear. A number of bold experiments, including bison-sized, bear-furred pantodonts, prospered briefly, then failed. There was

Top left: Rocks near Denning Spring, south of Pendleton, have produced a number of Paleocene plant fossils, including early citrus trees, bald cypresses, palms, and alders. The sandstones and shales that preserved these plants are mostly composed of particles of granitic rocks—weathered and eroded from the uplifted batholiths of Idaho, the Wallowas, and the Elkhorns—as well as smaller nearby intrusions.

Left: Fossils found side by side at Denning Spring and similar Paleocene localities include both serrate leaves (left), typical of temperate climates, and smooth-edged leaves (right), characteristic of more tropical environments.

Right: Tuffs and silica-rich volcanic rocks, including these dacites along the East Fork of Bridge Creek, may represent sporadic Paleocene or early Eocene volcanic activity.

some ecological cross-dressing. Early carnivores (*Oxy-claenus*) had hooves. (Or, perhaps, early ungulates ate meat.) Mammals had never before tried to dine on one another. Until they disappeared in a puff of meteoritic smoke, dinosaurs were the principal carnivores. But now the model for predation was gone. Mammals emerged from the shadows and tried out new roles. They developed canine teeth. They experimented with new reproductive strategies. Marsupial animals, including a wide variety of opossums, proved popular. Paleocene animals tended to be low-slung; they lumbered, crept, or climbed. In the thick Paleocene forests, running was a waste of energy. Long, graceful legs led to entanglement rather than escape.

While some of the animals that lived in Paleocene forests seem awkward, verging on comical, they were well adapted to their environments. But like many animals and plants today, they faced changing habitats and weather patterns. The climate continued to warm. The seas were rising. The forest was thinning. Many could not adapt to onrushing global change or the immigration of new animals from Asia. Genera and families vanished. And like all species that fall victim to extinction, they would never return.

In the future, volcanoes would blossom in Oregon, building the continental edge farther westward. The Eocene would rank among the warmest times in Earth's history and was certainly the warmest period of the Cenozoic. Apparently, many species that lived during the temperate Paleocene survived in dwindling numbers into the Eocene. In this greenhouselike world, new mammals—ancestors of horses, cows, pigs, and dogs—would emerge, making the Eocene the dawn of life familiar to us today.

CHAPTER 7

Eocene

Oregon's first native volcanoes

In Oregon, volcanoes seem to have been absent during most of the Paleocene. But beneath the calm veneer of the Paleocene's dense forests and tranquil lakes, plate motions were changing. North America had overridden the principal Pacific coast subduction zone in the Cretaceous. In the late Paleocene, about 60 million years ago, the Pacific seafloor buckled downward, and subduction began off Oregon's coast.

The legacy of the Eocene, the epoch of time from 56 million to 34 million years ago, is as grandiose as the Paleocene heritage is sparse—an IMAX movie compared to a video. Eocene volcanic rocks sweep across the Oregon landscape from the Blue Mountains in the northeast to the Klamaths in the southwest. Eocene mudflows, or lahars, dimple hillsides in the Greenhorn Mountains and the western foothills of the Elkhorns. We find the remnants of forests and the animals that lived in them in central Oregon near the John Day River, and a muddy lake near Mitchell. And there are a beach and a deep-sea fan, now the foundation of the Coast Range. Offshore, a chain of seamounts that would

Black Butte, just west of Mitchell, is a remnant of a Clarno volcano's vent. During the Eocene, 40–50 million years ago, much of the landscape around Mitchell looked like the volcano-studded high-elevation rain forest of Central America or southern Mexico today.

one day form the base the Coast Range erupted. At the very end of the Eocene, the first of what would become the Cascade eruptions dribbled out near Ashland. When the Eocene began 56 million years ago, Oregon's coastline ran from somewhere just west of Pendleton south to Ashland. (This shore may have originally been north–south in its orientation. Much later tectonic movement shoved the Klamath block—and the remains of Eocene shorelines—farther to the west.) In the ensuing 22 million years, volcanic eruptions and sediment deposition would build Oregon's coast westward to the Willamette Valley. The Eocene was a time of major investment in Oregon's future.

Early Eocene Coal Beds and Rivers

Tucked into an obscure corner of the Blue Mountains about 20 miles south of Heppner, sandstones and coal beds mark early Eocene coastal wetlands and riparian areas. Known informally as the Herren formation, for Herren Meadow on Arbuckle Mountain, these sandstones, shales, and interlayered soft, brown coal seams are among Oregon's earliest Eocene relics. In fact, the oldest of these rocks are considered to be Paleocene in age. The lignite coal beds, at most a few feet thick, supported coal mining in the late nineteenth century. Ultimately, the mines extracted about 100 tons of lignite coal, mostly from beds a few feet in thickness.

This coal, and the surrounding sandstone and shale, say Mark Ferns and Howard Baker of the Oregon Department of Geology and Mineral Industries, was deposited in a delta, perhaps similar to the modern Mississippi. The mineral grains in the sandstones include chert as well as both white (muscovite) and dark (biotite) mica. Although the chert might have come from the older rocks of the Blue Mountains, the micas are from a far different source. The muscovite is extremely rare in Oregon rocks but abundant in granites from the continental core: eastern Idaho, Wyoming, and even a few of the older rocks of north-central Washington. The presence of this shiny, clear or white mica suggests that a large river traversed Idaho, cutting through the

low, eroded remnants of the Cretaceous Blue Mountains that were now a low-lying plain.

Clarno Volcanoes
Oregon's own native arc

Our most exquisite view of the Eocene is provided by the Clarno Formation. These largely volcanic rocks range from about 50 million to 40 million years old. They extend from northeastern Oregon to Prineville. They erupted from a chain of stratovolcanoes—mountains similar to Mount Hood—generated by the new Eocene subduction zone. Beyond just providing a record of eruptions, these volcanoes preserved evidence of ancient ecosystems in their mudflows, and of the Eocene climate in their soils.

The Clarno volcanoes, like the older volcanoes of the Blue Mountain island arc and the modern Cascades, were stratovolcanoes: individual mountains built of many layers of ash, lava, and mudflows. Rocks produced by the Clarno volcanoes are mostly dark gray andesites. Their composition resembles that of the rocks of Mount Hood, the Aleutians, and the Andes (for which andesite was named). These andesites are abundant in the rocky, juniper-clad canyons of Wheeler County, a landscape that, stretched flat, might rival Texas in size. Other Clarno andesites, their dull and dingy gray tainted a faint pink, purple, or green by hot volcanic waters, line road cuts from metropolitan Mitchell east to the summit on U.S. Route 26. They buttress Round Mountain and Lookout Mountain outside Prineville. They are found as far west as the Mutton Mountains on the Warm Springs Indian Reservation north of Madras and as far east as Unity. Generally, wherever there are Clarno andesites, Clarno mudflows and debris flows are close by. And wherever they are found, we are close to a volcano that resembled Mount Hood rising above a tropical forest.

Burnt Rock, along the John Day River, marks the vent of a small Clarno volcano.

The Clarno volcanic arc was a complex igneous system. Most eruptions built traditional stratovolcanoes. But some vents, where the new crust was under tension, spewed out mostly basalt. A few others disgorged rhyolite. The volcanic nature of the Clarno Formation is familiar to anyone who drives Route 26 through Mitchell. Pointed peaks rise 800–1,000 feet from the Mitchell valley floor like giant pyramids: Black Butte, White Butte, Marshall Butte, Bailey Butte. To some, they resemble small volcanoes, and that is exactly what they represent. However, these modern buttes are not complete volcanoes. Most are volcanic necks and plugs, the frozen conduits that once conveyed lava to the sur-

face hundreds of feet above their present summits. They reveal the guts of the Clarno volcanoes that erupted here 42–52 million years ago. Their carapace of lava, ash domes, and mudflows was eroded long ago.

You can still climb the flanks of these old volcanoes in many places across northeastern Oregon. Along the Middle Fork of the John Day River and in the alpine meadows where the Malheur and Burnt Rivers rise, knobby pinnacles poke from cobbled soils. The outcrops are a somber gray and lumpy, the lumps aligning in layers. On closer inspection, the lumps prove to be rounded volcanic rocks, often light in color. They are held in a hard, ash-rich, sandy matrix. Similar but softer

and much younger rocks are found today on the slopes of Mount St. Helens, or along the Lost Creek Nature Trail on the trail way to Ramona Falls, or up the White River on the southern flanks of Mount Hood. These deposits of rounded rock and fine ashy sand are the remnants of lahars, or volcanic debris flows. The white rocks that create the lumpy look are dacites, lightly colored lavas of volcanic summits and domes, washed down from high on the volcano by rushing water and melting snow.

The dissected throat of a nameless Clarno volcano, 43 million years old, yawns open on the western slopes of Round Mountain, 30 miles east of Prineville. Once

Left: Ash beds, lava flows, and volcanic vents of Clarno eruptive centers characterize the landscape along the John Day River about 20 miles northwest of Mitchell.

Above: Tawny ash beds and ancient soils lie beneath Clarno lava flows near Mitchell.

Above: Rainbows arch above irrigated fields
along the John Day River and Amine Peak,
a 42-million-year-old Clarno eruptive center.

Top right: Solidified Clarno debris flows
form castlelike palisades near the Hancock
Field Station. Debris flows like these often
preserve plants, and sometimes animals,
trapped near the volcano.

Right: Dikes that fed a series of Clarno
eruptions form canyon walls along
Cherry Creek northwest of Mitchell.

Rounded clasts the size of baseballs or basketballs form much of these mudflows along the Middle Fork of the John Day River near Bates.

it was a steaming and explosive vent. Today, it is merely a bizarre and barren terrain of steep rocks and precipitous cliffs. Shattered by volcanic explosions and baked by lava, this vent has eroded into a square-mile-sized kingdom of 100-foot cliffs and coagulated spires. It is a hostile place whose landscape seems to remember its eruptive ferocity.

More than 40 million years ago, volcanic debris flows rushed down the slopes of Clarno volcanoes. Like the flows of Mount St. Helens or Mount Hood, the Clarno lahars were generated when water from an erupting stratovolcano mixed with ash and rock on its flanks and poured downslope from the summit, sweeping trees, animals, and other rock with them.

Today, Clarno debris flows overlook the Hancock Field Station near the John Day Fossil Beds National Monument. Their many-spired cliffs resemble great stone temples and castle parapets. In the Eocene, these mudflows entombed trees, tiny horses, and rhino-sized titanotheres—they were not to be trifled with. To sit quietly on these rocks today is to invoke memories of hot muds and turgid waters flowing across a vine-laden, thickly forested landscape, sweeping up squat, shallow-rooted cycads, palm trees, avocados, ferns, and small horses, then logging trucks and Toutle River bridges.

The mind flips into fast forward, then to reverse, merging images, sounds, destruction, and chaos like a digital video cut. The past is present. The present is past. Time is circular. Process continues.

Ecosystems and the Clarno Landscape

The plants and animals that lived among the Clarno volcanoes endured a hazardous life, a lifestyle that we, who also dwell in the shadow of active stratovolcanoes, share with our Eocene kin. Their remains—caught in lahars, preserved in ashfalls, covered by streams, or buried in lake bottoms—provide an elegant tale of life from 52 million to about 40 million years ago. Our understanding of this time comes from fossil plants and animals, and soils. The fossils provide information about the ecosystems, and the ancient soils provide solid data about temperature and rainfall. Greg Retallack, a "soils paleontologist" at the University of Oregon who has examined the clay mineralogy of Clarno soils, has diagnosed Oregon's Eocene climate as a subtropical paradise where winter snows fell only on the volcanic summits.

What did the Clarno landscape look like? Imagine modern Costa Rica or the tangled, leafy forests on the slopes of Volcán San Martín in Veracruz, Mexico. Volcanoes emerge steaming from a chaotic web of green. Tapir root for buried seeds in red, clay-rich soils thick with decaying vines. Deer browse. Panthers prowl. Fish cruise through shallow, shaded, mud-bottomed lakes. In this subtropical climate there is no summer, no winter. Annual temperatures average 70°F (21°C), and only rarely does the thermometer dip below 50°F (10°C).

These landscapes are similar to those of Oregon's Eocene. Like modern landscapes, the Eocene forests varied with elevation, rainfall, slope, and substrate. A detailed record of the trees, vines, and animals that lived near one volcano was captured in the sediments of a stream about 44 million years ago. Today, the deposit is known as the Clarno Nut Beds. More than 170 different species of plants and 12 of animals, representing both upland and lowland habitats, have been preserved in the fine, ashy clays here. Clarno paleosols (ancient soils) preserve insect burrows, termite mounds, fecal pellets, worm burrows, and dung beetle larvae.

During the middle Eocene, notes paleobotanist Steven Manchester, the lowland forest was subtropical and vine-infested. The plants that he and others have identified among abundant specimens at the Clarno Nut Beds near the Oregon Museum of Science and Industry's Hancock Field Station include palms, magnolias, and moonseed as well as sycamore, oak, chestnut, elm, and kiwifruit. An understory of dogwood, rose, and hydrangea, with pondweed and lotus in wetter places, is also preserved. A similar though less diverse assortment of plant fossils has been found in Clarno mudflows near Granite. Early models of coffee trees, figs, cinnamon, and cashews grew in wet soils at the base of volcanoes. There were bananas in the lower-elevation forests, too. These were small bananas, about 2 inches long, with three rows of large, barrel-shaped seeds. These plants were members of the genus *Ensete*, a banana that was, obviously, native to the Americas but that grows only in Africa now.

Vegetation varied with rainfall and elevation. In the wettest and most humid forests, identified as 43–44 million years old, more than 80 inches of rain fell each year. The mean annual temperature was about 75°F (24°C). At higher elevations, where gravelly soils were common, deciduous trees dominated the forest. Sycamores, katsuras, laurels, and maples flourished. The understory consisted mostly of ferns and horsetail rushes.

Although some Clarno plants seem like holdovers from earlier ages, the animals were decidedly modern. They included several extant genera and represent many orders of animals that live among us today but were rare in North America's Paleocene landscape. The modernization of North American animals seems to have been abrupt. In less than 100,000 years, the Paleocene faunal experiments disappeared. They were supplanted by well-developed and well-adapted creatures, most of whose descendents have remained here. They included early lemurs and early horses. This switch was the most dramatic biotic change since dinosaur extinction, notes Gabriel Bowen and other scientists at the University of

Top: Eastern Oregon's subtropical Eocene landscape included both mountains and lowland forests. Palm trees, magnolias, figs, grapes, sycamores, horsetail rushes, and cycads grew. Crocodiles lurked in lowland basins while *Orohippus,* an early, three-toed, dog-sized horse, browsed on vines and shrubs. Larger animals included rhino-sized brontotheres and a large, catlike predator, *Patriofelis.* Painting by Doris Tischler from the John Day Fossil Beds National Monument.

Above: The smooth edges of Eocene leaves could shed water quickly and are one piece of evidence for a warm, wet Eocene climate.

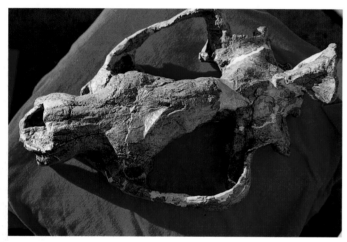

Top: An Eocene fig, preserved in the Clarno Nut Beds near the Hancock Field Station, is not very different from today's version.

Above: The skull of *Patriofelis* found in the John Day Fossil Beds is about 18 inches long. This animal was a type of creodont rather than a true cat.

Right: The deep red soils beneath the Eocene rain forest are preserved in the northwestern part of the Painted Hills in the John Day Fossil Beds National Monument at The Brown Grotto. Lighter-colored soils above record the cooling and drying climate of the late Eocene and early Oligocene.

California, Santa Cruz. It was partly due to rapid migration of animals from Asia to North America across tectonically crafted land links between Siberia and the newly accreted terranes of Alaska. The migrations were spurred, notes Bowen, by climate change—rapid warming as the Eocene began.

On a larger and more palpable scale, the animals found in the floodplain deposits of the Clarno Nut Beds included large tortoises that browsed on lowland ferns. There were buffalo-sized titanotheres as well as small, fleet-footed rhinos about the size of a modern mule deer. Early horses were about the size of a Labrador retriever.

With this variety of herbivores, it is no surprise that something was around to eat them. There were land-dwelling crocodiles capable of running. A superpredator lurked in Oregon forests: *Patriofelis*. A low-slung, heavy-bodied, tiger-sized, catlike animal, *Patriofelis* probably relied on ambush to make its kills. Not a true cat, *Patriofelis* was a creodont, an animal unrelated to modern cats though its body type and design slightly resemble today's large felines. An adult *Patriofelis* may have weighed 250 pounds and likely was equal in predatory merit to the modern tiger.

The first horses in the Oregon landscape, *Orohippus*, browsed in the Eocene Clarno forest. But we would not immediately recognize it as a horse. If *Orohippus* scampered across our lawn, we might think that we had glimpsed a stray Labrador retriever. Two feet high (6 hands) at the shoulder, with slender legs, four toes on the back feet and three on the front, *Orohippus*, like most early horses, was a forest-dweller. Its teeth were designed to mash stout ferns and the succulent leaves of shrubs. Likely, the horses lived alone or in pairs, a lifestyle suited to the dense forest. Wild horses would not gather in herds until the Miocene, when forests receded, grass-covered savannas and plains dominated the North American landscape, and equine teeth had adapted to cutting and chewing the tough stems of grasses.

The animals whose remains lie in the Clarno Nut Beds and in other Clarno deposits are among the first that are truly Oregon's own. In contrast, the ancient landscapes of the Paleozoic and Mesozoic Klamath and

Blue Mountain islands are curiously inanimate. We have no fossils of land-dwelling, air-breathing animals. There is no record of terrestrial vertebrates (or invertebrates) from the land that would be Oregon in the 300-million-year span from the Devonian to Paleocene, though fauna ranging from dragonflies to dinosaurs plodded, ran, scurried, and flew elsewhere in North America and around the globe. In all of Oregon's previous history, the only land-dweller is a Cretaceous pterosaur (in addition to the immigrant Californian hadrosaur), and from the single specimen we have only a fragment of arm bone and a single vertebra. Like an albatross or frigate bird, the pterosaur's stay may have been fleeting.

But in the Eocene, Oregon had warm, fuzzy, and sometimes ferocious land animals that are distinctly North American. They ranged across what would be the United States. *Patriofelis* hunted in a verdant Nevada. *Orohippus* browsed in northern Florida. Brontotheres lumbered across Wyoming. So they were not Oregon's sole property, our exclusive Eocene zoo. They are the first solid ties to the rest of North America, and in fact, to the rest of the globe, for similar fauna ranged across Japan, China, and Siberia and may have spread to North America across an ancient land bridge. Oregon's landscapes would be isolated no longer.

That is true not only of mammals and reptiles but of fish as well. Stranded just below Ochoco Summit there are the remains of a lake. Our cars slalom through a steep-sided gouge that exposes sternly striped outcrops at about milepost 53 on U.S. Route 26 from Prineville en route to Mitchell. The thick stack of black shale and fragile gray sandstone contain wood chips and leaf fragments. The darkest layers sequester the scales, skulls, and vertebrae of bowfin, catfish, and suckers. These same fish occupied contemporary Wyoming lakes and,

Top and far left: Thinly bedded sandstones and shales of an Eocene lake bed, yielding catfish, bowfin, and plant fossils, are exposed in road cuts near milepost 53, 3 miles east of Ochoco Pass on U.S. Route 26.

Left: Eocene leaf from shale near Ochoco Pass.

in fact, freshwater bodies and slow-running streams across western North America. So even in the lakes and streams, by the middle of the Eocene, Oregon was indisputably part of the continent.

The middle Eocene coastline ran south to Roseburg. There, it swung north and then west around the massive block of older rocks in the Klamaths. The apparent and pronounced southwest–northeast alignment of the Eocene coastline is mostly the result of later tectonic rotation of Oregon's coast. The original coast more likely ran north–south, much like today's. Regardless of the coast's exact orientation, we do know that the southern Willamette Valley was a deep bay, and it would remain so for the next 25 million years. Today, southern Willamette Valley towns like Eugene, Springfield, Harrisburg, Brownsville, and Albany sit atop a mile or more of soft sedimentary rocks deposited in this Willamette Bay. Oil companies and optimistic prospectors have drilled for oil or natural gas here for years—all to no avail except for a single and profitable reservoir of natural gas in the modern Coast Range at Mist. The natural gas at Mist occurs in the Keasey Formation. It is the product of decaying leafy vegetation and decomposed clams, crinoids, and snails, all of whom gave their lives so we might one day heat our homes, cook their descendents, and unwittingly warm the climate back to Eocene levels.

To create the complex hydrocarbons in oil and natural gas, there must be an abundance of building blocks: organic molecules from decaying plants and dead animals. This organic material must be heated to the right temperatures ($300–480°F$, $150–250°C$) for the right amount of time (a million years or more) at the right pressures (burial of no more than 4 miles). And there must be structures that trap and concentrate the resulting hydrocarbons: anticlinal folds that bulge upward to collect the rising oil or gas, with impenetrable caprocks to hold the petroleum in reservoirs below the surface. Some of the prerequisites for economic deposits are lacking in the sedimentary rocks deep beneath the Willamette Valley. There is neither enough heat nor enough organic matter to cook the rare remains of life into petrochemicals we might deem useful.

97

Eocene Coastline and the Klamath Mountains

Throughout the Eocene, the Klamaths were a rugged highland. There were no Eocene volcanoes here. Instead, streams dutifully eroded the landscape, carrying sediment to the sea. The coastline lay just north of the Klamaths, and rivers built thick accumulations of sandstone offshore. Today, these constitute the Empire Formation and other sandstones exposed near Coos Bay and Cape Arago. At Riverton, south of Coos Bay, there are remnants of coastal Eocene forest ensconced as coal beds. The forest included figs and palms at lower elevations and deciduous trees, including laurel and walnut, inland at higher elevations on drier sites. Clams, oysters, and marine snails lived in the estuarine sands. Long-legged auklike birds (*Hydrotherikornis oregonus*) patrolled the coastline while a flightless pelican (*Phocavis maritimus*) swam and dove for fish offshore.

Sediments from the erupting volcanoes and eroding remnants of the Blue Mountain island arc coursed down an ancestral Columbia River system, building a 2-mile-thick delta at its mouth. Today, those sediments form the low foothills of the Coast Range around Vernonia and Keasey. Clams, some more than a foot long,

gastropods (snails), and even crinoids (starfish relatives with elongate arms atop a long single stalk attached to the seafloor) are found in the sediments of the Keasey Formation. The waters here were about 2,000 feet deep, and at a temperature of about 45°F (7°C), relatively warm compared to those of the modern Pacific Northwest. Farther south, in the Eola Hills southwest of Salem and in the coastal foothills at Dallas, there are Eocene limestones composed of untold billions of miniature clamlike crustaceans that are called ostracods. These quiet, lime-rich reefs once harbored crabs and fish. Today, they nurture vineyards for some of Oregon's best Pinot Noir.

Left: Wave action has eroded the Eocene sandstones of the Coaledo Formation at Shore Acres State Park near Coos Bay into spectacular patterns.

Above: The coarse bedding of Eocene coastal sandstones suggests they were deposited close to shore. The dark, round, cannonball-sized concretions result from local concentrations of iron and calcium that collected and cemented portions of the rock into a harder, rounded, ball-like shape.

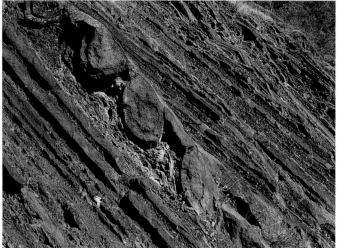

Above: Turbidite sandstones at Marys Peak southwest of Corvallis. Sediment eroded from the Klamath Mountains now makes up the foundation of Oregon's Coast Range and the Willamette Valley. These rocks (Tyee, Flournoy, and Lookingglass Formations) were deposited as a deep-sea fan in the ocean north of the Klamath uplift. Although they have been explored for oil and natural gas, most of these rocks have as yet proven of little economic value.

Left: Load casts in Tyee Sandstone along the Rogue River. These structures develop where soft, clay-rich sediment is pressed down as heavier sands are deposited above them.

By the Eocene, the accreted exotic terranes of the Klamaths were mountains in their own right. Faulting had lifted their granitic rocks, greenstones, sandstones, and limestones into a hilly landscape. With uplift comes erosion. The rain and streams and rivers that washed the Eocene Klamath Mountains carried tiny pieces of them—eroded sands and silts—back to the sea. Thicker beds of sediment accumulated in the embayment north of the Klamaths. Today, this massive fan of sands and siltstones extends the length of the Coast Range. Known as the Tyee and Flournoy Formations, the sands are tiny fragments of the old Klamath terranes and granites. Each sand grain of the Tyee Formation carries the heritage of its parent rock. Tiny, rounded fragments of feldspar can be traced to a precise granite intrusion. This grain came from Ashland. That one from the Grayback pluton that rises south of Cave Junction. The sediments include turbidites, layers of sediment initially deposited quickly and unstably at the top of a submarine fan and later shaken loose by an earthquake or other disturbance and redeposited. The hundreds of turbidites in the Tyee Formation suggest an active and quake-prone shore.

Seamounts and the Siletz River Volcanics

Oregon's last exotic terrane

There was good reason for seismic activity. Not only was subduction necessary to feed the active Clarno volcanoes, an extensive line of submarine volcanoes and seamounts lay offshore. And westward-moving North America was closing in on them. In another 10 million years, in the late Eocene, North America would collide with these seamounts. This was North America's last major collision, and its last major land acquisition. By the end of the Eocene, 34 million years ago, the seamount chain was being uplifted to form the Coast Range. Today, the basalts and interbedded sediments of Paleocene and Eocene seamounts occur on Marys Peak (4,097 feet), the highest summit in the Coast Range. They form the dark basalts along the Umpqua River at Roseburg and the Siletz River northwest of Philomath.

Top: Pillow basalt on Marys Peak in the Coast Range southwest of Corvallis is a component of the chain of Paleocene and Eocene seamounts that collided with Oregon between 40 million and 30 million years ago, building the coastline to its present position. The glassy rims and radial fractures are diagnostic of these quickly chilled, submarine lavas.

Above: The lumpy basalts of Waverly Heights southeast of Portland near Milwaukie rank as the easternmost exposure of the Eocene seamount exotic terrane.

They appear on Tillamook Head. They crop out on Waverly Heights west of Milwaukie and underlie most of Tryon Creek State Park near Lake Oswego. They occur in Washington as the rocks of the Willapa Hills and the Crescent Formation along the western shore of Hood Canal.

If a basalt is found on a mountaintop, or in a road cut on Interstate 5, or along the banks of the Columbia River, how can we tell it originally erupted underwater? It's simple. We look for a certain amount of marine sediment—sandstones and shales—interbedded between flows. And we look for pillows. These are not the kind of pillow you would sleep on. Basalt pillows are the rounded result of hot lava erupting into cold water and chilling to glassy stone, like hot sugar syrup congealing into balls when dropped into cool water. As lava erupts into the sea, the water chills the outermost part of the flow into glass almost instantly. The result is a rounded tube that serves as a conduit for more lava. But seawater is a powerful coolant; the lava in these tubes finally solidifies and stops flowing altogether. The lava's advance underwater resembles Medusa's hair: a lot of small round tubes wrapping over and past one another.

Millions of years later, when a road is cut through these now-solid lava conduits, we see them in cross section. The cross sections are round; they are often a foot or two in diameter, about pillow-sized. Each pillow has a glassy rim and radial cracks, or joints. Their centers may be almost hollow or filled with secondary minerals. Often, there is sand or sediment or a yellow, clay-rich basaltic ash called palagonite between pillows.

Oregon's climate in the early and middle Eocene was subtropical (or, more technically, paratropical) by all methods of measurement. The fossil record of western North American plants suggests that the climate fluctuated during the latter part of the Eocene. By 40 million years ago, average annual temperatures had dropped to about 60°F (16°C). By 38 million years ago, temperatures had risen to about 70°F (21°C). The soils and fossil plants of the Clarno Formation provide evidence of these fluctuations. They also suggest that during the Eocene, temperatures never plunged below freezing.

There was no winter in Mitchell in those days, no skiing at Spout Springs or Anthony Lakes, though in winter, volcanic summits may have sported snow. In the late Eocene, the climate would begin to change more drastically, driven by the changing positions of continents and changing patterns of oceanic circulation. Perhaps the most significant event was the opening of the Norwegian Sea between Greenland and Norway. Cooler Arctic waters flowed into the Atlantic, and the circulation of bottom waters shifted. Slowly, Oregon became a little drier and a little colder. The animals and plants that had thrived in subtropical conditions began to disappear, to change, and to adapt.

Last Days of the Eocene
Clarno, Cascades, and catastrophe

Not far from the Clarno Nut Beds, where middle Eocene plants and animals are preserved, there is another Eocene graveyard. It is somewhat younger than the 44-million-year-old nut beds. Known as the Mammal Quarry, it reveals a slightly different life amid quiescent volcanoes 39 million years ago. The plants of this time were subtropical but adapted to cooler average annual temperatures of 60–65°F (16–18°C). Dogwoods, sycamores, cashews, and moonseeds are present. Palms are gone. There are fewer vines. The animals include crocodiles. Modern crocodiles cannot survive freezing temperatures, so the cooling climate had not yet experienced a first frost. *Patriofelis* has been replaced by a new model: a large, saber-toothed, more catlike predator called a nimravid. Another large creodont, the bearlike predator *Hemipsalodon grandis,* has appeared on the scene. There are titanotheres and tapir as well as rhino-like brontotheres and entelodonts, early versions of wild pigs on steroids. Two different genera of horses browse in the forest: *Epihippus* and *Haplohippus.* The proliferation of equines, similar to the proliferation of modern antelope species in modern Africa, with many niches to fill and many species to fill them, will accelerate in the middle Miocene.

As the erupting Clarno volcanoes built central and eastern Oregon's landscapes, other volcanoes pioneered the coast. As the Eocene faded and the Oligocene dawned, 34–35 million years ago, coastal volcanoes that were actually the early Cascades erupted near Scotts Mills, Stayton, and Molalla. Somewhere south of Ashland, a small volcano, precursor to the much more extensive Oligocene Cascades that would follow, disgorged ash, lava, and steam into shallow lakes and thick, moist forests. This buried wood today forms thin, supple coal deposits in what is called the Colestin Formation. These first proper patriarchs of the Cascades would reach their full size and strength in the Oligocene and, like the modern Cascades, were unquestionably generated above a subduction zone.

By the end of the Eocene, 34 million years ago, Oregon's climate had cooled to nearly temperate conditions. Animals and plants adapted to tropical habitats had either gradually moved away or slowly died out. The subduction zone that produced the Clarno volcanoes had stopped, probably choking on the chain of seamounts that were now Oregon's new Coast Range. The tall volcanic peaks that shed mudflows and lava into the Mitchell Basin, Prineville, and Clarno quieted. They erupted occasional ash, and little else. In place of the Clarno volcanoes, the earliest Cascades erupted. Only one more event, all too familiar, was needed to chill the Earth a bit more and flip the climate in Oregon to truly temperate: meteoritic impact.

Buried 1,000 feet beneath Chesapeake Bay about 125 miles southeast of Washington, D.C., there is a circular structure about 50 miles wide and ½ mile deep. It is a crater, 35 million years old. A second, slightly larger crater of the same age is located in Siberia. Those who fancy cataclysm as a principal agent of change believe that the two strikes, at almost the same geologic instant, produced dust that blocked the sun for months and cooled the climate below the threshold of recovery. Snow settled permanently on Antarctica for the first time. Plants died. At the portal to the Oligocene, about 35 percent of all marine life died. This extinction pales in comparison with the Permian and Cretaceous extinction events. But it was very significant to the animals who disappeared and those who filled new niches in the coming age. Whatever the cause of the Eocene–Oligocene extinction, the geologic clock was reset in a big way. Oregon was at last approaching modern times.

The columned pinnacle of Pilot Rock as well as andesites and layers of tuff near Ashland are part of the Colestin Formation, the oldest rocks of the Cascades, erupting about 35 million years ago at the end of the Eocene and the beginning of the Oligocene.

CHAPTER 8

Oligocene

A familiar landscape takes form

It seems a shame that we cannot visit the Oligocene, a pity that we cannot charter a plane to take us there, or step off a schooner onto its shores. Its landscapes would be familiar, its trees like old acquaintances. The coastline would lie close to where it is now, albeit without a rocky reach of sea stacks to catch and hold the sinking sun. The huge bay that covered the Willamette Valley would provide a sunset vista more like Seattle's than Oregon's modern coast. The Cascades erupted, though their closer proximity to the coastline might seem odd. The Oligocene is so near to us in time, beginning 34 million years ago and ending a mere 24 million years ago, that it taunts us—so nearly tangible, yet visible only as a mindscape, a dream world woven of scientific fact and inspired fancy. If we could just move a little faster, reach a little farther, we might snatch it for a moment.

In contrast to the Eocene's tropical symphony, the Oligocene played jazz. Its climate was more varied, its life-forms more bold. The Oligocene kept a diary of sorts in the ancient soils now preserved as the Painted Hills and Blue Basin of the John Day Fossil Beds. In these layers of antiquated earth, the transition from Eocene to Oligocene is clear—the deep red clays of the Eocene

Painted Hills in the John Day Fossil Beds
National Monument. These Oligocene soils
record the drying and cooling climate
as well as changes in the vegetation.

change abruptly to Oligocene pastel. The Eocene–Oligocene boundary, says University of Oregon geologist Greg Retallack, records "an abrupt paleoclimatic and paleofloristic dislocation." Radiometric dates from soil horizons and estimates of the time required for drier soils to form indicate that the switch from tropical to temperate savanna took less than a few hundred thousand years, he says.

The Cooling Climate

About 33.5 million years ago, the Earth's tropical climate changed significantly. It grew cooler and slightly drier. Humidity in the forested landscape of the Oligocene John Day Fossil Beds averaged about 80 percent, in contrast to the oppressively tropical 90 percent of the Eocene. Geologists once thought that the change in Oregon's forests, plants, soils, and animals was related to the eruption of the Cascades—the rise of the mountains—and the consequent rain shadow. Precipitation, they hypothesized, was captured on the west-facing slopes of the nascent Cascades, leaving the eastern side drier.

But now it is evident, says Retallack, that the transition to a drier, temperate Oligocene climate was global. He has linked the worldwide climate change to change in vegetative types. Grasses became more dominant. Plates shifted, changing oceanic circulation patterns. Although Oregon's shift to a drier eastern side is partly linked to the Cascades' rain shadow, it was also driven by global change.

Some geologists link the advent of global cooling to the impact at Chesapeake Bay 35 million years ago, near the Oligocene's beginning. Centered at the southern tip of the Delmarva Peninsula, the Chesapeake crater measures about 50 miles in diameter. The impact, says U.S. Geological Survey geologist C. Wylie Poag, shattered bedrock to a depth of 5 miles and threw enough dust into the stratosphere to mute the sun. It is likely that several other bolides struck the Earth at almost the same time, including one in Siberia. The consequences were widespread forest fires that left a layer of charcoal in formations near the Chesapeake Bay, obscuring the sun and accelerating the global cooling that was already under way.

Whatever the cause of the global cooling, tropical vegetation that had covered virtually all of North and South America retreated to the equator early in the Oligocene. Middle latitudes, Oregon included, became temperate and seasonal. For the first time, snow and ice collected at the poles and stayed there. Polar ice would never completely melt until, perhaps, the global warming we are experiencing now.

Near the South Pole, almost 2½ miles beneath the surface of the Antarctic ice, there is what some scientists regard as an early Oligocene lake. It is Lake Vostok, a body of fresh, liquid water 140 miles long and 30 miles wide, about the size of Lake Ontario, buried completely beneath the ice. Vostok, in fact, is one of the fifteen largest lakes in the world. But Vostok is more than just a buried lake; it is likely the remnant of a 30-million-year-old lake that froze over on a cold night in the Oligocene and never thawed again. Some scientists have suggested that Vostok may still hold viable Oligocene life-forms: diatoms, algae, and other small plants and animals. (The alternative hypothesis is that Vostok was created by ancient snow and ice melting in a newly developing volcanic rift zone.) At the very least, bacteria, viruses, and other life have been imprisoned under 2 miles of ice since the early Pleistocene almost 2 million years ago, and very likely for at least the last 20 million years, growing and evolving in the cold, chill darkness of a totally isolated world.

Oregon's Oligocene remnants are not as viable as Lake Vostok's possible relict fauna may be, but here, the Oligocene is more accessible.

John Day Fossil Beds
The Oligocene's Eden

In Oregon's Oligocene 33 million years ago, the landscape resembled today's open-canopy, mixed conifer and deciduous forests near Oaxaca, Mexico, says Steven Manchester, a paleobotanist who has chronicled Oregon's early plant communities. There were recognizable seasons. The average temperature was about 50°F (10°C).

Rainfall totaled 25–30 inches a year. Fossil wood from Oregon shows strongly developed annual growth rings, similar to the cross-sectional rings in trees of temperate forests worldwide, where bands of summer wood are light and wide, and those of winter wood dark and dense.

One of the best, most accessible places to find the beginning of Oregon's Oligocene today is in the Painted Hills northwest of Mitchell. This improbable, striped landscape is a geological library. It houses a record of eastern Oregon's Oligocene forests and floodplains,

Red bands in the Painted Hills record soils that developed in wetter Oligocene climates, and yellow bands, under drier conditions. Black dots and streaks are manganese nodules that may have been created by manganese-fixing plants.

creatures and climate. Like the leaves of a book, each layer reveals a tale of temperature, humidity, soil acidity, and organic material, together with the forest plants and their root structure, and the burrows of mice, ground squirrels, gophers, and rabbit.

Most of the red and yellow bands in the Painted Hills, and similar but less accessible formations 40 miles northwest near the Hancock Field Station and in the John Day Fossil Beds National Monument, represent individual soil layers. The raw material for the paleosols (or ancient soils) of the Painted Hills was the weathered detritus of Clarno volcanoes, or later, volcanic ash from the Cascades. As the Cascades grew during the Oligocene, they hurled enormous quantities of ash into the sky. This ash was transported east by prevailing winds. It fell into the John Day Basin, accumulating considerable thickness. With time, rain, and plant activity, ash was transformed into soil. Each soil layer took between 10,000 and 200,000 years to develop before its ecosystem was temporarily snuffed out by an ash-rich volcanic eruption or a change in climate, according to Greg Retallack.

The earliest soils of the Painted Hills are late Eocene in age, about 39 million years old. They form the striped hills found in the Brown Grotto about ¼ mile west of the popular overlook point. They are deep red-brown and bear vestiges of long development in a tropical climate—perhaps as long as 1 million years for each soil horizon. Later soils, developed in the early Oligocene as the climate became drier and more temperate, are yellow, though a few reddish layers are interbedded. A geologically brief period of warmer climate in the early Oligocene is marked by a return to red colors in about 30 feet of Painted Hills paleosols that were mapped by Ted Fremd, Erick Bestland, and Greg Retallack. Oligocene soils, developed as the climate stabilized during drier conditions, harbor faint hexagonal patterns, evidence of mud cracks crafted about 30 million years ago when a lowland basin was flooded by early spring storms, then parched under blistering summer sunlight.

Small lakes and rolling hills occupied this landscape. Where the Painted Hills stand today, wetlands and even small lakes developed, persisted, and finally vanished as stream courses changed through time and the climate dried. Throughout most of the 4 million years represented by Painted Hills soils, the area was wooded or marshy. But it was not an old-growth forest, says Retallack. Walnut trees, horse chestnuts, pecans, cashews, and laurels were common. Sycamores, basswoods, oaks, elms, and beeches occupied high, dry, open woodlands. Shrubs included sumac, serviceberry, hawthorn, raspberry, and Oregon grape as well as a variety of wild-rose-like plants. There was even poison oak! Insects, including leaf miners, nibbled on the foliage and munched scribbling paths across the leaves. Oregon grape, rose, and hawthorn, along with a variety of smaller shrubs formed the understory. The charred wood found in early Oligocene soils is a vestige of forest fires that torched the dry summer savanna. Where fire or flood disturbed the ecosystem, alder trees took root, just as they do today.

Oligocene Plants

In the drying climate of Oregon's Oligocene, conifers were far less abundant than deciduous trees. Conifers grew best in moist lowlands like the Painted Hills marshes. This was the age of the dawn redwood, *Metasequoia occidentalis,* whose closely related cousin *M. glyptostroboides* is still living. The modern trees grow to 150 feet tall and 6–8 feet in diameter in the easternmost part of central China's Sichuan province. Oligocene *Metasequoia* needles, cones, and pollen are abundant throughout Oregon's fossil record.

Twenty-five million years ago, *Metasequoia* trees were somewhat smaller than their modern descendants. *Metasequoia* is, and likely was, deciduous. Its short needles turn golden in the fall and are shed entirely in winter, much like the tamarack or western larch that grows in eastern Oregon today. Then, as now, dawn redwood grew in riparian areas and valley bottoms, often at the base of steep slopes. Its presence indicates lakes or streams. Horsetail rushes, hydrangeas, cattails, early grasses, sumacs, and birches prospered along with a few alder and walnut trees in environments that Greg Retallack has termed a "swampy, permanently water-logged floodplain."

The fossil remnants of similar forests occur between Prineville and Madras at Gray Butte. Some plant assemblages represent wetlands. Others are upland forests that grew on volcanic slopes. Dated at about 31 million years in age, the plants preserved in volcanic ash deposits at Sumner Spring include abundant conifers. The forest here included pine, spruce, and true *Sequoia* (not *Metasequoia*). Walnuts, maples, and sycamores also grew. The oak trees were live oaks, evergreen trees that prosper in California-like climates where there is little seasonal variation in temperature and the winters are mild.

Grass First Appears

If the Oligocene has one claim to evolutionary fame, it is the development of grass. Before 30 million years ago, grass was rare and there were no grasslands, with little for grazing animals to eat except ferns, weeds, or woody shrubs. Grasses would change the course of evolution, and they probably contributed to global climate change as well (Chapter 10).

The fossil leaves of grasses (*Graminophyllum*) found in two Oligocene soils in the Painted Hills indicate that very early in the Oligocene, grasses had taken root in wetland areas here. They would spread across an increasingly open landscape until by the end of the Oligocene and advent of the Miocene, 24 million years ago, they were perhaps the most diverse, universal, and elegantly adapted elements of Oregon's flora.

No other plant has so critically supported subsequent ecosystems, provided opportunities for ecologi-

Top right: *Metasequoia* was a common conifer in wetlands and along stream banks. Like the modern tamarack, *Metasequoia* shed its needles in the fall and sprouted new ones in the spring.

Middle and bottom right: Alder leaves and fruits are preserved in ash-rich sediments along Bridge Creek in Wheeler County.

cal expansion, and nurtured the rise and success of important (to humans) orders of animals: the grazers, especially the horse. Grass is prolific in its ability to support grazing. No other plant can as readily regrow its nutrient-rich leaves after they have been nibbled off. Most other plants—the daisies, the legumes, the dicots in general—retreat and regroup after an injury as stressful as having an entire set of leaves and branches cropped off. Grass relishes the challenge. It rises to the occasion and resprouts. Fires inspire it to root more deeply, produce stronger and more chlorophyll-rich leaves, and double its seed production. Periodic trim-

ming, whether by hungry ungulates or lawn mowers, keeps it healthy. It can cover vast areas with a relatively uniform blanket of readily available forage. Humans rely upon grasses for most of their daily bread. Wheat, rice, and corn are all grasses. So are bamboo and sugarcane. Most of the animals we depend on for food are,

---

Blue Basin, John Day Fossil Beds National Monument. The blue-green soils of the John Day Formation are younger than the soils at Painted Hills. They are part of the John Day Formation and indicate that the climate grew cooler and drier throughout the Oligocene.

like us, grass eaters. In a world without grass, cattle, horses, antelopes, buffalo, and most other ungulates might have taken very different evolutionary paths. Worse yet, there would be no milk, no ice cream, no bread, no cake, and no cookies.

The spread of grasses would, by the Miocene, allow early horses to change from solitary forest browsers to social grazers on open land, living in herds, and with size and swiftness their greatest defense. But in the Oligocene, the horses that lived in the John Day Basin were only just beginning to discover this new food. Horse teeth did not fully adapt to eating the silica-rich stems and leaves of grass until the Miocene, about 20 million years ago. Those species of horses that adapted from woodland browser to grassland grazer persisted. Others, though successful during their moments, ultimately took a dead-end turn along evolution's interwoven paths.

Oligocene Animals and the Tuffs of Turtle Cove

It is fairly easy to visualize the John Day Basin's Oligocene landscape about 30 million years ago — oaks and sycamore, hawthorns and Oregon grape, clustering across a gentle, grassy landscape; maples hugging wet meadows; squat, fat-needled evergreens, thick-stemmed grasses, and horsetail rushes hunkering along streams and in wetlands. Rainfall averaged about 30 inches per year, about twice the precipitation of the John Day Valley today. Winter frosts were common. The overall appearance may have been something like the grassy open hills of the central California coast around San Luis Obispo.

But the animals were a different matter. The fossil-rich soils and lake beds in the John Day Basin record an Oligocene fauna that challenges our imagination. The evidence comes from the Blue Basin (also known as the Turtle Cove Member of the John Day Formation for the abundance of fossil turtles) of the John Day Fossil Beds and from thinly bedded ash along Bridge Creek, several miles from Mitchell.

The green-tinted, suede-textured rocks of Turtle Cove, 24–30 million years old, are slightly younger than the red-banded soils of the Painted Hills. Like the Painted Hills, Turtle Cove's steepled exposures represent ancient soils. They exhibit, Greg Retallack notes, the "root traces, diffuse contacts, and mineral segregations typical of soil horizons." These soils, like those of the Painted Hills, are composed predominantly of volcanic ash that has been reworked by streams and mixed with clays and other sediments. But unlike the marshy environments of the Oligocene Painted Hills, the environment here, 40 miles and 4 million years removed, was a floodplain of a meandering stream, a landscape that occasionally flooded but that also dried out for much of the year, says Retallack. Annual precipitation varied from about 20 to 30 inches, similar to rainfall on today's Kansas plains or California's San Joaquin Valley.

In the green layers of Turtle Cove, the ash particles are still largely composed of glass shards, 29-million-year-old glass shards. This ash came mostly from the Cascades, a range then characterized by eruptions that were much richer in silica than those of the modern High Cascades. In the Blue Basin, the Turtle Cove beds still have the approximate composition of a rhyolite or rhyodacite ash. The ash was reworked by rainwater or deposited by water washing across unconsolidated soils, then colonized by plants, including alder and hackberry, and possibly grass. Each blue-green layer in Turtle Cove represents between 10,000 and 50,000 years. Interspersed brown paleosols correspond to somewhat shorter intervals of only 2,000 to 10,000 years of soil development, according to Retallack.

Twenty-nine million years ago, the open oak-sycamore savannas of eastern Oregon supported a bizarre assortment of animals, including entelodonts: pony-sized, pig-shaped animals with rhino-sized heads, and teeth to match. Discoveries by John Day Fossil Beds paleontologist Ted Fremd and colleagues have revealed an animated, diverse fauna. There were chalicotheres, lumbering, dog-sized herbivores that resembled a long-tailed bear with a horse's head. Their larger European cousins (*Moropus*) had padded paws with remarkable claws up to 2 inches in length. But despite this fearsome weaponry, their teeth

Above: Turtle Cove, John Day Fossil Beds National Monument. The soft beds of Turtle Cove, and most of the John Day Formation, are composed of volcanic ash erupted from silica-rich volcanoes of the early Cascades.

Top right: Sheep Rock towers above the John Day River. It is composed mostly of John Day Formation soils and ash flows, and is capped by a topknot of Columbia River basalt.

Bottom right: Cast of an entelodont skull. Similar in design to modern peccaries, but much larger, these animals may have been truly omnivorous, catching prey or eating plants opportunistically.

Bottom far right: An Oligocene watering hole at what is now Turtle Cove, John Day Fossil Beds National Monument. With the advent of grass, the landscape was more open and savanna-like, with oaks, maples, and other deciduous trees abundant, and *Metasequoia* shading the wetlands. Foreground, browsing horses (*Miohippus* and *Mesohippus,* eating hawthorn and hackberry); midground, oreodonts and early dogs; background, *Diceratherium* (horned rhino) and tapir. In the tree, *Dinictis,* a saber-toothed nimravid (catlike predator), holds an oreodont. Painting by Doris Tischler from the John Day Fossil Beds National Monument.

were strictly those of an herbivore. Chalicotheres likely used their height and claws to strip leaves and fruit from branches, and may have dug insects from logs and termite mounds. Whatever their strategy, chalicotheres were successful. Chalicothere fossils are found in Oregon from Oligocene into Miocene time, from about 25 million to 15 million years ago.

The Oligocene fauna also included tapir the size of large house cats, and four types of large rhinoceroses, including *Diceratherium,* a two-horned animal about the size of a modern black rhino. There were three types of goat-sized, thin-legged, fleet-running camels. Tragulids, deerlike animals whose closest modern relative is the Chinese water deer (*Hydropotes inermis inermis*),

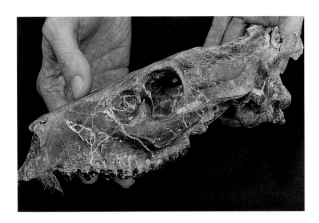

Top: Oreodonts were sheeplike in size
but had much more impressive teeth.

Above: Fossils of turtles and tortoises are abundant
in the wetland soils preserved the John Day Fossil Beds.

represent one of the most abundant Oligocene animals. Oreodonts—rounded, fur-clad animals about the size of a modern hog but with larger, sharper teeth—were so common that the Blue Basin holds the remains of ten genera, a situation similar to the variety of antelopes on the modern African savanna. Where there are oaks, there are squirrels; the John Day Fossil Beds have yielded the fossil remains of two species. Turtles, tortoises, and salamanders lived along streams and lakes. Crayfish lurked in the water. Fish included those adapted to warm shallow water: mud minnows and the progenitors of colder-water trout. Waterbirds, including grebes and gulls, settled on shallow lakes. Pheasants clucked through the underbrush. There were plenty of field mice and gophers. Pocket gophers gathered the first grasses. Two species of early rabbit hopped. And by the end of the Oligocene, *Ekgmowechashala,* a foot-tall, lemurlike creature and the only primate native to North America, hung out in an increasingly temperate and deciduous forest.

Horses

The animals from which the modern horse descended, continued to develop, experiment, and proliferate through the Oligocene. The variety of horses increased from the Eocene's *Orohippus, Haplohippus,* and *Epihippus,* three distinct genera of multitoed, Labrador retriever-sized animals, to four genera that roved the John Day Fossil Beds area during the Oligocene. The two most abundant and successful of these Miocene horses were *Miohippus* and *Mesohippus.* These two protohorses were small, standing only about 24 inches (6 hands) at the shoulder. They were less doglike in appearance. Their backs were flatter, their faces longer, and their brains bigger. They looked more like today's steed. Although *Mesohippus* and *Miohippus* still had multiple toes, they had only three (rather than four) on each back foot, and three on each front foot.

Like earlier horses, the Oligocene horses of the John Day Fossil Beds were forest-dwelling leaf browsers. But *Miohippus,* a horse who survived into the Miocene, had made one sudden change, one evolutionary gamble that its woodland-dwelling brethren lacked: its teeth were able to cut and chew grass. In the Miocene, more horse species would develop teeth specialized for eating grass. *Miohippus* was the first to adapt. Its contemporary, *Mesohippus,* kept shrubs on the menu as its main diet. These two close relatives would share the John Day Basin for at least 4 million years before *Miohippus's* new-found capacity for eating grass ensured its survival into the drier, prairie-rich Miocene time.

Ever since Yale paleontologist Othniel C. Marsh diagrammed it in 1874, we have tended to think of horse evolution, and in fact, all evolution, as a linear process —a sort of ladder, says Stephen Jay Gould, that leads to the ultimate final product: modern horse, modern human, or modern whatever. But evolutionary change is much more complex than that. It is, notes Gould, a trial-and-error process with no goal other than adaptation and serendipitous survival. Marsh's view (which was simplified by a dearth of specimens) was that from its Eocene origins (*Orohippus*), the horse grew gradually larger, fused its four toes into a single hoof, and produced larger teeth that could chew tougher grass. But like our everyday lives, the process of evolution is anything but linear. Our best plans are waylaid by external events. There are traffic lights and detours, side-road shortcuts, and new highways that we navigate each day. Horses, we now know, tried many branching paths. Some of these evolutionary routes allowed genera such as *Miohippus* to continue. Others, such as *Mesohippus,* were detoured onto an evolutionary dead end. So horses and most other living things (including us) have arrived at this point in time by using the back roads. Evolution is not a tree or ladder of straight ascent, but a bush, a set of anastomosing detours around ecological obstructions.

Predators and the fossil record

In the Oligocene, predators came into their own. The John Day Fossil Beds have yielded what Ted Fremd terms "an astonishing number of diverse carnivores." Saber-toothed, catlike animals called nimravids ambushed larger prey. The nimravid clan included bobcat-sized animals such as *Hoplophoneus,* with 6-inch-long, scimitar-like teeth, and *Dinictis,* with more manageable 2-inch sabers. The first dogs appeared, low-slung and weasel-like. In the John Day Fossil Beds, seven different dog genera are present, and it is likely that they all lived at about the same time and hunted in similar terrain. There were three genera of bear in the John Day Basin. And there were eight different kinds of bear-dogs (amphicyonids): thick-bodied, trap-jawed predators ranging from fox-sized to wolf-sized, according to Fremd. For herbivores, especially those who lived in woodlands, the Oligocene world was a dangerous place.

If it seems that the Oligocene bestiary was overpopulated, it was not. Although wildlife populations were dense and extremely diverse compared to modern wildlands where humans have decimated animals and habitat, the Oligocene animals mentioned did not all occupy the same snippet of John Day landscape at the same time. The deposits that contain these fossils represent millions of years. The multiple layers of soil at the Painted Hills each required 10,000 to 200,000 years to form. The stacked, blue, ash-rich beds of Turtle Cove and Blue Basin represent at least 2 million years of time: 2 million summers, 2 million winters, many storms, many droughts. Two million years is a short time geologically but a long time in *Miohippus* years. Fossils in adjacent layers are the remains of animals who never saw one another and who are a thousand generations or more apart. There is a lot of room for change in a thousand generations.

With an imposing set of sharp canine teeth, nimravids were catlike predators, probably very efficient.

Animals migrated in the seasonal Oligocene world, just as they do today. Habitats changed; fauna adapted to fit. Streams meandered, their channels moving. Volcanic eruptions blanketed the landscape with ash, resetting the ecological clock. During all this, animals came and went, lived and died. But though not all the fauna documented in the Turtle Cove beds lived there at the same time, the species richness and diversity of this locality far surpass anything that late Pleistocene humans likely witnessed or that we will ever experience in the future.

Paleontological records are soundless and come to us in shades of gray and tawny stone rather than color. Did nimravids roar and wear a tiger's coat? Were oreodonts spotted? Did *Mesohippus* have zebra stripes or a dark streak down its back? We can only assume, in the spirit of uniformitarianism, that the present is the key to the past and that animals then, as now, tended to blend with their surroundings. Only recently have artists used a full box of crayons when drawing dinosaurs. For dinosaurs, we do, indeed, have a few tattered impressions of skin texture. But the colors remain pure conjecture. Perhaps nimravids were pink, like a flamingo. Perhaps *Miohippus* wore a long woolly coat like a mammoth. Unlikely, yes, but we may never truly know.

Despite its general blindness to color and pattern, paleontology does provide some insight into the lifestyles of the extinct. Fossils reveal broken and healed bones, birth defects, and disease. One fossil of an early dog found at Turtle Cove bears a broken and healed lower jaw. The skull, with its lower teeth slightly askew, provides clues; we must unravel the story. Perhaps kicked by its intended prey, the young canid would have lived in pain, relying on softer foods, carrion, and perhaps even fruits to survive until its lower mandible healed. If early dogs, like modern wolves, had a strong social group, other members of the pack may have shared their kills for a time, perhaps even regurgitating food for the injured animal. Or perhaps the injury made the dog a liability to the pack and it was driven away until the wound healed and the animal could hunt successfully with the pack again. Other, more gruesome tales of Oligocene death and intrigue include the *Miohippus* whose head was snapped back so far that its spine

punctured the rear of its palate. These stories, told by seemingly mute fossils, weave the past into a palpable fabric, a tapestry that we can feel more fully in our hearts as well as see in our mind's eye.

Volcanoes

Oregon's Oligocene volcanoes erupted predominantly in two locations: the eastern interior and the Western Cascades. Although the Cascade eruptions are related to subduction, the dwindling middle Oligocene eruptions in eastern Oregon may have been the last cough of the Clarno. At the northern end of the Elkhorn Mountains, about 20 miles from Granite by Forest Service back roads, lie the vents and flows of silica-rich volcanoes. They range in age from 33.3 million to 28.8 million years and generally coincide with the volcanic ash-rich layers of the Painted Hills (33.3 million years) and Blue Basin (28.8 million years). These eastern Oregon volcanoes may have contributed to the ash-rich soils of the John Day Fossil Beds and the Painted Hills.

Eruptions in northeastern Oregon

Around Granite in the northern end of the Elkhorn Mountains, lightly colored volcanic rocks breach the surface. Dated about 33 million years in age, they erupted at the beginning of the Oligocene and continued to produce ash and silica-rich rhyolite for several million years afterward. This small and nameless set of volcanoes was an anomaly. There is no good geologic rationale for their presence. They may have been the last of the Clarno, a pustule of melted crust that burst after the major Clarno volcanoes had ceased activity and the subduction zone had moved on.

The largest area of Oligocene volcanic rocks in eastern Oregon occupies Tower Mountain, a promontory that sports a fire lookout tower on its 6,850-foot summit. The rocks here, dated at about 28.8 million years, are mostly light-colored rhyolites. They are the stuff of explosive eruptions, of ash flung into the stratosphere, of pumice, tuff, and searing nuées ardentes (glowing clouds of hot volcanic ash and gas, the expression from the French *nuée*, cloud, and *ardente*, glowing). The ini-

tial vents for this volcanic complex erupted about 10 miles north and west of Granite, producing rhyolite flows along with ash and gases. Most of the volcanic activity here produced thick, slow-moving lava. Geologist Mark Ferns, who mapped the area in 1995, found only one ignimbrite, an 80-foot-thick package of glassy rock and crystal-lined vugs, or cavities. Ignimbrites (the word from the Latin *ignis*, fire, and *imbris*, storm cloud) are the rocks formed from nuée ardente deposits. There is no way of telling how much ash erupted from the Tower Mountain vents. And we do not know how much of it fell into the John Day Fossil Beds, but some probably did, adding to Oregon's geologic record and contributing to the variegated colors of the Painted Hills.

Carroll Rim, above the Painted Hills, is capped by a 28.7-million-year-old ash-flow tuff (fragment also shown) erupted from a vent in eastern Oregon.

In the Painted Hills and throughout the John Day Formation, there is ample evidence that ash-flow tuffs and small basalt flows periodically covered some of the John Day Basin's temperate landscape. Welded tuffs cap ridges, including Carroll Rim (28.7 million years old) above the Painted Hills, forming important Oligocene time markers. Oligocene volcanic vents produced economic deposits of mercury and minor gold at the Horse Heaven Mine and other locations between Ashwood and Mitchell. Dark basalt dikes angle across some multicolored layers, and in some places, dark, wall-like outcrops jut to the surface. Basalt layers appear in John Day Gulch and on the Burnt Ranch near the John Day River. Basalt clasts rest in the tuff-laden soils of the Blue Basin. These basalt flows were not very abundant, and they did not cover much territory. But they do hint at some significant tectonic activity. These basalts are dark, dense, and laden with the mineral olivine. They are also enriched in the element titanium. Together, this suggests that these basalts erupted during faulting and ex-

tension—pulling apart—of the John Day Basin about 30 million years ago.

To geologists, this scenario makes perfect sense. The subduction zone off the Oregon coast had shifted into high gear, pushing sediment and seafloor into the mantle beneath the continent. All this raw material fueled vigorous eruptions in the Oligocene Cascades. Rapid subduction also stirred the deeper mantle. Currents of magma rose to the surface behind (east of) the Cascade volcanoes. As often happens in such circumstances, the crust east of the main line of Cascade volcanoes began to pull apart, extend, and let the new basalt lavas erupt as linear vents and small cinder cones. This volcanic ac-

Above: Orange-brown ash-flow tuffs of the Oligocene John Day Formation line the canyon of Trout Creek near Ashwood.

Right: The Western Cascades viewed from high on Mount Hood are a muted range of older volcanoes.

tivity was sporadic, and it would cease near the end of the Oligocene. But the John Day eruptions perhaps served as a relief valve for the hot and fluid basalts that would build the early Western Cascades.

Cascade eruptions

The persistent volcanic action of the Oligocene would be found in the Cascades. But these Cascade volcanoes were not the familiar peaks that punctuate today's skyline. The volcanoes of the Oligocene long ago eroded to become the western foothills of Mount Jefferson, Three Sisters, Diamond Peak, and Crater Lake. Thirty million years ago, the rugged topography along the North and Middle Santiam, the McKenzie, and the upper Willamette Rivers consisted of volcanoes that erupted farther west than the modern Cascades.

This broad and ragged line of low peaks is called, simply, the Western Cascades. Their rocks are found today in the Coburg Hills east of Eugene and interbedded with marine sediments at Scotts Mills. Their eruptions formed the cliffs above McKenzie Bridge, the high rocks above Opal Creek's old growth, and the round-rocked, slide-prone lahars at Tidbits Mountain. Farther to the south, they are the pinnacle of Pilot Rock and the layered ash and lavas at Siskiyou Pass. Their hot, acid waters deposited gold at Quartzville, Lucky Butte, Mineral, Bohemia, Gold Hill, and Blue River. Judging from the abundance of mudflows and andesites, the Western Cascades were predominantly a range of stratovolcanoes, similar to the Clarno volcanoes that preceded them and the modern High Cascade peaks like Mount Hood that followed. Their eruptions may have been more explosive and produced more ash than the average stratovolcano, for they are cited as the source of the ash that filled the John Day Basin some 100 miles to the east.

The Western Cascades may have begun erupting about 40 million years ago at the end of the Eocene. Evidence for these eruptions is scanty, best found in southernmost Oregon and northern California. These Eocene rocks include the Payne Cliffs Formation: sandstones, tuffs, and sediments exposed in the Medford–Ashland area, and vents such as Pilot Rock.

The Western Cascades reached their greatest size, distribution, and power during the Oligocene. In southern Oregon, multiple volcanoes produced the rocks of the Colestin Formation: ash as well as basalt, andesite, and rhyolite lavas. Erick Bestland of Flinders University, South Australia, notes at least three separate episodes of volcanic activity in the Oligocene Colestin volcanoes of southern Oregon: a basaltic shield volcano, a small stratovolcano, and a rhyolite vent. This Oligocene volcanic activity is similar in scope to the modern volcanoes of Three Sisters, which also include vents of all three compositions. Ash and rocks eroded from these volcanic centers are more than 3,000 feet thick and include lignite coal beds—the remains of coastal wetlands buried by eruptive materials, mudflows, and shallow flood deposits as the embayment that was the Willamette Valley filled, folded, and retreated northward.

Left: Close-up of Western Cascade volcanic rocks exposed along Oregon Highway 22 west of Detroit. Lichens and weathering impart a pinkish hue to these Oligocene tuffs of the Breitenbush Formation.

Right: Remnants of an Oligocene vent form cliffs above the North Umpqua River east of Glide.

Left: The only Oligocene rocks in the Columbia River Gorge are found at the trailhead to Latourell Falls. These Western Cascade andesites of the Skamania Volcanics are a telltale gray in contrast to the darker, somber browns of the surrounding and much younger Columbia River basalts.

Above: The South Santiam River rushes through the 30-million-year-old, dark brown Little Butte Volcanics near Shot Pouch Butte. These are part of the Western Cascades, a range of Oligocene and early Miocene volcanoes that erupted to the west of the present Cascades.

Farther north, Oligocene volcanic rocks occupy the landscape around Detroit Lake and the Santiam River. There, the dark brown rocks are known as the Little Butte Volcanics and Breitenbush Formation. The volcanoes constituted almost a coastal range, and much of their eruptive material is interbedded with marine sediments of the Scotts Mills Formation. Like those of the Colestin Formation, they erupted a variety of lavas and probably produced an abundance of ash. Most of their pyroclastic material was transported east on the prevailing winds to become the ash-laden soils of the John Day Formation's Painted Hills and Turtle Cove (or Blue Basin). Tuffs along Bond Creek and at Spores Point near Eugene have been dated from 34 million to 31 mil-

CHAPTER 9

Early and Middle Miocene

Lavas blanket Oregon

You cannot travel anywhere in Oregon without encountering the Miocene, from 24 million to 5 million years ago. It lines the Columbia River Gorge, layer upon layer of dark, columned basalt. It is the pockmarked, honeycombed face of the Owyhee Mountains, the filigreed parapets of Hells Canyon, and the speckled underpinnings of Mount Hood. We can walk its beaches along the shell-studded cliffs of Astoria or hike its rock-shaded grasslands at Succor Creek. The Miocene appears in the undulating coastal summits of Saddle Mountain, the red basalts of the Salem Hills, and the tawny cliffs of Smith Rock. Its eruptive power glowers from the dark faces of Steens Mountain, Hart Mountain, and Abert Rim. It is Table Rocks near Medford and Table Rock near Mount Hood. Strawberry Mountain, Dooley Mountain, Glass Mountain—in Oregon, the Miocene is inescapable. In the nearly 20 million years of the Miocene, more lava probably flowed across the Oregon landscape than had erupted here in all the time before and all the time since.

The 23-million-year-old, light-colored, ash-rich lake beds near Alvord Creek seem out of place on the dark face of Steens Mountain. These sediments contain the leaves of a mostly deciduous wetland forest, including maples and walnut trees. A conifer forest grew at somewhat higher elevations.

Elsewhere around the globe, the Miocene is known for its quiescence. The climate grew generally warmer and drier. The Tethys Sea narrowed, closing its link to the Atlantic and shrinking to form the nascent Mediterranean Sea along the belly of Europe. As the Mediterranean became more isolated from the Atlantic, its water evaporated faster than the inflow of seawater. Isolated from the oceanic circulation, and destitute of large rivers in an arid world, the Mediterranean dried up. Where Phoenician ships would sail and Odysseus would make his mythic voyage, in the Miocene there were only sand dunes and salt flats.

In the Miocene, mountains were uplifted as continents merged. The Alps and the Himalaya began to rise, squeezed skyward by the collision of Africa with Europe, and India with Asia. North and South America connected, providing a bonanza of new habitats for animals of both continents, initiating rapid migration and interchange along the new Isthmus of Panama. Movement began along the San Andreas Fault. The world inched closer to its present form. But nowhere was volcanic activity as prolific as in Oregon.

Early Miocene
The land before lavas

Yet the Miocene did not begin as an epoch steeped in lava. At its onset, 24 million years ago, eruptions were rare. A few volcanic centers in the Cascades produced lahar-mantled stratovolcanoes. In southeastern Oregon, ash-laden rhyolites erupted. As the Miocene began, Oregon's landscape was a rolling, savanna-like plain from Burns Junction to Bend, Enterprise to Estacada, Rome to Redmond, Succor Creek to Sisters. Eastern Oregon was hardly a place we would recognize. There were no Elkhorn Mountains, no Wallowas, no Strawberries, no Steens Mountain, no Abert Rim—no familiar mountains of any size or significance in eastern Oregon. The Clarno volcanic peaks that erupted 20 million years earlier in the Eocene had eroded into hills. There were no High Cascades, only a range of lower peaks 20 miles to the west of today's Cascade crest.

Where Mount Hood rises today, the ancestral Columbia River followed a gentle valley. The Coast Range was still a mounded lump of low hills. The Willamette Valley floor had just emerged from the sea.

Twenty million years ago, Oregon's early Miocene landscape might have resembled the rolling hills of Ohio. Grass, a comparatively new arrival in the plant kingdom, grew in clearings and provided ground cover amid a hardwood forest dominated by ginkgo, oak, and maple. The best records of Oregon's early Miocene plants come from two very disparate places: the ash-rich claystones and cobbled lahars along Eagle Creek in the Columbia River Gorge, and the steep, arid eastern face of Steens Mountain.

A stroll along the first half mile of the Eagle Creek Trail will take you deep into a Miocene forest. Broken stumps and roots, now turned to stone, poke out of mucky claystone stream banks. Scraps of fossil leaves sometimes appear on the trail. Rounded cobbles and knobs of volcanic rock indicate that you are walking through the relicts of a 20-million-year-old forest that grew on ancient mudflows and debris flows at the base of a Miocene volcano.

The forest preserved in the early Miocene Eagle Creek Formation in the Columbia River Gorge included oaks, maples, ginkgoes, sycamores, and sweet gum trees, which likely grew on upland slope. Willow, yew, and cottonwood shaded nearby streams. Wetlands to the south, at the junction of the Clackamas and Collawash Rivers, supported swamp cypress, tupelo, and *Metasequoia*.

The mudflows of the Eagle Creek Formation came from small, nameless stratovolcanoes that erupted west of today's Cascade crest as part of the Little Butte Volcanics. These early Miocene Cascade volcanoes, like the sediments of the Eagle Creek Formation, extended north into Washington and south to Oakridge, southeast of Eugene. Soda Mountain and Rooster Rock in the Menagerie Wilderness east of Sweet Home are early Miocene volcanic centers that oozed rhyolite lava and a little ash. They were a holdover from Oligocene volcanoes, the last gasp before a new regime would assert itself. There is no record of the animals that lived in the forests around these peaks. The forests likely sheltered early forms of deer, browsing horses, canids, cats, and beaver, but we do not know. The fauna evidently escaped the mudflows that entombed the forest.

Evidence of the animals that may have lived here, says Ted Fremd, comes from the Warm Springs fauna, fossils found southeast of Mount Hood in tuffs and sediments that are coeval with the Eagle Creek Formation. They include, Fremd notes, the rabbit *Hypolagus,*

About 20 million years ago, mudflows from a long-vanished volcano just north of Mount Hood's present position entombed a forest of ginkgoes, sycamores, oaks, and maples. This tree stump along Eagle Creek, about 3 feet in diameter, probably remains in the original growth position where it died.

the mountain beaver *Rudiomys,* the "horned rodent" *Mylagaulodon,* a new species of ursid (bear), a chalicothere, three genera of horses—*Parahippus, Archaeohippus, Merychippus*—and the camel *Oxydactylus.*

How representative is the fossil record?

It is difficult to know which trees and shrubs were in a Miocene old-growth forest. Most plants preserved in mudflow deposits or volcanic ash, including those of Eagle Creek, Maupin, and the Alvord Desert, are early successional species; they represent the first plants to sprout and grow at a site where previous plant life was wiped out by volcanic eruption, catastrophic flood, or other high-energy event. A glimpse of plants growing on modern Mount St. Helens mudflow deposits, or the trees that sprout first after a devastating, canopy-destroying forest fire, prove that this disturbance forest is different from the more stable forest that will eventually replace it and inhabit the area for thousands or tens of thousands of years. The early successional forest includes a large proportion of trees like alders whose ecological design makes them the botanical equivalent of modern-day emergency medical technicians: the first to arrive at a disaster scene and try to heal wounds. Their role is to stabilize and enrich the soil and provide shade for the growth of replacement conifers. The old-growth native forest adjacent to the mudflow or other disturbance may be quite different in species composition and character from the plants that first colonize a landscape swept barren by flood, fire, or eruption. But it is the disturbance forest that is more likely to be overrun by the next mudflow—and hence preserved.

Some paleoecologists, including Ralph Taggart of the University of Idaho, worry that most of the fossil record of trees is richer in deciduous species that thrive through disturbance and whose leaves would most likely be preserved at the top of a fresh mudflow, whereas native conifers that prosper in old-growth forests on undisturbed uplands would hardly be represented. There is much to be said for this argument. Many trees in the fossil record, including the Eocene katsura tree entombed—trunk, roots, and all—in an Eocene mudflow at the Hancock Field Station, grew atop earlier mudflows and likely were part of early plant succession.

Most of the fabulous fossils found at Hancock grew on a disturbed site that was inundated by another mudflow. There are few old-growth forests in Oregon's fossil record. This is not because they did not exist; it is because few were in the right place for preservation.

Of course, not all plant fossils represent disturbance events. In eastern Oregon's Eocene and Oligocene rocks, the colorful layers of the Painted Hills and Clarno Formation hold records of ecosystems that remained undisturbed for long periods of time—tens of thousands of years or more. The fossils found in these ancient soil horizons suggest that at least in Oregon, the plants that grew on mudflows and other disturbed sites represent the generally deciduous character of regional lowland forests in the Eocene, Oligocene, and Miocene. Swampy Oligocene soils contain the remnants of *Metasequoia,* alder, ferns, grasses, and basswood. Seasonally dry Oligocene soils supported alder and oak. Plants on these stable sites are similar in composition to those preserved on adjacent sites such as mudflows, but not exactly the same. Taggart's point is worth considering. Few fossil records represent all plants and animals that lived in an area.

First signs of the flood

At almost the same time that the early Miocene Cascades erupted, explosive eruptions began in Oregon's southeastern corner near what is now the Alvord Desert. These were mere warm-ups, practice sessions, crustal stretching exercises for much more extensive eruptions yet to come. But the rocks, named the Alvord Creek Formation for the small, steep stream where they are well exposed, built a foundation for Steens Mountain and much of the surrounding desert.

The Alvord Creek beds seem out of place on Steens Mountain. Lightly colored and soft, they dangle beneath the dark, columned bodice of Steens Mountain like a faintly festive Victorian petticoat, there to be admired and foundational to the multiple layers of somber garment above. This light-colored formation differs from the volcanic rocks that compose the rest of Steens Mountain. It is sedimentary rock, the ash-laden beds of a 23-million-year-old lake. The beds preserve the leaves of a deciduous wetland forest. Maples, wal-

nut, serviceberry, and sumac clustered around the lakeshore. Conifers, notably Douglas fir, true firs, and hemlock, grew on the drier heights of a hilly terrain. (The rocks of Steens Mountain were yet unborn, and the fault that would lift its summit more than a mile was not even conceived, though faulting would tilt the lake beds slightly before a series of rhyolite eruptions laid the foundations of the mountain 22 million years ago.) The remnants of this shady woodland, with its inviting lake, seem sadly abandoned in the desert setting, where, uplifted by faulting, an ancient forest has only the desiccated, mud-cracked playa of Alvord Lake to contemplate.

The volcanic ash that lined this Miocene lake came from small but explosive eruptions. These would continue and increase during the next 2 million years as rising magmas lifted and tilted the old lake beds. Between 22 million and 20 million years ago, a volcanic center, erupting ash and pasty rhyolite lavas, developed on a rolling and forested landscape where Steens Mountain rises today. The result was a vent system of flows and tuff about 15 miles long and 2,000 feet thick.

About 19 million years ago, another type of lava appeared in the eruptive cycle: andesite. With more iron but less silica than the earlier rhyolites, these lavas cloaked the landscape in tawny browns and somber gray. The andesite eruptions built at least three cinder cones exposed today as light-colored rocks low on the eastern face of Steens Mountain. By 18 million years ago, 1,500 feet of andesite flows known as the Steens volcanics had accumulated. All had come from the mantle, with little contamination by the crust. They were the advance guard for major eruptions, the more fluid basalts that were poised to erupt across southeastern and northeastern Oregon, as well as the calderas that would engulf the Owyhee Mountains.

Middle Miocene

Lava floods the landscape

Seventeen million years ago, Oregon was poised at the beginning of the middle Miocene. This time period would have the warmest climate since the greenhouse conditions of the Eocene. Sea level rose. South America abandoned its tenuous connection to Antarctica, opening the Drake Passage and allowing warmer Atlantic waters to mingle with cold polar currents. Milder ocean temperatures moderated the temperatures on land, changing weather patterns across the planet.

The reasons for climate change are obscure, but some geologists and paleoclimatologists suggest that carbon dioxide, carbon monoxide, and other gases released in the extensive middle Miocene volcanic eruptions created a short-lived greenhouse effect, raising temperatures globally and melting a substantial percentage of polar ice. Throughout western North America, the cuticles and stomata of middle Miocene fossil plant leaves are exceptionally large, indicating rapid transpiration and suggesting warmth (average temperature 75°F, 24°C) and humidity (relative humidity 75 percent, about the average humidity of North Carolina, according to Greg Retallack of the University of Oregon and Matthew Kohn of the University of South Carolina).

Despite their special adaptations, middle Miocene plant communities would have looked familiar: alders shaded streams; grasses floored oak and maple savanna. The principal requisite for plant life was that it thrive on heat, humidity, and disturbance.

The middle Miocene was also a time when almost half of Oregon's landscape was inundated by the products of volcanic eruptions. Basalts covered the Columbia Basin and much of southeastern Oregon. Calderas produced the ash-flow tufts found throughout the Owyhees. Volcanoes erupted ash and andesites near John Day and Baker City. Cascade volcanoes were active.

Did eruptions in Oregon contribute to climate change and the sharp warming that occurred between 17 million and 14 million years ago? In the middle Miocene, when the vents of the Columbia River basalts, the Owyhees, and Steens Mountain were most active, sea level rose and average global temperatures were the warmest of the Miocene epoch. This time, known as the Miocene Optimum, saw warm-water Asian mollusks periodically invade Alaskan waters. While we cannot point unequivocally to our own eruptions as the culprits, we can comfortably view them as likely accomplices.

Sources of Pacific Northwest Flood Basalt

In the middle Miocene, 16.6 million to 15 million years ago, lavas flooded two parts of the Pacific Northwest: the Columbia Plateau and what is now Oregon's Basin and Range, including Steens Mountain. The basalts in each area are among the most thoroughly studied rocks in the Pacific Northwest. They are similar in composition as well as age. They were thought to have separate origins. But in 2002, Peter Hooper, of Washington State University, and colleagues suggesed that the basalts of Steens Mountain and the Columbia Plateau shared a common source: the Yellowstone hot spot in its first location, beneath eastern Oregon.

For a very long time, the source of the Columbia River basalts seemed a mystery, though there were many hypotheses. The ideas ranged from plausible to presumptuous. They included proposals that Oregon overran a mid-oceanic ridge that continued its activity. Or that a meteorite crashed into eastern Oregon. Another model suggested that the crust of southeastern Oregon began to rift open, allowing mantle-derived lavas to seep out like blood oozing through an open wound. Some of the ideas had merit. The West Coast of North America did, in fact, override the Farallon mid-oceanic ridge from about 50 million to 25 million years ago, an event that shut off the eruptions of the Western Cascades. The Basin and Range has extended, allowing some magmas from the mantle to erupt as basalts. The meteoritic suggestion, however, has always lacked credible scientific evidence. There are no shocked minerals, geophysical sightings of buried circular structures, or anomalies of meteorite-induced chemistry in regional middle Miocene soils.

Peter Hooper has studied Columbia River basalts for most of his long academic career. Along with his graduate students and colleagues, he has mapped their extent, analyzed their chemical composition, and scrutinized their origins via isotope geochemistry. Hooper's work offers a succinct explanation. Using precise dating and calculations of Miocene tectonics, Hooper can place the plume of magma and rising heat that today powers Old Faithful at Yellowstone National Park, known to geologists as the Yellowstone hot spot, beneath the site of Steens Mountains 16.6 million years ago, precisely when the eruptions at Steens first began.

The Yellowstone hot spot, like other magmatic hot spots, including Hawaii, is a source of hot, melted rock that remains stationary while the Earth's tectonic plates move above it. As the rising magma erupts onto a continental or oceanic plate, it traces the plate's movement. To demonstrate this, you might hold a pencil or marker (the hot spot) stationary and move a piece of paper (the continental or oceanic crust) past it. The resulting line records the paper's movement. The hot spot has not moved. Instead, it has left a line of volcanoes, a trace of the plate's movement.

About 16.6 million years ago, a vigorous plume of basalt magma rose from the mantle, erupting where Steens Mountain is today. The magma source in the mantle remained fixed. But North America, the continental plate above the hot spot, moved westward at a relatively steady pace of several centimeters per year. Magmas continued to erupt, creating a series of volcanic centers, but generally, each new set of eruptions was farther to the east. This series of eruptions during the past 16 million years crafted the Snake River Plain, a gently curving volcanic plateau that arcs across southern Idaho from Oregon to Wyoming, tracking the motion of North America above a fixed point in the mantle. The farther east you go along the Snake River Plain, the younger the volcanic rocks. The youngest and most active volcanic center is now located at Yellowstone National Park. In fact, Yellowstone is a potentially dangerous eruptive center, driven by the same energetic plume of mantle magmas that generated the Columbia River basalts 16.6 million years ago.

Steens basalts

About 16.6 million years ago, a broad shield volcano stood where Steens Mountain is today. The very first of the Columbia River basalts, says Peter Hooper, were the lavas that form the dark cliffs on the upper half of Steens and line the canyons of Kiger Gorge, Little Indian Gorge, and the Donner und Blitzen River. At Steens Mountain, where rhyolites and andesites had erupted

in the early Miocene, the pressure of the rising Yellowstone mantle plume forced fissures to open. These elongated cracks began to erupt fluid torrents of basalt.

Lava spread north and west, flowing rapidly, spreading dark basalt across the flat landscape from vents at Steens east to what today are the Trout Creek Mountains (east of Alvord Lake) and west to what would become Hart Mountain and Abert Rim, beyond Lake Abert to Summer Lake. Although these basalts have a chemical composition that is more similar to rift-zone lavas than to lavas from a mantle plume, their eruption early in the Yellowstone hot spot's history may be related to this somewhat different composition.

These exceptionally fluid lavas spread quickly into thin but extensive flows, averaging less than 20 feet in thickness near the linear source vents. Like the Columbia River basalts, most of the vents were elongate fissures. Many are still visible, cutting like dark vertical ribbons through Steens Mountain's precipitous face. At least seventy distinct flows erupted from the vents at Steens over the course of about 1 million years, amassing a thickness of about 4,500 feet of basalt. The mountain's faulted face reveals that little time passed between flows. As each successive lava flow cooled and solidified, new fissures opened, providing avenues for more lava to erupt.

Similar lava erupted from vents just to the south of Steens Mountain in the Pueblo Mountains. The Pueblo basalts flowed across the landscape from about 16 million to 15.5 million years ago. Both sources contributed to Basin and Range rimrock on Abert Rim, Poker Jim Ridge, Hart Mountain, and other uplifted ridges across southeastern Oregon's Basin and Range.

Columbia River basalts

Between 16.6 million and 15 million years ago, eastern Oregon sat above the nascent Yellowstone hot spot's rising jet of basalt. The power of lava ascending 5 miles to the surface from a seething, 150-cubic-mile magma chamber opened a series of long, northwest-trending fissures. Today, the solidified remnants of these fissures (intrusive bodies called dikes) have been mapped across much of northeastern Oregon. One cluster of dikes, known as the Monument swarm, is centered near the

Above: Little Indian Gorge on Steens Mountain reveals more than forty basalt flows. The lavas erupted quickly, beginning 16.6 million years ago. These eruptions, and the Columbia River flood basalts that followed, may have marked the inception of the Yellowstone hot spot.

Right: Many of the last basalts that erupted at Steens Mountain, Abert Rim, and other Basin and Range locations have huge feldspar crystals. The biggest (to 3 inches in diameter) and most colorful crystals, found on the eastern slopes of Abert Rim near Plush, are Oregon's official gemstone, the sunstone.

community of Monument along the North Fork of the John Day River. Another group (or swarm) of feeder dikes is exposed near Huntington, in the Wallowa Mountains, in canyons north of Enterprise, and across the Blue Mountains to Walla Walla, Washington. Known as the Chief Joseph swarm, these elongate vents

Left: In Big Indian Gorge, eroded canyon walls reveal the vertical dikes that fed flows of Steens basalts.

Below: Many sea stacks along Oregon's northern coast, including Haystack Rock at Cannon Beach, are remnants of Columbia River basalt flows.

served as the major conduits for upwelling lava. Basalts literally flooded from these 10- to 25-mile-long cracks, at first ponding in low places, then gradually filling and leveling the landscape, much like cake icing fills the imperfections in the surface.

The Columbia River basalts are a world-class example of continental flood basalts—lavas that erupt rapidly in a geologically short period of time and inundate vast areas. Worldwide, other continental flood basalts have erupted at least eleven times throughout geologic history. Most are associated with the inception of mantle plumes, according to Steve Self of the University of Hawaii. They include the Deccan Traps of India (65

million years ago), the Karoo basalts of southern Africa (183 million years), and the Siberian basalts (248 million years). The Columbia River basalts are the youngest of these major continental flood basalt outpourings.

The major Columbia River basalt eruptions continued for more than 1 million years, covering 62,000 square miles of Oregon and Washington to depths of as much as 3 miles (more than 15,000 feet) of basalt and producing lavas so hot, voluminous, and fluid that they surged to the Pacific Ocean. The sea stacks off Newport, Cape Lookout, Cannon Beach, and Astoria are the remnants of Columbia River basalt flows.

The Columbia River basalts (officially the Columbia River Basalt Group) erupted in several phases and in several places. Each phase and locality bears its own name and characteristic mineralogy and chemical composition, rather like each person in a family has a different first name and slightly different genetics though all share the same surname. The earliest of these basalts are known as the Imnaha Basalt: 26 lava flows erupted 16.6 million years ago in northeastern Oregon. The most voluminous and most rapidly erupted of the Columbia River Basalt Group are the 120 flows of the Grande Ronde Basalt, also erupted mostly from linear fissures in northeastern Oregon, southeastern Washington, and western Idaho. These flows line much of the Columbia River Gorge; some surged all the way to the Pacific shore. The 61 lava flows erupted near Monument are part of the Picture Gorge Basalt, 16 million years in age. Later series of eruptions produced 36 flows known as the Wanapum Basalt (14.5 million years old) and about 19 mostly smaller flows, the Saddle Mountains Basalt (from 12 million to 6 million years; Chapter 10).

Generally, the most voluminous eruptions—those of the Grande Ronde Basalt—coincided with other types of eruptions elsewhere in Oregon. So, about 16 million years ago, when the Columbia River basalt eruptions were at their maximum, vents in the Owyhees and the Strawberry Range were active along with eruptions in the Cascades.

The canyon of the Imnaha River,
where Columbia River basalt flows
form most of the landscape.

Left: The view from Hat Point, on the rim of Hells Canyon, reveals that Columbia River basalts form the upper canyon walls.

Above: Where basalt erupted in northeastern Oregon, it covered older rocks of the Blue Mountain island arc. Here, along the canyon of the Imnaha River, 16-million-year-old basalt rests directly on 230-million-year-old Triassic greenstones, leaving a 214-million-year gap in the geologic record.

While the middle Miocene landscape of Oregon was flooded by geologically contemporary eruptions, on a human timescale the eruptions were more leisurely. There were hiatuses between individual flows. On average, Columbia River basalt eruptions occurred about every 10,000 years, with some more than 25,000 years apart. In the warm and relatively moist climate of the Miocene, this was sufficient time for soils to develop, forests to grow, and complex ecosystems to develop. From our perspective, 100,000 years is a very long time—much longer than, for example, the 23,000 years since glaciers covered New England or the estimated

15,000 years since humans first migrated to North America. In contrast, today we live during a giddily active volcanic regime, with Mount Hood erupting barely two centuries ago, and Mount St. Helens only decades ago and still steaming.

Imnaha basalts

The first lavas that were truly part of the Columbia River basalts erupted 16.6 million years ago in the northeastern corner of Oregon, according to dates from Peter Hooper. Where today the canyons of the Snake and Imnaha Rivers plunge thousands of feet from rimrock to bottom, 17 million years ago the landscape consisted of gentle valleys. The Imnaha Basalt poured out of long fissures like hot molasses onto a waffle. The flows filled valleys. They smothered 19,000 square miles of the landscape in a uniform brownish black that may have looked like today's Diamond Craters in Harney County or Craters of the Moon National Monument in southern Idaho. There were twenty-six major flows during the 500,000 years of volcanic activity—on average, one every 20,000 years.

The Imnaha basalts are distinctive. Chemically, they are what geologists call primitive. Rich in magnesium and poor in silica, they mimic the composition of their parent mantle. Many flows bear large white crystals of feldspar, clumped together into groups that look like the tracks of big birds and loosely termed "turkey track basalt," a feature the Imnaha basalts share with some of the basalts of Steens Mountain and Abert Rim. Because

Many Columbia River basalt feeder dikes form streaks of reddish brown rock that crosscut the granitic and sedimentary rocks of the Wallowa Mountains. These dikes slice through the granitic rocks of Cornucopia, north of Halfway.

their rocks are hard, somewhat more resistant to erosion than the basalts above them, today they form the lower benches along the Imnaha and Snake Rivers where Wallowa County stockmen found premium grazing for sheep and cattle in the late nineteenth century and early twentieth.

Grande Ronde basalts

The most voluminous eruptions of Columbia River basalt are known as the Grande Ronde basalts. These eruptions lasted less than 1 million years—from 16.5 million to 15.6 million years ago—and covered almost 60,000 square miles. The total volume of the 120 Grande Ronde Basalt flows is estimated as 35,000 cubic miles. (Yes, 35,000 cubic miles: enough to circle the Earth twice at the equator with a tube of basalt 1 mile in diameter, or construct a 7-foot-thick, 100-foot-wide basalt freeway to the moon.)

These rocks are called the Grande Ronde Basalt because they are well exposed in the canyon of the Grande Ronde River. The lavas inundated the landscape of eastern Oregon and southeastern Washington, from linear vents up to 10 miles in length near today's towns of Enterprise, Joseph, Troy, and Walla Walla across eastern Oregon and Washington. Other eruptions poured from fissures near Monument, creating the basalts along the John Day River and found in today's Picture Gorge. The Grande Ronde lavas generally flowed toward the west. As they cooled and solidified, they left a Colum-

View from Lord Flat northward, Hells Canyon National Recreation Area. The Grande Ronde basalts are the most extensive of the Columbia River basalts. They traveled as far as the Pacific Ocean, more than 300 miles from their vents. In northeastern Oregon, deep canyons reveal their extent and thickness.

Top left: The layered walls of the Columbia River Gorge are composed of Columbia River basalt flows. These cliffs above Ainsworth State Park showcase at least eleven Grande Ronde Basalt flows, about 15.6 million years in age. Those at the top are Frenchman Springs basalts, about 14. 5 million years old.

Bottom left: The White River plunges over Columbia River basalts at White River Falls near Maupin.

Above: The fanning basalt columns of many Columbia River Gorge cliffs are the result of patterns that develop as hot lava cools, solidifies, and shrinks.

Right: Soils that developed atop a lava flow were usually baked and oxidized to a bright red by the heat of the next flow several thousand years later. Ancient, baked soil and the oxidized flow top are exposed in Picture Gorge, about 5 miles west of Dayville.

bia Basin landscape covered with dark, heavy rock. So much basalt accumulated in the lowlands of south-central Washington, where the Hanford Reservation is today, that the Earth's crust sagged under the weight, allowing even more lava to pond there. Beneath the nuclear reactors at Hanford, more than 2 miles of basalt flows are stacked one atop another.

When Washington's Hanford site was chosen for Manhattan Project nuclear research and plutonium production in January 1943, its thick pile of basalt was considered an asset, a guarantee of stability. Then, having established the place, scientists decided they needed to know more about it. Years of mapping, seismic and borehole exploration, geochemistry, and paleomagnetic studies have provided an exquisite portrait of the Columbia River basalts there. We know the details of the eruptions, the parts-per-million chemical composition of individual flows, and their volume and mineralogy. We have fathomed their thickness and mapped their distribution. But 60 years of study have also revealed that Hanford's thick stack of basalts is cut by active faults, complex joint patterns, and highly permeable layers that channel groundwater toward the Columbia River—not a good place to store nuclear waste.

The Grande Ronde Basalt flows covered enormous areas. They poured across the flat Miocene landscape at speeds of 1–2 miles per hour. Some individual flows extended more than 300 miles from eastern Oregon or western Idaho to the Pacific coast. The truly great flows erupted at the rate of more than a cubic mile of lava per day from linear vents sometimes more than 10 miles long. Some eruptions lasted for weeks.

Individual flows of Grande Ronde Basalt compose most of the layered cliffs of the Columbia River Gorge. In some places, the lava encountered lakes or river channels, which it dammed. Where these dryland lavas encountered water, they chilled into rounded pillows rather than forming stalwart columns. The rounded forms in the top basalt layer at Multnomah Falls or the lumpy basalt outcrops at The Dalles provide evidence that some of these basalt flows encountered lakes or large streams along their path.

The lavas ran into forests and wetlands as well as lakes. In Oregon's far northeastern corner, Miocene wetlands were overrun and buried beneath thin basaltic flows. On the slopes above the Wenaha River, dark seams of organic material, compressed between the flows, are potentially commercial deposits of lignite coal. Elsewhere, the lava flattened forests, knocking over trees, setting them afire, then recorded their presence, sometimes even their bark, in empty molds. Along the Columbia River at Vantage in south-central Washington (Ginkgo Petrified Forest State Park), the petrified remnants of swamp cypress, upland conifers such as hemlock and spruce, and the oak and ginkgo trees of a deciduous forest that grew along a lake are preserved in the wetland soils sandwiched between lavas along with lake-bottom sediments.

Basalts Reach Portland and the Coast

Once they had filled and flattened the Columbia Plateau, lavas used broad valleys and the ancestral channel of the Columbia River as a westbound, downhill highway. Sixteen million years ago, the Columbia River's channel turned southwest near The Dalles. Its course followed a 25-mile-wide valley that angled toward the southwest, leading toward the location of Portland and the wide plain that would become the Willamette Valley. The Columbia River flowed through a lowland where Mount Hood rises now; the Miocene Cascades apparently did not contain any prominent volcanic peaks and, in fact, were part of a subsiding lowland according to work by Marvin Beeson and his students at Portland State University.

The first Columbia River basalts to reach western Oregon were the extensive flows of Grande Ronde

Top right: Saddle Mountain and other northern Coast Range peaks are composed of Columbia River basalt that flowed from vents in eastern Oregon and Idaho all the way to the Pacific Ocean.

Right: Peak of Saddle Mountain.

Far right: The lavas also deformed the sediments at Hug Point.

Basalt. Some followed the ancestral Columbia's broad valley. Others may have flooded through low places in the Cascades. Today, Grande Ronde flows are exposed along the Clackamas River, and at least four can be counted at Silver Falls State Park. In some places the lava invaded forests. If you stand in the basalt-ceilinged grotto behind North Falls and glance upward, you will see rounded holes—molds of trees surrounded and burned by lava. Some of the lava covered portions of the Willamette Valley and what would one day become Portland. Today, about eight flows of Grande Ronde Basalt have been mapped in the West Hills (or, as they are also known, the Tualatin Mountains) where they form the bulk of Marquam Hill. They underlie Hoyt Arboretum and the steepest slopes of Forest Park. The dark, columned rocks along Balch Creek Canyon and Cornell Drive are Grande Ronde Basalt. All these rocks originated more than 200 miles to the east and arrived here as fluid lavas.

At Hug Point State Park, basalt lavas threaded their way down into soft sediments, creating dikes and stringers of lava.

The first basalt that reached the Willamette Valley encountered a set of hills close to where Portland's West Hills are now, as well as farther west near Newberg. For a time, this topography diverted the flows northward. But once the basalt had partly filled this area, some flows followed a valley or structural lowland southward past Lake Oswego and Sherwood, then west to the Oregon coast near Mount Hebo. Others worked their way to the north, following a path similar to the modern Columbia's course. And some may have flowed through valleys in the low hills between the Willamette Valley and the coast. In the Miocene, notes Marvin Beeson, the Coast Range provided only a leaky barrier for these lavas.

When it reached the coast, the heavy Columbia River basalt tended to sink into soft mud. The shattered appearance of many basalt headlands and sea stacks today, including Haystack Rock near Cannon Beach, Hug Point, and the northern side of Cape Lookout, attest to the explosive interactions as hot lava met cold seawater. As the flows sank into the sands, they often disrupted the layering and took on the appearance of intrusive dikes. For years, this camouflage deceived geologists, who believed that Miocene coastal basalts

came from local vents along the Oregon coast or in the Coast Range. But the chemical compositions of these so-called intrusive rocks—the ring dikes at Otter Rock, the stacked basalt columns of a dike exposed at Fish-hawk Falls, and the fragmented, dark apophyses of basalt at Hug Point—are identical to Columbia River basalt flows farther east. Gravity studies show that the coastal basalt "dikes" extend only a few hundred feet into the sand, not thousands of feet into bedrock as an intrusive body should.

These basalt flows, which reached the coast, rank among the longest on Earth. They surged 300 miles from eastern Oregon and Washington. The dark brown rocks of Saddle Mountain are not native to the Coast Range. Like similar rocks on Onion Peak and other basaltic northern coastal mountains, they are eastside interlopers, bareheaded, dryland immigrants peering over the shoulders of the tree-shrouded, rain-sodden Coast Range.

Next Generation of Columbia River Basalts

The Wanapum flows

About 14.5 million years ago, a new series of basalt eruptions commenced from linear vents between Pendleton and Hanford, Washington. They followed the route of the earlier Grande Ronde Basalt flows westward. Known as the Wanapum Basalt, they were also part of the Columbia River Basalt Group. Although these rocks are almost identical in appearance to those of earlier, more extensive flows, they are younger, and their chemistry is subtly different. Hence, these flows merit a different name. Most of the Wanapum Basalt found near Portland, in the Columbia River Gorge, at Silver Falls State Park, and near Salem is part of a voluminous subgroup called the Frenchman Springs Member of the Wanapum Basalt.

The Frenchman Springs basalts line the canyon of the upper Clackamas River and bolster the hills south of Oregon City. They occupy the hilltops north and west

Above: South Falls at Silver Falls State Park plunges over several flows of Grande Ronde Basalt.

Top right: The dark rocks and red soils of Salem's Eola Hills are remnants of Columbia River basalts.

Right: Where the basalts flowed into a large body of water, pillow lavas formed. At The Dalles, rounded pillows and yellow palagonite mark the Priest Rapids lava's encounter with a long lake about 14.5 million years ago. As basalt continued to fill the lake bed, pillows gave way to columns in the upper part of the flow.

of Marylhurst and West Linn. They are rarer than the Grande Ronde Basalt flows partly because they have been eroded from hilltops or buried by later sediments where they lie in a valley. And overall, this new generation of basalt was not as voluminous as the preceding Grande Ronde.

A few of these flows continued all the way to the ocean. The bedrock beneath the slippery red clays of the Salem Hills and the grape-covered slopes of the Eola Hills include Frenchman Springs basalts. The basalt headland at Cape Foulweather represents the westernmost reach of these lavas. Perhaps the best known of the entire Wanapum Basalt is a flow called the Priest Rapids Member. Today, all 1,100 vertical feet of Crown Point is composed of this single basalt flow and the products of its explosive interaction with a lake.

About 14.5 million years ago, the Priest Rapids basalts erupted from vents in western Idaho. Some flows spread north and west. Near Dry Falls in north-central Washington, one Priest Rapids flow entombed an 8-foot-long rhinoceros (*Diceratherium*), preserving a body mold complete with skin texture. Similar animals are found in the Miocene John Day fauna. But much of the basalt lava followed the ancestral channel of the Columbia River. Somewhere east of The Dalles, earlier lava flows had dammed the river, creating an extensive but shallow lake. As the Priest Rapids flows moved down the river's course, the hot lava encountered lake water. The interaction was explosive, sending surges of hot ash and mud ahead of the advancing lava. This interaction continued for miles as hot water carried sediments downstream, ultimately filling the lake, according to Terry Tolan and Marvin Beeson of Portland State University, with about 2 cubic miles of glassy shards and turgid yellow clay (palagonite). The lava flows and sediments completely choked the Columbia's channel. At Crown Point, the Priest Rapids basalt filled and overtopped the channel, and finally cooled sufficiently to simply stop in its tracks. Today, the pillow lavas at The Dalles represent the Priest Rapids basalt flow as it entered the shallow lake; Crown Point is the terminus of the same lava.

With its channel blocked, the Columbia River had to move. It shifted north, establishing a course that would last for the next 10 million years. This channel, known as the Bridal Veil channel for its exposures at Bridal Veil, Oregon (or sometimes called the Pomona channel for the last major Columbia River basalt flow that would travel through it 12 million years ago; Chapter 10), was steeply walled and canyonlike in places. Today, its mudflow-filled cross section can be found between Coopey Falls and Bridal Veil Falls at the western end of the Columbia River Gorge, and at Mitchell Point near Hood River.

Above: Close-up of pillows.

Right: The Priest Rapids Flow of the Wanapum Basalt forms Crown Point.

Dooley Mountain and the Strawberry Volcanics

In the Blue Mountains to the south and east of the Columbia River basalt vents, different kinds of volcanoes coughed to life about 16 million years ago. Dooley Mountain, 20 miles south of Baker City, is mostly a thick stack of beige tuffs and ignimbrites. Some carry clasts as big as 6 feet in diameter. These ash flows probably erupted from vents just west or southwest of Dooley Mountain itself, says U.S. Geological Survey geologist James Evans. In the last stages of these eruptions, rhyolites oozed from the ground, serving as a harder and protective caprock for the older and softer ash. These rocks, dated at 14.7 million years, now form the summit of Dooley Mountain. Evans thinks it likely that Dooley, like other large rhyolite volcanoes of the past, was an active volcanic center for at least 2–3 million years. Its silica-rich lavas are an anomaly in a Miocene world that bled basalts. So it is possible, Evans thinks, that these odd, quartz-rich, light-colored lavas were generated by melting a small and exotic piece of continental crust deeply buried under the edge of North America.

At the same time, south of Prairie City, small stratovolcanoes developed. These scale models of Mount Hood covered 500 square miles of the Grant County landscape with thick gray andesites and occasional mudflows. You can hike through the interior of one of the main volcanoes that has been dissected by Pleistocene glaciers at Strawberry Lake and Rabbit Ears in the Strawberry Range.

Dooley Mountain and the Strawberry volcanoes produced rocks that were very different from the contemporary Columbia River basalts. Their sources and means of generation remain problematic. Some models

suggest that Dooley Mountain's rhyolite lava represents crustal rocks melted by the onslaught of Columbia River basalt magma. The Strawberry andesites may come from a deeper source, however. Although they may have been produced by the mixing of lower crustal melt with rising basalt magma, they were more likely produced, says Tom Robyn, by lavas related to subduction. The Strawberry Volcanics may, in fact, be distant though displaced cousins of the Cascades.

Left: The eastern half of the Strawberry Range, south of John Day, contains several vent areas where the Strawberry Volcanics erupted about 14.7 million years ago. Most of these lavas are andesite.

Right and below: Ash-flow tuffs from Dooley Mountain's eruptions, 16 million till about 14 million years ago, form hills near Hereford in the Burnt River Valley.

Andesites and the Grande Ronde

Last hurrah of the Columbia River basalts

Between 14 million and 13 million years ago, the character of lavas erupting in northeastern Oregon changed drastically. Instead of dark, hot, fast lavas that spurted from long, linear vents, the flows were more pasty and more deliberate. They tended to erupt from single volcanoes or lines of cinder cones. Many of these lavas were not true basalts. They generally were andesites and dacites (the latter with more silica and often lighter in color): gray rocks with compositions more reminiscent of the Cascades than the Columbia River basalts. They are known, regionally, as the Powder River volcanics for their abundance along the Powder River north of Baker City and the town of North Powder. Geologists, including Tracy Vallier of the U.S. Geological Survey, have speculated that some of the vents and tuffs on the south-ern flanks of the Wallowa Mountains near Richland may be as young as Pliocene, only 4–5 million years old.

The andesite and dacite lavas moved slowly and traveled only short distances. This slow movement allowed the lava to separate into layers or laminations, a structure the flow preserved as it cooled and solidified. Today, these gray rocks break readily into thin layers and plates. They are often mistaken for sedimentary shale though they are a wholly igneous rock.

These deliberate Powder River lavas were especially abundant near La Grande; 13–14 million years ago they oozed across a flat landscape. Since that time, the landscape has been faulted into valleys and mountains. To-

---

Powder River volcanics are mostly andesites and dacites that stretch from the southwestern flank of the Wallowa Mountains near Keating to the Grande Ronde Valley, also appearing on the northern side of the Wallowas near Enterprise.

day, Miocene andesites and dacites are evident in the steep faces of Mount Emily, Mount Fanny, and Mount Harris, which overlook the Grande Ronde Valley. The andesites that form the cliffs of Mount Emily are about 13.4 million years old. Similar-age lavas erupted as cinder cones near Union, at Pumpkin Ridge, and north of Elgin. They appear at Sawtooth Crater, Point Prominence, and the uplands above the Minam River along the western fringe of the Wallowa Mountains. At Craig Mountain, south of Union, the gray, shingled rocks are about 13.1 million years old.

How were these dacites and andesites generated? For 3 million years, the deep bedrock of northeastern Oregon was heated by great volumes of basalt. Inevitably, says David Bailey of Hamilton College, who mapped and studied the Powder River volcanics, some of this crust melted. Some of the melt rose to the surface and erupted as dacites, such as the rocks at the very summit of Mount Emily. But most of this silica-rich melt mixed with basalt magma, creating a variety of intermediate rocks—andesites.

Calderas Erupt in the Owyhee Mountains

At the same time that basalt lavas spread across the Columbia Plateau 15.5 million years ago, two types of eruptions, explosive rhyolite and quiet basalt, began in the Owyhees. (Geologists call this schizophrenic, Janus-like volcanic activity, which produces light-colored rhyolite and dark-colored basalt, bimodal volcanism.) Like the Columbia River basalts, one phase of Owyhee erup-

Tuffs from Three Fingers caldera form reddish, variegated cliffs above the Owyhee River.

tions produced basalt, mostly from single vents rather than from elongate fissures. Some of these lavas bear the same chemical composition as Columbia River basalt flows and are likely from the same magma source. In contrast to the quiescent basalt eruptions, other volcanoes of the Owyhees erupted with bombastic explosiveness. They produced ash, tuffs, and rhyolite. These were calderas, the most volatile of volcanoes.

Few of us would recognize a caldera as a volcano. Calderas lie low and flat against the landscape. Their only acquiescence to volcanic form may be a circular depression where eruptions have evacuated much of the volcano's liquid lava, leading to collapse of the low, subtle summit. Yellowstone Lake is such a depression. Few visitors to Yellowstone National Park ever consider that they are on the flat slopes of a huge, dangerously active volcano. Yellowstone Lake seldom gets the same respect

as Mount Hood even though Yellowstone's eruptions will be far more powerful. Yellowstone, like other active calderas, including the Long Valley Caldera near Bishop, California, simply does not look like a volcano.

Instead of building a cone, calderas spread their eruptions far afield as a turbulent cloud of hot gas and ash that often moves at 60–100 miles per hour. Such eruptions produce flat and extensive ignimbrite deposits. Calderas do not build mountains *up* as do the pasty lavas of most stratovolcanoes, but they are far

---

Above: Rocks of the Owyhee Mountains, including those of Leslie Gulch, are predominantly ash-flow tuffs.

Right: Along Pine Creek, tuffs erupted by the Mahogany Mountain caldera have been sculpted into strange forms by wind and water.

more dangerous and destructive. In 1902 a relatively wispy ignimbrite-forming cloud from Mount Pelée wiped out every living soul but one on the island of Martinique. And a mild-mannered nuée ardente from Vesuvius extinguished Pompeii in A.D. 79.

When the basalts of Steens Mountain and the Grande Ronde Basalt eruptions waned, at least six calderas (Three Fingers, Mahogany Mountain, Castle Peak, Mc-Dermitt, Pueblo, and Whitehorse) developed in Oregon's Owyhees and Basin and Range during the middle Miocene, 15 million years ago. They included the flat desert floor east of Pueblo Mountain and the eroded, pine-covered highlands of Mahogany Mountain. The ash and ignimbrites from these volcanoes covered several thousand square miles. The rocks are soft and easily sculpted, but the topography is rugged and unforgiving.

The rosy golden cliffs of Leslie Gulch are ignimbrites erupted from the Mahogany Mountain caldera. An ignimbrite is also called an ash-flow tuff or welded tuff. At Leslie Gulch, the soft yellow stone of the ash-flow tuff is more than 1,000 feet thick. The rocks are soft, sculpted by water and pockmarked by the escaping gases of their eruption. Larger holes reveal that sometimes chunks of solid rock are torn from the caldera's throat during eruption, entrained in the turbulent nuée ardente, and held closely in the ash flow until time, erosion, and weathering pry the clast from the soft ash-flow tuff's grasp.

Interlayered lava flows, tuffs, and coarse-grained river sediments are typical of Oregon-Idaho graben deposits in the Owyhee Mountains.

Smaller vents erupted rhyolite as well as ash. The Honeycombs, a reticulate mass of yellow-gray rock near Lake Owyhee, represent a minicaldera that produced tuffs and rhyolite flows too viscous to be blown away. Instead, the gas-charged lava froze above its conduit, piling up a mass of soft, cavity-ridden stone like a giant sponge. Fifteen million years of unceasing labor by wind and water eroded the softer stone, leaving rocks that look as though a shotgun-toting, Paul Bunyan-sized cowboy thought they were local road signs.

Oregon-Idaho Graben

The Owyhee caldera eruptions pumped a lot of magma and molten rock from beneath the surrounding landscape. About 14.5 million years ago, the crust just west of the main calderas began to subside along shallow faults. The resulting down-faulted basin is called the Oregon-Idaho graben. Lakes developed along the valley floor. Ignimbrites and a few basalts erupted periodically from near the edges of the basin.

The faults served one other purpose: they engendered gold deposits. The faults along the edges of the graben tapped into the remnant magma chambers below. As water seeped downward from the surface through the fault, it heated and interacted with the remaining minerals and magmas. It became acidic, dissolving precious metals from wall rock and from subsurface deposits. Then, heated to temperatures above boiling, highly acid and carrying a load of dissolved metals, it rose to the surface at hot springs. The boiling action changed the water's chemistry, and it dropped its load of gold, silver, and mercury in cavities and tiny pores within the rocks just below the surface of the hot spring, creating a gold deposit.

Grassy Mountain, Red Butte, and Quartz Mountain, a series of peaks just west of the Owyhee River near Leslie Gulch, all sit atop large deposits of gold so finely divided that the metal can barely be seen in an electron microscope. The deposit at Grassy Mountain has been mapped out as 1.05 million ounces of gold contained in 17.2 million tons of rock, or 0.061 ounces (1.7 grams) of gold per ton of rock to be mined. Known

as no-see-um deposits or, more formally, Carlin-type deposits after Carlin, Nevada, where they were first recognized and mined, these accumulations of gold are very fine-grained, intimate mixtures of rock and gold particles less than 30 micrometers (about a thousandth of an inch) in diameter. The technique of extracting the gold calls for large-scale open-pit mining. The gold is extracted from millions of tons of crushed rock by spraying or injecting a cyanide solution onto or into heaps of it and leaching the gold out. Known as cyanide heap-leach mining, the technique uses the cyanide to dissolve gold from the stone, then recovers both cyanide and gold. The process requires holding ponds of cyanide-laced waters. While an economical method of mining gold, cyanide heap-leach mining carries grave risks and leaves deep scars on fragile arid landscapes.

Breccias throughout the Owyhee Mountains attest to an explosive eruptive history.

east of Succor Creek near Picture Gorge. The Mascall beds are associated with the eruptions of Columbia River basalts rather than the Owyhee calderas. Both the Mascall beds and Succor Creek record vegetation that grew during the warmest portion of the Miocene, and some geologists have suggested that the raging diversity of plant life was in part due to the high levels of atmospheric carbon dioxide at the time. At the Mascall localities, as at Succor Creek, swamp cypress, alder, and *Metasequoia,* a tree that would disappear from the North American landscape in another 5 million years, grew in wetlands. Oak, sycamore, maple, and ginkgo held the high ground along with cedar trees.

In fact, says paleontologist Ted Fremd, Succor Creek fossils are part of the same, temporally and geographically extensive ecosystesm represented by the slightly younger Mascall beds near Dayville and other middle Miocene fossil and rock units across Oregon and the Pacific Northwest. Geologists can trace these units from central Oregon to the northern edge of the Owyhees: "You can walk this stuff out, working from Seneca through Drewsey across Drinkwater Pass or through Unity," Fremd notes. "And to the west, Lake Simtustus is the Mascall. Sure, they can be associated with different volcanics, but they overlap . . . they should simply be considered different members of the same unit as we do everywhere else."

The Miocene ecosystem was resilient in the face of volcanic disaster. In Succor Creek's ash beds, a layer of scorched pine needles and charcoal records a searing volcanic blast. In subsequent layers, vegetation returns, first as grasses, daisies, legumes, and mallows, then a pine-studded parkland, and finally a mature conifer-laden forest.

The middle Miocene, with its varied habitats and vegetation, produced the greatest diversity of hooved animals that have lived at any time in the past, according to paleoecologist Christine Janis of Brown University. Whereas the grass-floored woodlands of the middle Miocene, 15–16 million years ago, became more open and deciduous, the lumbering fauna of the Oligocene evolved toward swifter creatures with longer legs. The climate became drier. Trees gave way slowly to grasslands. More nimble legs would serve middle Mio-cene animals well. In the Miocene's open landscapes, grazing and running replaced browsing and plodding as the preferred mode for herbivores.

Middle Miocene Animals

In the increasingly open savanna of central Oregon, new animals that were better adapted to open forests and expanding grasslands prospered. The once-abundant oreodonts of the Oligocene vanished. *Dromomeryx* (a deerlike animal) and peccaries explored grasslands along with rhinos and seven genera of horses comprising at least fourteen species or subspecies. Two of the genera, *Hypohippus* and *Parahippus,* were older forms of horses; though somewhat adapted to eating grass, they still relied heavily upon shrubs for food. There was also a medium-sized horse whose diet consisted of at least 80 percent grass: *Merychippus.*

Merychippus appeared about 17 million years ago. It stood about 40 inches (10 hands) tall at its shoulder and sported three toes on each foot. Although it still had multiple toes, the central toe was larger and cusp-shaped, resembling a modern hoof. *Merychippus* had thus developed a pastern of sorts and ran with the spring-footed, toe-balanced stride of modern equines. Its legs were adapted for fast running over hard ground. It was among the first ancestral horses to sport the high-

Top right: The Miocene Nestucca Formation is exposed at Oswald West State Park.

Right: Mascall flora and fauna. The grassy, open middle Miocene landscape of central Oregon, 12–15 million years ago, included swamp cypress, ginkgo, sassafras, and serviceberry. Animals included dogs (*Tomarctus*), giraffe-deer (*Dromomeryx*), camels, rhinos, early mastodons, and a pony-sized horse (*Merychippus*). Painting by Doris Tischler from the John Day Fossil Beds National Monument.

Far right: The Nestucca Formation is similar though finer-grained than the Astoria Formation farther north. It represents muddy offshore shoals and harbors fewer fossils than the Astoria Formation.

crowned, densely enameled teeth needed to crop and chew grass, and it was probably the first horse that fully abandoned shrubs and relied on grasses for its food. *Merychippus* moved the horse out of wooded retreats and onto open prairies where speed, size, and living in ever-watchful herds would ensure survival.

Merychippus is, generally speaking, a name that includes four or more species—at least two that are well represented in the Mascall beds. A number of other horses in the Mascall beds, for example, *Hypohippus* and

Below: An unnamed waterfall plunges over Miocene volcanic rocks of the Sardine Formation. Miocene Cascade volcanoes erupted the basalts in the dark cliff, as well as ash, the light-colored outcrop in the foreground.

Right: The soft brown cliffs of Smith Rock that rise above the Crooked River are a porous tuff produced by steamy and probably explosive eruptions about 14 million years ago.

Above: At Smith Rock State Park, the rimrock
just south of the Crooked River is much younger basalt
from Newberry Crater, about 1.8 million years in age.
The dark pinnacle across the river, a rhyolite dike,
is composed of harder rock than the rest
of Smith Rock's Miocene tuffs.

Left: Smith Rock includes flow-banded
rhyolites that fed the eruptions.

Kalobatippus, are truly significant to equine evolution, says Ted Fremd. They illustrate not just adaptive radiations, but seeming reversals. For example, some get smaller and develop a more browsing dentition as characterized by increasingly V-shaped anterior palates.

Perhaps the most impressive animals in the middle Miocene woodland were the elephants. A compact pachyderm called *Zygolophodon* rooted for its food, at least part of the time, in forest soils, using its elongated jaw and protruding lower teeth as a sort of shovel. These animals were about the size of a yearling Asiatic elephant today. A fossil jaw was found in ash-laden Miocene sediments near Unity.

Like modern ecosystems, the forests, wetlands, and mountains of the middle Miocene supported animals of all shapes, sizes, and orders. Wetlands and beaches provided bird habitats. There were ducks and sandpipers, as well as quail that thrived on seeds of the newfangled grass plants. The Miocene woodland sheltered small mammals and reptiles: beaver, rabbit, flying squirrels, opossum, turtles and snakes, shrews, field mice, bats, and gophers with large gun-sight-shaped appendages on their noses. These animals served as walking lunch pails, for where there is prey, there are bound to be predators. Oregon's woodlands harbored bear-dogs and hyena-like canids with bone-crushing jaws.

In the Cascades and Coast Range, the record of middle Miocene life is sparse. But life on the beach and just offshore thrived. The Astoria Formation, best exposed in sea cliffs at Beverly Beach and other localities between Lincoln City and Newport, showcases an abundance of marine life. Altogether, almost 100 species of mollusks have been cataloged, including clams, scallops, and turban-shaped gastropods. They once lived, says U.S. Geological Survey paleontologist Ellen Moore, in warm ocean waters on a muddy bottom at a depth of about 500 feet. Oregon's shoreline has generally moved west since the Miocene. Or more accurately, it has been uplifted, hauling these mollusks out of the water and into geological dry dock where we can view them today, barnacles and all.

The Cascade volcanoes seem to have quieted in the early Miocene. But as the tide of flood basalt subsided about 14 million years ago, the Western Cascades increased their activity. Eruptions included basalts and andesites.

The Sardine Formation in the central Western Cascades is the best representative of these renewed eruptions in the waning middle Miocene. Its dark rocks frame Cougar Reservoir east of Eugene. Lighter-colored tuffs, also from Miocene eruptions, are found west of Spencer Butte near Eugene. Miocene volcanic rocks also surround Detroit Lake reservoir and compose the rugged topography from McKenzie Bridge north almost to the Columbia River. South of McKenzie Bridge, the Miocene rocks are less abundant than Oligocene volcanics.

The Cascades would find renewed energy in the late Miocene, erupting from low-lying, silica-rich, explosive vents. Some eruptions also occurred to the east of the Cascade crest. Smith Rock, a climber's Mecca, represents one of these vents and is part of a larger group of vents called the Gray Butte Complex, which erupted between 18 million and 10 million years ago. Most of Smith Rock is composed of welded tuff and the clayey palagonite produced by steam-drenched explosive eruptions. This softer, tan rock is intruded by a younger rhyolite dike that forms the darker red points and veins that cut through the tuffs. By the time eruptions ceased at Smith Rock, the major basaltic eruptions of the Miocene were ending. But there would be more eruptive violence before the Miocene ended.

CHAPTER 10

Late Miocene

Mountains rise, the climate cools, and grass reigns supreme

In the latter part of the Miocene, from 12 million to 5 million years ago, the landscape of Oregon began to take its modern form. Folding and faulting lifted mountains and dropped valleys. Rivers established familiar channels. Eruptions dwindled. Without the periodic influx of volcanic carbon dioxide, the global greenhouse effect diminished. The late Miocene climate was cool and temperate, with average annual temperatures probably similar to those in Portland today but with lower humidity (65 percent) and only about 25 inches of rain per year.

By 12 million years ago, volcanic activity had diminished. Most of the major eruptions of the Steens and Columbia River basalts were over. In the Owyhees, a new round of eruptions began. These new calderas (Star Mountain, Pole Creek Top) were less explosive than those of the previous generation. But unlike the earlier generation, they produced two kind of lavas: thick, pasty rhyolites and hot, fast-moving basalts.

Life in the late Miocene included deciduous forests of oak, alder, redbud, and elm, which shaded lakes near Juntura in southeastern Oregon and streams at The

Basin and Range faulting has lifted Hart Mountain more than 1,000 feet above Warner Lakes.

Dalles. The climate was cool and temperate. Conifers apparently were rare—there are few conifer fossils. Animals included large beaver, small camels, short-trunked elephants (*Mammut*), and shovel-tusked mastodons. The landscape was generally rolling and grassy east of the Cascades. Precipitation was more abundant, the climate slightly cooler, the grasses more lush, and the junipers nonexistent.

Late Miocene Tectonics

Imagine the rolling hills and open-canopied, oak-dominated woodland of central Missouri. Twelve million years ago the landscape of eastern Oregon exhibited a similar topography and vegetation. There were few distinctive landforms except for the low, and dormant, calderas of the Owyhees, and the isolated and eroding pimples of the Strawberry and Dooley volcanoes. But about 12 million years ago, things began to change. The Cascades became active again. The slanting subduction zone off the Oregon coastline stirred the mantle, continuing the movement of the Cascades and Coast Range westward. North America overran not only the Pacific Ocean floor but what is called a triple junction—a tender, volatile place that joins three arms of a mid-oceanic ridge. As North America moved west, the Pacific seafloor was shoved underneath the leading western edge. Instead of meeting the Pacific seafloor head-on, the collision became more of a side-swipe. And this angular motion began the rotation that is still going on now, facilitated by northwest-trending fault systems.

Driven by a complicated set of tectonic interactions that would have made Rube Goldberg proud, Oregon's crust began to shift. In Nevada and southeastern Oregon, the crust stretched in a geologic taffy-pull between the stable continent and the northward-rotating ocean floor, creating the stark topography of the Basin and Range.

Brittle rocks cannot stretch gracefully. Instead, they fracture. So, as the crust stretched, faults developed in the broad plateau of Steens basalts, breaking the landscape into huge blocks of thin crust. And like isolated pieces of pie crust atop a custard base, the crust sank unevenly into the puddinglike mantle below. The result is the landscape we see today: mountains created by tilting, with a steep face on one side and a long slope on the other. There are other analogies for these crustal blocks that, broken apart, begin to sink lopsidedly into the mantle. John McPhee likens them to foundering ships. Others think of them as flat-topped ice flows tossed on a viscous sea, a sort of spring breakup in slow motion. Whatever the analogy, the crust of southeastern Oregon, and all of the Basin and Range, is being stretched and broken.

The flat floors between mountain ranges, the Alvord Desert or the Klamath Basin, exist where the ranges have been pulled apart, leaving a basin that collects eroded sands from the mountains' summits. Throughout the Basin and Range, uplift and down-dropping are active even today. The crust is still extending, still being stretched. Buy land in Nevada today, or at Plush or Lakeview or Fields, and your fifth-generation descendents will hold property an inch longer than what the original deed specified. The Basin and Range, a landscape that writer John McPhee has called "a soundless immensity with mountains in it," is big country that is slowly getting bigger, courtesy of a long-vanished mid-oceanic ridge.

Brothers fault zone

The northern end of the Basin and Range halts abruptly along a little-known and practically invisible fault zone. This zone traces a diagonal path across the middle of Oregon like a giant zipper, allowing the Basin and Range crust to expand. This obscure band of faults is known as the Brothers fault zone. It extends from the north end of Steens Mountain through Burns, metropolitan Brothers (its namesake), and continues west to and beyond Bend, terminating between South Sister and Mount Bachelor. Drive U.S. Route 20, Burns to Bend, and you are following the Brothers fault zone and the northern limit of the Basin and Range.

Like the Basin and Range faults that it accommodates, the Brothers fault zone first became active 8–10 million years ago. In contrast to the Basin and Range faults that have uplifted and down-dropped crustal blocks thousands of feet, movement in the Brothers fault zone is mostly lateral. Its faults allow rocks to the south to move westward while those to the north remain stationary.

The purpose of a zipper is to open and close things. In the case of the Brothers fault zone, the primary function is to open. As a result, it creates an easy pathway for molten rock to reach the surface. The volcanoes that have erupted along the zone are progressively younger toward the west, the direction of opening or propagation of the faults. To see how this works, place your hands side by side in front of you. Now overlap your index fingers. Rotate your left hand away from you, keeping its fingernail firmly connected to the index fingernail of your right hand. The resulting wedge-

shaped opening has permitted, and even encouraged, progressive eruptions across the High Desert landscape—the volcanoes progressively younger toward the west—for the last 10 million years.

The oldest volcano that leaked through the Brothers fault zone is Duck Butte, a pile of 9.6-million-year-old rhyolite north of Steens Mountain. Related vol-

---

From Wildhorse Lake, near the summit of Steens Mountain, Basin and Range faults extend to the south, uplifting Steens Mountain, Pueblo Mountain, and other ranges, and down-dropping the Alvord Desert below. The steep face of Steens Mountain has been uplifted almost a mile along the Steens fault.

canic centers, from east to west, include Glass Butte (4.9 million years), Newberry Crater (where the oldest lavas are dated at almost 2 million years), and Quartz Mountain (1.1 million years). The most recent inductee of the Brothers fault system may be the rising plume of lava just west of South Sister, for the Brothers fault zone terminates in the Cascades at almost that exact spot.

To the south of the Brothers fault zone, another zone of faults, similar in function but less pronounced in expression, extends from Denio, Nevada, and the southern end of Steens Mountain west across the Cascades to Eugene. Known as the Eugene–Denio lineament, its faults became active at about the same time as

Below: The Brothers fault zone cuts across Oregon's High Desert between Bend and Burns. Although each of its small faults may have only a few tens of feet of offset, collectively they have allowed the Basin and Range to extend more than 30 miles westward in the past 8 million years.

Right: The Grande Ronde Valley, near La Grande, is a graben, bounded by faults of the Olympic–Wallowa lineament. Rocks that lie more than 2,000 feet beneath the valley floor were part of Mount Harris (far peak) when faulting began about 8 million years ago. Like most faulting in eastern Oregon, the faults near La Grande, Baker City, and Enterprise are still active.

The northern portion of Oregon's Cascades apparently was quiet during the middle Miocene. There were no high peaks or ridges to block the flow of basalt from eastern to western Oregon. After the Columbia River basalts stopped erupting, faulting uplifted the Western Cascades. The mountains cast a stronger rain shadow across central Oregon. They also became the site of renewed eruptions, with fairly explosive lavas reaching the surface and building small volcanoes.

This is especially true of the area around Mount Hood. The winding drive up U.S. Route 26 from Zigzag to Government Camp transects this buried, older volcanic terrain. Named the Rhododendron Formation after the nearby community of Rhododendron, these volcanic rocks include tuffs, lavas, and mudflows from small stratovolcanoes that erupted about 9 million years ago. The main vents are likely buried beneath Mount Hood. Other Rhododendron volcanic vents may have erupted at today's Burnt Lake near the summit of Zigzag Mountain. Most of Zigzag Mountain and the lower western slopes of Mount Hood along the road to Lost Lake are composed of Rhododendron andesites, mudflows, and tuffs. The rocks are dark and deeply weathered. Their minerals have been transformed to clays by intense weathering during the late Miocene.

The intrusive roots of the Rhododendron Formation compose much of Laurel Hill, a steep-sloped mountain where Oregon Trail pioneers roped wagons to trees and winched them downslope. Today, road cuts along the highway expose the light-colored, 8.4-million-year-old Laurel Hill diorite, an intrusion that may have fed some late Miocene eruptions.

Slightly younger basalts and andesites, from 7 million to 5.5 million years old, surround much of Mount Hood. They include the gray fissile andesites along Oregon Highway 35 near Polallie Creek, and the columned cliffs above the Hood River. Rocks of similar age, erupted from small volcanoes and vents to the south of Mount Hood, form a broad base for the High Cascades from Mount Jefferson to Crater Lake.

The late Miocene volcanoes that underlie the modern peaks tended to be low-slung models that belched

Above left: On Laurel Hill (left), where pioneers winched wagons down steep slopes on the last leg of the Oregon Trail, the underpinning of Mount Hood (in the background), a late Miocene diorite of the Laurel Hill pluton, is exposed.

Above: The Ship, a rock formation composed of interbedded ash-flow tuffs and coarse-grained fluvial (river) sediments, is a landmark at Cove Palisades State Park. The tuffs are dated about 7 million years old.

Right: Pipe vesicles at the top of a basalt exposed at Cove Palisades State Park bend in the direction that the lava flowed 7.2 million years ago. A second flow covered the first shortly after the lower basalt cooled.

ash rather than building cones or exuding lava. Much of their ash blew to the east. It descended onto a flat and arid landscape. This xeric system—the gravels deposited by flood-prone desert streams, and the ash and lava of nearby volcanoes—is exposed today at Cove Palisades State Park southwest of Madras. There, layers of gravels, coarse volcanic sands, and tuff-laden silts have been deposited by water that was released in sudden floods. Some floods may be related to storms, others to eruptions and the sudden runoff of melted snow. The earliest basalts in the Cove Palisades area are those near Pelton Dam. Dated at 7.42 million years, they are contemporaries of the Polallie Creek lavas of Mount Hood and just a bit younger than the diorite of Laurel Hill.

Volcanic rocks interbedded with the sediments attest to the proximity of volcanic vents. The most scenic of these formations include The Ship, a sculpted stack of welded tuffs and interbedded lava flows. Some lavas exposed in Cove Palisades spread east from Cascade vents; others erupted locally. Round Butte, a low shield volcano, is about 4 million years old. Tetherow Butte, a small volcano just north of Redmond, is 5.3 million years.

The eruptions of Round Butte and Tetherow Butte coincided with faulting that would change the configuration of the Cascades. Beginning about 5.4 million years ago, the central Cascades sank into an elongate, fault-bounded valley—the High Cascades graben. Diminished eruptions of lava and ash were generally contained in the broad valley along the Cascade crest and no longer reached the Deschutes Basin. Faulting continued for at least 100,000 years. By about 4.5 million years ago, the eastern side of the Cascade Range (the area between Redmond and the Cascade crest) had been down-dropped several thousand feet along the Green Ridge fault, just east of Mount Jefferson. This crustal stretching may have been related to the rotation of the Cascades or the onset of faulting that would create the Basin and Range.

We can still see the vestiges of the High Cascade graben. Its eastern side is represented by the Green

Ridge fault scarp that looms above the Metolius River just north of Black Butte. Its western boundary is marked by a series of faults that control the north–south direction of the upper reaches of the McKenzie and North Santiam Rivers. The late Miocene vents that occupied the High Cascade crest are now almost completely covered by younger, Pliocene basalts and Pleistocene lavas of the modern High Cascades. The sole exception is the base of Green Ridge itself—a layered stack of late Miocene basalt punctuated by long-extinct volcanic vents.

Harney Basin Volcanism

Devine, Prater, and Rattlesnake ash-flow tuffs

While volcanic eruptions gathered strength in the Cascades, they had become quite rare in eastern Oregon by 10 million years ago. But volcanic activity was not extinct, and those eruptions that occurred were memorable. During what may have been only a week or a few days in the late Miocene, 9.7 million years ago, a series of sequential eruptions shook southeastern Oregon. Today, the soft rocks it left behind are called the Devine Canyon Ash-Flow Tuff, named for early Harney County rancher John Devine. The Devine tuff appears throughout much of Harney County as yellowish to greenish, softly columned outcrops. But its eruption was anything but soft.

During a short period of time even by human standards, 46 cubic miles of hot gas and ash poured from vents near Burns in repeated eruptions. The Devine tuff blanketed virtually all of southeastern Oregon in a cloud of ash and fine particles of molten stone as hot as 1,500°F (820°C). It eradicated plants and animals in its path. But as we have witnessed at Mount St. Helens, ecosystems can rebound quickly from catastrophe.

During the ensuing 2 million years, a few other ignimbrite eruptions clouded eastern Oregon. Most notable of these is the Prater Creek Ash-Flow Tuff, erupted about 8.5 million years ago. It was small, as Miocene eruptions go, producing less than 1 cubic mile of ash—

Mount Hood rises above the lavas, ash flows, and gravels from the late Miocene Cascades, exposed in Cove Palisades State Park and the Deschutes Basin.

Left: Although the precise locations remain unknown, the Harney Basin was the source of at least two enormous eruptions of ash-flow tuffs. The first, the Devine tuff, erupted 9.7 million years ago. The second, the Rattlesnake ignimbrite, erupted 7.1 million years ago, suffocating 13,000 square miles beneath a thick layer of welded tuff, from Mitchell to Frenchglen. Harney Basin sunsets may have been as red as this one observed over Malheur Lake, shortly after the 1991 eruption of Mount Pinatubo in the Philippines.

Above: The 9.7-million-year-old Devine tuff forms broad, irregular columns in many places across the Harney Basin.

Right: The Rattlesnake ignimbrite erupted from a vent in the Harney Basin, and formed relatively soft outcrops in places, where Native Americans carved petroglyphs.

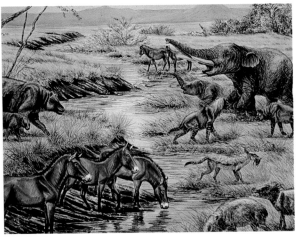

about the same volume as the eruption of Crater Lake about 6,850 years ago. Today, the Prater Creek tuff is found throughout the Harney Basin. It surrounds Malheur and Harney Lakes, and extends about 15 miles north of Burns, where it rises in 40-foot gray and awkwardly columned cliffs above U.S. Route 395.

Things were quiet for another million years. And then, 7.1 million years ago, hell broke loose. The biggest ash flow of Oregon's Miocene burst from a vent near Capehart Lake, 30 miles southwest of Burns. Called the Rattlesnake tuff, this huge ignimbrite is the result of a single eruptive event that produced about 70 cubic miles of ash in less than a week, probably erupting most of that in a single cataclysmic day. Research by Martin Streck of Portland State University has shown that the Rattlesnake coughed up almost 100 times the volume erupted from Crater Lake, and roughly 5 times the volume of ash produced by the eruption of Tambora (Indonesia, 1815), the most powerful and destructive eruption of modern times. In contrast, Mount St. Helens produced only 1/10 cubic mile of ash, approximately 0.1 percent of the volume of the Rattlesnake.

The Rattlesnake tuff erupted so fast and hot, says Streck, that the ash in the center of the flow remained plastic even after the cloud of ash and gas stopped moving. When it cooled, the molten ash welded together into a glassy and solid rock called welded tuff. Today,

much of the Rattlesnake tuff has a glassy texture. Where the ash was not completely molten, the rock may be porous, with elongate, flattened, collapsed pumice globes that have the appearance and dimensions of completely deflated soccer balls. Viewed from the side, these flattened pumice orbs are thin, wavy strips of glassy rock. They are called fiamme from the Italian *fiamma,* flame; Italians are familiar with these in the products of Vesuvius. Fiamme are common in ignimbrites worldwide; we just happen to have a world-class example here.

How fast did the Rattlesnake tuff ascend from its magma chamber 2 miles beneath the surface? At a speed of 10–15 miles per hour, says Anita Grunder of Oregon State University. This is stunningly fast for lavas rising through narrow conduits. The usual ascent rate for basalt is measured in inches or feet per hour, not miles per hour. Once it reached the surface, the eruption spread out, smothering 13,000 square miles of landscape beneath 10–60 feet of suffocating, torrid ash. From Burns to Madras, the landscape was suddenly barren.

The ash flow settled thickly on the John Day River Valley, about 90 miles north of the source vents. It buried the riverine ecosystem along the ancestral John Day River. For us, the eruption of the Rattlesnake tuff is fortunate for it preserved a snapshot of a day in the late Miocene.

Top left: Late Miocene eruptions in southeastern Oregon produced ash that was also deposited to the north, including the basin around Durkee.

Bottom far left: South of Burns, the Rattlesnake ignimbrite displays the elongate glassy clasts and pumice shards characteristic of major ignimbrites erupted at high temperatures. The area of rock shown is approximately 4 inches wide.

Left: About 7 million years ago, at the time the Rattlesnake tuff erupted, Oregon's landscape was predominantly grassland. Plants included elm, sycamore, and willow. Animals included the single-toed horse *Pliohippus* and peccaries (foreground), a variety of dogs and hyena-like dogs, and elephants as well as bearlike animals (*Indarctos*). Painting by Doris Tischler from the John Day Fossil Beds National Monument.

Life and Uplift at the End of the Miocene
Fish tales

The fossils preserved beneath the Rattlesnake tuff show that the late Miocene landscape was a temperate grassland where annual rainfall was only slightly more than the John Day River Valley receives today. By 5 million years ago, the plush deciduous forests of the early Miocene had been reduced to sparse clusters of sycamore, willow, and elm. To the south, in the Owyhee Mountains, lava flows dammed the ancestral Snake River, and faulting created a convenient basin for the water of the dammed river to accumulate in a deep and persistent

Grasslands similar to today's rolling topography south of Boardman, on the Nature Conservancy's Lindsay Prairie preserve, were abundant across Oregon's Miocene landscape 10–12 million years ago. The worldwide spread of grasses like these contributed to, and may have driven, global cooling.

rapidly into the void, filling what was then the landscape east of the Rockies.

The consequences were considerable. Animals that lived in forests found their habitat vanishing. Like the trees, they disappeared. Chalicotheres, gomphotheres, and a whole pantheon of browsing animals that lived in eastern Oregon 9 million years ago, including the browsing horses *Hypohippus* and *Parahippus,* were slowly erased, disappearing by about 6 million years ago, largely through lack of a home. In their place, grazers expanded their range and diversity. Camels and several species of grazing horses (*Plesippus, Merychippus*) increased in abundance. Ground squirrels similar to today's golden mantled ground squirrel replaced the tree-dependent flying squirrels of the early Miocene.

The advent of C_4 grasses did more than just fill in an open landscape. It forced the development of the modern horse. Along with a more efficient way of using carbon dioxide, the C_4 grasses also developed tough, silica-rich stems. Tough stems require tough teeth. The early *Merychippus* species found in Oregon had low-crowned teeth that wore down to their roots quickly when the animals were forced to chew grass. But the offspring that survived and produced subsequent *Merychippus* species had longer teeth and longer jaws, and thus could put more leverage into grinding up grass. Not only were they spring-footed and fleet, they also had more horselike heads and were smarter and longer-lived than their *Merychippus* ancestors (giving

the phrase "long in the tooth" a whole new meaning). Paleontologists who study the history of horses have used the carbon and oxygen isotopes in the tooth enamel of fossil horses to determine precisely when C_4 grasses became the dominant menu item for horses and also the dominant vegetation across North American landscapes. The date is 6–7 million years ago, according to Bruce McFadden, an expert in horse evolution at the University of Florida.

We normally assume that climate change modifies the vegetation. But in ecosystems, there is a powerful feedback mechanism that makes it hard for animals that are not well adapted to changing conditions to resist the slippery slope of extinction and climatic modification. Once vegetation has moved into new niches, it begins to drive the process of climatic modification further in its favor.

Take grass as a case in point. Greg Retallack suggests that once the expansion of C_4, hot-and-arid-climate-adapted grasses began in the late Miocene, the grasses themselves ensured their global expansion and acted as the major force in self-serving global climate shifts. Late Miocene grasslands, he notes, sequestered more carbon dioxide than the middle Miocene woodlands they replaced, ensuring that atmospheric carbon dioxide remained in a range optimal to their survival. And these grasslands, adapted to drought, promoted regional climatic drying by virtue of their higher albedo (sunlight reflectivity) and lower transpiration rate than woodlands of comparable regions. They supported a community of grazing animals (including grasshoppers) that dispersed their seeds, fertilized their soils, and kept trees at bay. "Long-term climatic cooling, drying and climatic instability," Retallack says, "may have been driven not by [tectonics], but by the coevolution of grasses and grazers."

CHAPTER II

Pliocene

Sculpting today's landscapes

Once, when geology was young and geologists were busy naming things, the Pliocene seemed an age when nothing happened. The word Pliocene comes from the Greek *pleion,* more, and *kainos,* new, and it attained the name because the epoch generally seemed just more of the same. To geologists in the nineteenth century, the Pliocene, from 5 million to 1.8 million years ago, was little more than 3 million years of breathing space between Miocene basalt floods and Pleistocene glaciation. But more recently, the Pliocene has taken on greater significance. Now, by applying computer models, isotope geochemistry, and remote sensing, we know that the Pliocene spawned an oscillating, schizophrenic climate that swung from cozy to chilly and led an unsuspecting planet into its third major Ice Age during the Pleistocene (Chapter 12).

The Pliocene began innocently enough. Five million years ago the climate was slightly warmer and wetter than today's, especially in the Arctic, according to Jonathan Adams of Oak Ridge National Laboratory. Arctic sea ice was rare. Trees like Douglas fir and hemlock extended their range far northward into Canada. Less

With Mount Hood obscured by May clouds, the Pleistocene and Pliocene volcanoes of the Boring volcanic field stand out across the Portland Basin. Mostly less than 1 million years old, the Portland Basin vents include Powell Butte, Mount Scott, Mount Tabor, and the youngest, Rocky Butte, dated at about 98,000 years.

ice, of course, meant more water. Sea level was 70–100 feet higher than today, inundating areas that would someday become Oregon coastal communities and driving the mouth of the Columbia inland to about Scappoose, where the river emptied into a huge bay.

This high stand of the sea occurred 3–4 million years ago when Pliocene temperatures reached their maximums. Evidence gathered from Greenland and other sites suggests that Arctic winter temperatures were warmer by 15–20°F (8–11°C) than today. Computer models of middle Pliocene conditions indicate that evergreen forests grew along the margins of the Arctic Ocean. The Sahara Desert shrank and was invaded by trees. And a small amount of deciduous vegetation grew at the edge of the Antarctic continent. For Ore-gon, average annual temperatures were likely warmer by 5–7°F (3–5°C), and in the middle Pliocene, eastern Oregon was likely a wetter place than today. Pollen recovered from a well near Vale by U.S. Geological Survey scientist Robert Thompson shows that a conifer forest covered at least part of southeastern Oregon about 2.9 million years ago. The forest expanded during wetter times and retreated during lengthy drier periods, giving way to a steppe grassland.

Pliocene lava flows of the Cascades and the Boring volcanic field, including this one exposed near Cascade Locks, are rare in the northern Cascades. Much of the Cascade's Pliocene rocks are covered by Pleistocene eruptions.

What drove the warming of the early and middle Pliocene? Atmospheric carbon dioxide levels were higher. The seaway between North and South America narrowed, shunting warm Atlantic surface water north toward the Arctic. This warmer water melted Arctic ice caps. With less snow and ice to reflect solar heat, the oceans and adjacent land warmed. Sea level rose. Because the seas were warmer, the greater volume of oceanic water retained more heat globally, leading to a warmer and more moderate climate. Like all climate changes, Pliocene warming was a cycle, a feedback loop that once set into motion gathered momentum, slowly accelerating for 1 million years.

Global temperatures would only begin to decline when the Isthmus of Panama solidly joined North and South America about 3 million years ago, shutting off the exchange of water between the Atlantic and Pacific. The Caribbean Sea, now essentially a closed basin where high temperatures engendered high rates of evaporation, became saltier and denser. As this dense, salty water moved northward in the Gulf Stream, it cooled. Because it was denser, it began to sink earlier, never reaching the polar region with its ice-melting warmth. Left without its source of tropical heat, the Arctic Ocean cooled. Ice began to form. Other factors, including the rise of the Himalaya and consequent disruption of atmospheric circulation, and the periodic changes in the Earth's orbit, also contributed to global cooling.

Like the global warming that preceded it, global cooling was a slow and highly complex process that took another million years, and then went overboard, leading into an Ice Age, the Pleistocene—a legacy of the Pliocene—beginning about 1.8 million years ago.

The Pliocene saw the rapid rise of the Himalaya, the boisterous eruption and growth of the Andes, the carving of the Grand Canyon, and the uplift of the Sierra Nevada. As Central America swung into place, it provided a land bridge between North and South America. Animals migrated, exploring new habitats and new continents. The first porcupines numbered among the early northbound immigrants, while camels—whose descendents would someday become llama, alpacas, guanaco, and vicuñas—hiked south. Ancestral dogs and cats, including saber-toothed, tiger-sized smilodons, reached South America for the first time, introducing new orders of efficient predators in an ecosystem that had been devoid of large carnivores. It was the largest American migration of fauna since the early Eocene's influx of mammals from Asia.

In Oregon, the Pliocene is perhaps best represented by its erosive and eruptive prowess. It built the foundations of the High Cascades, carved Hells Canyon, and excavated the steep-walled gorge of the Deschutes River. By the end of the Pliocene, most of Oregon's hallmark topography would be in place except for the highest pinnacles of the Cascades. Mount Hood, Mount Jefferson, Three Sisters, and their kin would not appear on Oregon's skyline until the middle of the Ice Age less than 1 million years ago. At the beginning of the Pliocene, the low and volatile volcanoes of the Cascades still erupted. They would continue to sling muds and ash flows, and occasional lavas, into the Deschutes Basin for another 500,000 years.

Basin and Range Faulting

Volcanoes were not the only action in Oregon. The crust was being stretched westward. In the southeast, Basin and Range faults down-dropped the Alvord Desert, Klamath Basin, and Warner Valley. In northeastern Oregon, motion on another set of faults, the Olympic–Wallowa Lineament, slowly crafted Baker Valley and Grande Ronde Valley and uplifted the Wallowas and Elkhorns several thousand feet.

In the Cascades, the ash-rich volcanoes that filled the Deschutes Basin found themselves dropping into yet another fault-bounded valley along the eastern flank of the range. This valley is called the High Cascade graben. (A graben is a valley created by faulting that lifts the sides up and drops the center down.) Today, the steep western slope of Green Ridge, east of Mount Jefferson, marks the High Cascade graben's most visible trace. Related faults continue north past Olallie Butte and turn west down the Clackamas River, likely merging into Portland's complexly faulted basin.

Portland's Volcanoes

The Boring volcanic field

Indeed, westward extension of crust that began in the Miocene increased in vigor throughout the Pliocene. By 4 million years ago, the area around Portland began to pull apart. Like the larger valleys of the Basin and Range, Portland lies in an extensional basin, stretched and down-dropped between the Portland Hills fault on the west and the East Bank fault that runs beneath the Lloyd Center and other fault systems farther east toward Gresham. This extension continues today, making these fault systems capable of producing significant earthquakes (Chapter 13).

While movement on the Green Ridge and other faults seemed to shut off the supply of lava to the Pliocene Cascades, it opened the spigots in the Portland Basin. Beginning about 3 million years ago, small volcanoes and cinder cones erupted across most of the

As the Portland Basin was stretched open by faulting, a series of small volcanoes known as the Boring volcanic field erupted throughout an area from Tualatin east to Sandy and north to Battle Ground, Washington. Eruptions began in the western Cascade foothills during the Pliocene, more than 3 million years ago, and continued at least until the late Pleistocene. The basaltic rocks in these columns on the northern side of Rocky Butte are only about 98,000 years old.

Portland Basin and the Cascade foothills north and west of Mount Hood. They spread basalts, ash, and cinders across a swampy, riverine landscape rich in lakes and wetlands.

The small volcanoes were the inevitable result of stretching thin crust above a restless mantle. Named the Boring volcanic field for the proliferation of vents around the town of Boring, the eruptions sprouted cinder cones, small shield volcanoes, and a few longer lava flows. The lavas were rich in gas. The resulting rocks are pockmarked with tiny, irregular holes. Viewed under a microscope, small crystals crisscross like tiny logs, jutting into the gas-molded cavities. Rub a finger across a freshly broken surface of most of these basalts and the surface feels as prickly as sandpaper. This texture is called diktytaxitic, and it makes the gray lavas of the Boring volcanic field easily distinguishable (for geologists) from the more conventional and much older Columbia River basalts. Differences between the Boring flows and the Columbia River basalt flows that reached Portland may be seen, if not felt, in the 16-million-year, 260-foot-long geologic core and time line displayed deep underground at the MAX light-rail station at Washington Park in Portland's West Hills.

The Portland Basin continued to widen, and the Columbia and Willamette Rivers carried heavy loads of sediment from rising mountains. Spring floods carried gravel from eastern Oregon and Washington into the basin, depositing it as the uppermost stratum of the Troutdale Formation. Today, this gravel-rich formation serves as a major aquifer for Portland and Clark County, Washington, funneling both river water and groundwater from surrounding highlands into the subsurface.

Other small eruptions dimpled central and eastern Oregon. Along the Brothers fault zone, eruptions produced isolated peaks, including Glass Buttes, 4.9 million years old, and Frederick Butte, about 3.7 million years. Near Burns, a vent unleashed a 7-mile-long lava flow that filled a small valley. Today, this lava sits atop a ridge known as Wright Point. More resistant to erosion than the tuffs of its valley walls, the rock of the flow remained while water and wind wore away the surrounding softer stone. Now what was once a valley bottom provides a

high, windswept view of the entire Harney Basin. The lava caps the ridge, protecting what remains of the soft, stream gravels it buried long ago. Wright Point is an outstanding example of reversed topography—the ancient channel, once the lowest point around, is now the highest part of the landscape.

In northeastern Oregon, Pliocene ash and tuffs, generally about 5 million years in age, are found near Keating east of Baker City and at Dooley Mountain. Ash dated at 3.1 million years is sequestered in sediments of the Grande Ronde Valley. Pliocene volcanic rocks are rare in eastern Oregon, but there were a few widespread and sporadic eruptions from vents that, even now, are poorly known.

Lake Idaho, Grande Ronde Valley, and Hells Canyon

South of the Owyhee Mountains, Lake Idaho, a vast body of water almost 1,000 feet deep and bigger than Lake Erie, stretched along the plain of the Snake River from Twin Falls, Idaho, to Ontario, Oregon. One arm of the lake extended west along the Malheur River Valley to Rome, Oregon. This lake had developed in the late Miocene when lava flows and uplift blocked the Snake River's southern outlet. After 3–5 million years, Lake Idaho was a fixture of the landscape, surrounded by sparse coniferous forests. The Snake River fed its waters. Freshwater limestones accumulated around its margins. Lake Idaho was full of fish, including an 8-foot-long salmon, *Smilodonichthys* (Chapter 10), proof positive of the large lake's connection to the Pacific.

The connection between Lake Idaho and the Pacific may have been through an ancestral Grande Ronde River, according to Jay Van Tassel of Eastern Oregon University and Mark Ferns of the Oregon Department of Geology and Mineral Industries. In the Pliocene, faulting uplifted the sides of the Grande Ronde Valley, transforming its floor into wetlands and small lakes. The fossils of four species of fish—pikeminnow, bullhead catfish, western sunfish, and whitefish, a member

Stretching across the High Desert south of Burns, Wright Point traces the path of a Pliocene stream channel that was filled by basalt and then became a high-standing ridge as the soft sediment adjacent to the channel-filling flow eroded away, leaving the harder and more resistant basalt as a ridge-top caprock.

of the salmon family—have been recovered from the old Pliocene lake beds about 400 feet below the valley surface by well-driller Wally Lowe and Van Tassel. The presence of the cold-water whitefish suggests that a significant stream ran through the Grande Ronde Valley at that time.

Along with the fish fossils, the well core contained tiny diatoms. Virtually the only other place the same type of diatoms have been found is in sediment de-posited by Lake Idaho near Glenns Ferry, Idaho. The presence of these microscopic plants suggests an aqua-tic link between the Grande Ronde's marshy landscape and Lake Idaho. The diatoms also hint that Lake Idaho's mysterious early Pliocene outlet to the sea may have flowed through Ontario, Durkee, Baker City, and the Grande Ronde Valley. So much faulting has oc-curred subsequently that these ancient channels and drainage patterns seem foreign to us today. But 3–4 mil-lion years ago the ancestral Grande Ronde River may have hosted 8-foot-long migrating salmon as well as whitefish in its cold-water streams, while catfish lolled in nearby marshes and shallow lakes.

But toward the end of the Pliocene, 2 million years ago, Lake Idaho's days were numbered. The landscape was about to change dramatically as an ambitious stream found the power to transform its unassuming valley into Hells Canyon.

A hundred miles north of Lake Idaho, the Salmon River had been cutting doggedly through the rising Bitterroots and Blue Mountains for a very long time. It flowed from Idaho and turned north to rendezvous with the Columbia. Its canyon was broad and probably no more than 1,000 feet deep. There was a smaller tributary stream that ran from hills near Lake Idaho north into the Salmon River. It was an ambitious stream with more power and a steeper fall in its channel than the river that drained toward the Grande Ronde Valley. One day, perhaps because of an earthquake, an extraordinarily high spring runoff, a great storm, or perhaps simply the reward of patient erosion, its headwaters tapped into the waters of the huge lake. At first, this overflow was probably not significant. But where there is a channel, water will flow.

Over time, the entire body of Lake Idaho began to drain down the ambitious little stream's steep channel instead of the ancestral Grande Ronde. The new river carried progressively greater amounts of water in its channel as it joined the Salmon River and followed the Salmon's course to the Columbia. The stream's course would become the new channel of the Snake River, and with the erosive power of Lake Idaho's water pouring down a steep gradient, much of today's Hells Canyon was carved out in its first million years. It took Lake Idaho a long time to drain completely down this new outlet, but it did empty completely. Today, its desiccated lake beds are exposed near Glenns Ferry, Idaho, and Ontario, Oregon, and form much of the fertile soils of the western Snake River plain.

Across Oregon and the rest of western North America, the Pliocene seems the time when most major canyons had their origins. The steep-walled canyons of the Deschutes and Crooked Rivers were initially carved about the same time as Hells Canyon. The most significant deepening of the Columbia River Gorge dates to the Pliocene. The Grand Canyon was incised into the Colorado Plateau about the same time. The reason for this continental paroxysm of canyon cutting has been laid at the feet of the great god Uplift: the rise of the Colorado Plateau, the rise of the Rockies, the

upwarp of Oregon's Coast Range and Blue Mountains. All this occurred during the last breath of the Miocene and through most of the Pliocene. But the exact reason for landscape uplift and Pliocene canyon cutting across most of the American West is still a geologic mystery.

Life in the Pliocene

During the late Miocene and throughout the Pliocene, from about 7 million to 1.8 million years ago, Oregon's climate became fully segregated into a dry east side and a westside rain forest. Oaks, wild cherry, alder, willow, and cottonwood formed a familiar riparian and upland community east of the Cascades.

In southeastern Oregon, around the shores of Lake Idaho and in the nearby highlands, the Pliocene landscape was generally a grassy plain dotted with deciduous trees and upland conifers. The trees would expand their range during the wetter, warmer climate of the middle Pliocene, then retreat again as Oregon, and the planet, grew cooler and drier at the end of the Pliocene.

Throughout this time, a diversity of animals flourished. Marshes, streams, and lakeshores supported muskrat, otter, and beaver. Two species of mammoths and one of mastodons grazed in the rolling hills west of Juntura. They were accompanied by wild peccaries, tapir, three different species of camels, including *Titanotylopus,* a large camel, and other camelids that more closely resembled the modern llama. A small, lighter-footed version of cow grazed along with the camels. There were bats, rabbit, ground squirrels, and shrews.

And there were horses. By 8 million years ago, *Merychippus,* the small, three-toed horses that first relied on grass as their primary food, were replaced by a much larger, hardier animal. Known as *Pliohippus,* this horse had developed a single large toe as a hoof but still retained a smaller, essentially nonfunctional toe on each side of it. These extra toes were similar to a dog's dewclaw. *Pliohippus* stood about 40 inches (10 hands) at its shoulder. Its head was elongate, similar to modern horses. The fossil remains of *Pliohippus* are found in tuffs and lakebed sediments about 40 miles east of Burns.

By Pliocene time, about 5 million years ago, the two

During the Pliocene, lakes occupied the widening basins of the Basin and Range and northeastern Oregon. The Grande Ronde Valley was a marshy lowland with shallow lakes that may been have drained by an ancestral Snake River that ran from Lake Idaho north to the Columbia River.

extra toes had disappeared from horses altogether. And by the onset of the Pleistocene, 1.8 million years ago, the horse had become *Equus.* In the sediments of Lake Idaho near Hagerman, Idaho, fossil horses that stood about 50 inches (almost 13 hands) have been found in abundance. Lake-bed sediments near Juntura contain similar teeth. The Hagerman horse is the Idaho state fossil and represents the extinct species *E. simplicidens,* a zebralike animal that has been compared to Przewalski's horse, a tough, 13-hand-high, dun-colored wild horse that lives on the Mongolian steppe.

Where there were horses, camels, peccaries, rabbit, and shrews, there were also predators of all sizes and abilities. In the 5-million- to 7-million-year-old ash beds near Juntura, the fossil remains of coyote-like dogs, marten, and weasel suggest a number of carnivores specialized in small prey. In other areas of southeastern Oregon, paleontologists have found the teeth of a large bear and saber-toothed cats. The larger herbivores had predators to match.

The Pliocene did not so much end 1.8 million years ago as shift into high gear. By that time, the cooling trends that had begun 1.2 million years before, as the Isthmus of Panama closed the Pacific–Atlantic connection and the Caribbean became more saline, spiraled into irreversible climate change. As glaciers grew, the polar ice caps reflected progressively more heat away from the Earth. The planet grew colder. The stage was set for the Pleistocene. The Ice Age was coming.

CHAPTER 12

Pleistocene

High Cascade volcanoes versus glaciers

Of all the things we know about geology, the Ice Age probably ranks close to dinosaurs in capturing our imagination. The idea of a world swaddled in snow, of shaggy mammoths roving a frozen planet, is at once appealing and appalling. And the Ice Age's chilling breath is close to us in time and space. There are mastodon bones beneath shopping malls, and glacial pebbles in our driveways. The Ice Age is only a moment away in the history of our planet, and it may be our future as well as our past. Today's comfortable temperate climate may be only a lull before the next glacial advance.

The Ice Age is known geologically as the Pleistocene. Although global cooling began about 3.4 million years ago, and many geologists now date the major climate shift at 2.6 million years ago, the Pleistocene proper represents a time from about 1.8 million until 10,000 years ago, when global climates cooled drastically and glaciers advanced periodically from their mountain strongholds like a marauding (but very deliberate) guerilla army. In Oregon, catastrophic floods scoured Hells

The major peaks of today's Cascades are all younger than 700,000 years. Mount Hood and Mount Jefferson continued to erupt throughout the Pleistocene, filling in glacial erosion. Three Fingered Jack and Mount Washington ceased their activity by 30,000 years ago and were extensively eroded by glaciers. Their broad bases indicate they were once much larger mountains.

Canyon as well as the Columbia River Gorge and transformed the Willamette Valley into a huge lake. Glaciers sculpted the highest peaks. Fish swam in desert valleys. But in Oregon, the Pleistocene is not just about floods and ice, it is about fire as well.

Before the Pleistocene, the skyline to the east of Portland was relatively vacant. Mount Hood was absent. There were no Three Sisters, no Mount Jefferson. Mount Rainier was not even a glimmer in a subduction zone's eye. The entirety of the High Cascades—the spired peaks etched in the Pacific Northwest's psyche—was crafted during the Pleistocene. For every volcano that we hold dear, every picture-postcard shot of a snowcapped volcanic peak, we owe a debt to Pleistocene eruptions.

For the almost 1 million years of the Pleistocene, an unremitting battle was fought between Cascade eruptions that sought to build a mountain range and Cascade glaciers that worked to wear it down. Older volcanoes and eviscerated peaks like The Brother, a sharp

knob of rock just west of North Sister, or Three Fingered Jack lost the glacial battles. Younger or more active vents like Mount Hood or South Sister survived with their forms more intact.

The causes of the Pleistocene's bitter climate and spates of ice have been linked to several factors. The closing of the Isthmus of Panama shut off the equatorial flow of warm waters. Antarctica moved into position at the South Pole, increasing the Earth's albedo, reflecting critical solar warmth back into space. Another

Below: Salt Creek Falls (near Willamette Pass), Oregon's second-highest, tumbles 268 feet over a 600,000-year-old andesite flow in the central Oregon Cascades near Diamond Peak.

Right: At Toketee Falls, the North Umpqua River cascades 120 feet over the columnar face of a Pleistocene basalt flow that filled a portion of the river's glacially carved upper valley.

factor in climate change is more remote: a rare conjunction of planetary orbital fluctuations. These perturbations are called Milankovitch cycles, first described in 1938 by Serbian astronomer Milutin Milankovitch. Three components of the Earth's rotation (axial tilt, precession, and orbital eccentricity) combine to affect the amount of sunlight reaching any point on Earth. When the three cycles (ranging in duration from 21,000 to more than 100,000 years) coincide, the climate cools. But these cycles alone are not enough to trigger global glaciation. Other factors, including atmospheric carbon dioxide, oceanic circulation, and continental configuration, are critical.

And each advance of glaciers may have a unique cause. The Pleistocene was only one of many times that the Earth's polar regions have been sheathed in ice. Altogether, there have been two other major Ice Ages in the last 700 million years of Earth's history, a total of five times that the poles have been covered with ice. We live in one of those times when, for now, ice covers both the North and South Poles.

Between 650 million and 600 million years ago, in the late Precambrian, the entire globe may have been entombed in snow and ice. This extensive Ice Age, called Snowball Earth, was likely triggered by increased precipitation over the scattered landmasses, extremely low levels of atmospheric carbon dioxide, and reflection of solar heat as the ice cover increased. Snowball Earth was probably reversed courtesy of volcanic eruptions that increased carbon dioxide far beyond today's levels, elevating average global temperatures above 100°F (38°C) about 600 million years ago, just before the sudden prolific expansion of life around the planet about 570 million years ago. Another, more moderate glacial episode occurred from 300 million to 280 million years ago during the Pennsylvanian and Permian, when ice advanced across what is now southern Africa and China.

In the Pleistocene, Oregon never developed huge ice sheets like those that covered the Midwest and New England. The demure Cordilleran ice sheets of the Pacific Northwest stopped just north of Tacoma and Spokane, Washington. In Oregon, the only Pleistocene glaciers were those that began rather locally, descending to lowlands from mountain strongholds.

The ice sheets may have advanced and retreated thirty times in the Pleistocene's million-year tenure. The two final advances that are best documented are named after the Midwestern states where they left specific evidence of glacial advance: Illinoisan and Wisconsonian, in chronological order. West of the Rocky Mountains, the last phase of glaciation is called the Fraser period, from its evidence along British Columbia's Fraser River. This last event lasted from about 22,000 to 12,000 years ago. Each of these cold periods was separated by a warmer period when glaciers melted back to a size we would recognize today. The climate became more temperate. During these interglacial periods (including the one we live in), the outsized woolly animals so well adapted to the cold retreated toward the Arctic. Plants tiptoed north as well. But when the ice returned, the flora and fauna moved south.

Throughout the Pleistocene's coldest periods, ice caps covered Oregon's highest elevations. A massive glacier smothered the Cascades. This large ice cap extended from the base of Mount Hood south about 170 miles to Mount McLoughlin. At its greatest extent, the ice may have been ½ mile thick. During the Fraser glacial maximum about 18,000 years ago, alpine glaciers on Mount Hood extended down to an elevation of about 2,500 feet, ending near Zigzag. Other mountains with extensive glaciers and ice caps included those in the Strawberry Range, Elkhorns, Wallowas, Steens Mountain, and the Klamaths. The U-shaped valleys of Oregon's mountains record the advance of alpine glaciers along almost every mountain stream.

It is difficult to measure the extent of the earliest glaciers because they have been thoroughly overprinted and eroded by the last, most extensive glaciation of the Fraser stage, from about 22,000 to 12,000 years ago. Understanding the early Pleistocene glaciers is about as easy as unraveling a crime scene after it has been bulldozed.

Many glacial features in the Cascades have been covered or filled by subsequent eruptions. Here, above Crater Lake, a set of striations carved by glaciers about 20,000 years ago survived Mount Mazama's cataclysmic eruption 6,850 years ago.

Top left: Glaciers eroded near-perfect U-shaped valleys into the gentle western and northern slopes of Steens Mountain, including that of Indian Creek, and Kiger Gorge.

Left: Near the summit of Steens Mountain, the Pleistocene ice cap ground rocks to a fine polish.

Above: In the Lake Basin of the Wallowa Mountains, glaciers sculpted peaks, scoured the bedrock, and left high-elevation meadows.

Early Pleistocene Cascades

The record of the early Pleistocene volcanoes is far easier to read than the glaciers that eroded them. At the onset of the Pleistocene, about 1.8 million years ago, the low-lying volcanoes along the Cascade crest were largely dormant. In the central Cascades, the vents that spewed ash and basalt lava eastward subsided into a troughlike faulted valley. One of the few relicts of these hump-backed volcanoes remains at Green Ridge, east of Mount Jefferson.

The volcanoes that would grow into today's High Cascade peaks began erupting about 1 million years ago. Tucked into the western base of Mount Hood, like a handkerchief in the mountain's pocket, there is a smaller volcano, the Sandy Glacier volcano. Its youngest rocks are dated at about 1.3 million years. This volcano erupted basalt and a few andesite lavas similar to those of the larger mountain that overshadows it today. Basalt flows from the volcano form Vista Ridge, a spur of dark rocks and Douglas fir forest that juts west from the base of Mount Hood above Sandy Glacier. Its central vent lies beneath the northern slope of Mount Hood.

Few other High Cascade volcanoes (the Cascade peaks that we hike and climb today) approach the Sandy Glacier volcano in age. This omission is likely the result of glacial erosion, which erased any sizable peaks while younger lavas covered the remnants. About 70 miles to the south of Mount Hood, between Mount Jefferson and Three Sisters, the remnants of another early Pleistocene volcano, 900,000 years in age, is known as Cache Mountain. Black Butte, the stately and symmetrical cone west of Sisters, is about 1.4 million years old, about the same age as the Sandy Glacier volcano. Black Butte seemingly escaped the ravages of glaciation because it lay east of the Cascade crest in a zone of low precipitation and was not quite tall enough to merit its own glaciers.

Lateral and terminal moraines of the Wallowa Mountains are among the best examples of glacial moraines in the world. These complex moraines record multiple glacial advances.

Pleistocene eruptions built shield volcanoes along the crest of the southern Cascades. The rocks beneath Pelican Butte are basalts of about the same age as the Sandy Glacier volcano and Black Butte. Other basalt and andesite eruptions produced peaks west of the Cascade crest, including Harter Mountain and Battle Ax (east of Quartzville), Foley Ridge (just northeast of Cougar Reservoir), and today's cliffs above the headwaters of the McKenzie River at the western edge of the Mount Washington Wilderness.

Middle Pleistocene

Cascades and other peaks mature

The familiar peaks of the Cascades are divided into two groups: those that began erupting between 700,000 and 250,000 years ago, and those that began erupting after 250,000 years ago. In these groupings, age is no guide to accomplishment. Some peaks that began erupting in the earlier generation rank among the Cascades' loftiest: Mount Hood (11,239 feet), with lavas dating to at least 600,000 years ago, and Mount Jefferson (10,497 feet), whose oldest eruptions are much younger, dating to only about 300,000 years. But other middle to late Pleistocene volcanoes, whose eruptions fizzled before the end of major glaciations, were virtually erased. These less fortunate volcanoes include Mount Washington (7,794 feet), Three Fingered Jack (7,841 feet), and some barely discernable peaks such as The Husband, west of Three Sisters. Before the final stage of the Pleistocene, these volcanoes were massive mountains that may have reached or exceeded 10,000 feet in height, but they lost the battle with Pleistocene ice.

At Mount Hood, the oldest lava flows have been dated at about 600,000 years; they are found in Zigzag Canyon. The gray andesites at Cloud Cap, on Mount

Three Fingered Jack, a Cascade stratovolcano, stopped erupting during the middle Pleistocene and was severely eroded by glaciers. It may have rivaled Mount Hood in size, but today only a portion of its flank, a jagged comb of layered ash and lava, remains.

Left: Ramona Falls, on Mount Hood's western flank, cascades over a Pleistocene andesite.

Above: Eliot glacier, on Mount Hood's northeastern slopes, is a reminder of the extent of Pleistocene glaciation.

Hood's eastern slope, may be even older. They are tentatively dated at 690,000 years. Unlike the basalt of the older Sandy Glacier volcano, most of Mount Hood is gray andesite. The two volcanoes—Mount Hood and its predecessor, the Sandy Glacier volcano—are very different in composition, and probably in the sources of their rock. Most of Mount Hood's early eruptions, from its inception until about 100,000 years ago, were the quiet productions of monotonously similar, slow, oozing lavas. But like all stratovolcanoes, Mount Hood is a geologic layer cake. About 30 percent of the cone consists of mudflows and ash, like soft layers of icing, interleaved between lavas. Many of these ash layers represent eruptive violence: ash that exploded into the air; mudflows that careened down mountain slopes and streams.

During the Pleistocene, repeated debris flows of mud, sand, rocks, and uprooted vegetation from Mount Hood traveled far down the Sandy River and Hood River Valley. Most mudflows, according to the U.S. Geological Survey, likely began as rockfalls high on the mountain and incorporated snow and glacial meltwater as they accelerated down the slope. Some were catastrophic. Between 100,000 and 50,000 years ago, part of the northern face of Mount Hood collapsed, creating a monstrous debris avalanche. A torrent of rock and mud raced down Hood River, burying the lower Hood

Top left: The lateral moraines of Mount Hood's Eliot Glacier are reminders of its former extent.

Left: North Sister, a stratovolcano composed of basalt and basaltic andesite plus cinders and ash, is the oldest of the Three Sisters volcanoes.

Above: Rose-colored tuffs along Tumalo Creek erupted from the Tumalo volcanic center, a broad and explosive volcanic system that now underlies Broken Top and other central Oregon volcanoes.

River Valley in mud and rock to depths of more than 120 feet, creating a 100-foot-high dam across the Columbia River, and only stopping after it had traveled 2 miles up the White Salmon River. Much of the town of Hood River is built on the gravels and muds deposited by this event.

The major edifices of many High Cascade peaks were built during the middle Pleistocene, from about 700,000 to 130,000 years ago. At the Three Sisters volcanic complex, North Sister erupted dark, iron-rich, fluid basaltic lavas and cinders. Nearby, Middle Sister produced more explosive eruptions of andesite. Mount Bachelor and South Sister would not appear until much later, after most of the Pleistocene glaciers were gone.

But just northwest of Bend, a powerful, low-lying volcano erupted huge volumes of ash and ignimbrites. Known as the Tumalo volcanic center, its activity began about 600,000 years ago, the same time as the first eruptions of Mount Hood. Today, the Tumalo volcanic center is truly extinct; its last eruptions were about 280,000 years ago. Rather than building a cone, the Tumalo eruptions spread ash across most of central Oregon, depositing thick beds of tuff that today support upscale homes on the western slopes at Bend. The soft rocks from the Tumalo vents form broadly columned cliffs at Tumalo State Park and loosely bedded ash along the Deschutes River at Cline Falls. The Tumalo eruptions built the base for Broken Top, a glacially eroded volcano east of Three Sisters. Broken Top's eruptions began about the time that Tumalo activity waned. Without this platform of tuffs to stand on, Broken Top would be a smaller volcano, one with less glacial sculpting.

Mount Mazama

And to the south, Mount Mazama (which would erupt explosively, creating Crater Lake, well after the Ice Age was over) built a massive and complex cone of andesite and basalt that rose to 12,000 feet before its cataclysmic eruption. Mazama, more than any other Cascade volcano, was a series of overlapping shield and composite volcanoes rather than a single system. The oldest lavas we know of are the dark basalts that form the Phantom Ship, a truncated vent that rises ghostlike from the southeastern side of Crater Lake. Andesites and basalt of similar age form Mount Scott to the east of Crater Lake, one of the few remaining vestiges of the original volcano. The andesites, dacites, and ash of Danger Cliffs, the crumbly, precipitous western shore of Crater Lake, were erupted about 340,000 years ago. The next series of eruptions produced the solemn gray andesites of Dutton Cliff through a long series of eruptions from 340,000 to 190,000 years ago.

From 70,000 to 10,000 years ago, during the last part of the Pleistocene, Mount Mazama's eruptive style grew progressively more explosive. While other Cascade peaks erupted stout andesite lavas, Mount Mazama produced ash and gas, hot tuffs, and only a few small lavas. These eruptions included the soft rocks

that form Pumice Castle, from an eruption of tuff and pumice about 50,000 years ago. Small eruptions of sticky dacite lavas occurred about 20,000 years ago at the beginning of intensive glaciation. Mazama would lie in wait more than 12,000 years before its cataclysmic blast (Chapter 13).

Eruptions in the Portland Basin

The Boring volcanic field began erupting about 3 million years ago as the Portland Basin opened initially during the Pliocene. These eruptions continued through the Pleistocene, and faulting widened the basin still farther. Basalt flows built small shield volcanoes, lava fields, and cinder cones.

Today, the vents of the Boring volcanic field provide much of the Portland area's scenery. Mount Scott, Rocky Butte, and Powell Butte are all small Pleistocene volcanoes. The Oregon Zoo is perched atop a shield volcano, Mount Sylvan. Farther south, the Sylvania campus of Portland Community College hugs another vent, Mount Sylvania. Cooks Butte, above Lake Oswego, was once a tiny volcano. At Mount Tabor Park, the outdoor basketball court occupies the excavated guts of a cinder cone. A scenic lake occupies the crater of a 100,000-year-old shield volcano at Battle Ground Lake State Park in Washington. Willamette Falls pours over a Boring lava flow that filled the Willamette's ancestral channel and forced the river's channel south. Eruptions from Boring volcanic vents persisted through the late Pliocene and into the Pleistocene. Many small shield volcanoes, cinder cones, and lava flows in the Portland Basin have been dated at less than 1 million

Top right: The Phantom Ship in Crater Lake is the oldest remnant of Mount Mazama, about 340,000 years in age.

Right: Mount Tabor is a Boring volcanic field vent that erupted basaltic cinders, and a lava flow that extends northward. Now, a picnic area and basketball court occupy the volcano's vent area.

years by Robert Fleck and colleagues at the U.S. Geological Survey. Basalts near St. Vincent's Hospital erupted about 170,000 years ago. The youngest known vents in the Portland Basin, including Rocky Butte (98,000 years), are less than 100,000 years old. Altogether, more than 100 Boring volcanic vents have been identified, and many are regional landmarks. Some geologists think that as the Portland Basin continues to expand, there is the potential for future eruptions to the north and west of the existing volcanoes.

Newberry Crater

Volcanic activity was by no means limited to the Cascades or the Portland Basin. To the east, the Pleistocene saw the first development of Newberry Crater south of Bend. These eruptions began with thin, fluid basalt flows that moved north, slipping into Deschutes Canyon and the canyon of the Crooked River about 1.2 million years ago. These rocks today form the dark cliffs and rimrock of Cove Palisades State Park and the southern rims of Smith Rock State Park. Newberry would grow rapidly during the Pleistocene. Too low and too far east to collect glacial ice, Newberry expanded by erupting ash about 510,000 years ago. Like most volcanoes, Newberry's eruptions were discontinuous, punctuated by vacations while the complex magma sources regrouped.

Although Newberry Crater is generally the same age as the High Cascades, the sources of its lavas are very different. Newberry's lavas are not related to subduction. Instead, they are a mixture of melted mantle rock and melted crust that rose through fractures of the Brothers fault zone. Newberry's early Pleistocene eruptions consisted of explosive ash alternating with calm basalts. Basalts constitute about 75 percent of Newberry's volume and account for its low, shield volcano profile. The violent eruptions of ash crafted a series of calderas, large circular depressions in the vent area, now occupied by East Lake and Paulina Lake. Activity built Newberry sporadically, with the best-dated eruptions at 510,000 (Tepee Draw tuff) and 400,000 (West Flank

Dome) years ago. Late in the Pleistocene, additional eruptions would shake Newberry again with a flurry of eruptions about 12,000 years ago. These eruptions included basalt that started in lava tubes high on Newberry's north-facing flank and spread northward toward Prineville. These rocks today form a malpais (from the Spanish *mal pais,* bad land), a rugged and jumbled landscape of lava flows about 10 miles east of Bend named the Badlands. A thin coating of Mazama ash indicates that the Badlands' flows are older than 7,500 years, but their pristine condition argues that they are not much older. Eruptions would continue at Newberry until about 1,200 years ago when obsidian oozed from vents near the volcano's summit.

Fort Rock and Related Vents

About the time that Mount Hood was building its main edifice and Newberry Crater pumped out its main basalts, smaller volcanoes erupted in southeastern Oregon. These early Pleistocene vents include Hole in the Ground, Fort Rock, Four Craters, and Table Rock near Christmas Valley. Altogether, about forty small volcanoes erupted here in the early Pleistocene. Most of these eruptions produced small amounts of gas-charged, silica-rich magmas. The resulting material was a hot, fast-moving froth rather like the foam from a latte spilling over the edge of the cup.

Fort Rock is the best known of these desert tuff formations. It is a kind of tuff ring: ashy, gassy lava that boiled from a circular vent, creating a donut-shaped extrusion. On Fort Rock's steep, water-washed, sand-blasted walls, you can see layers. These represent pulse after pulse of sticky, frothy, at times explosive ash. As this material bored its way to the surface, it picked up chunks of subsurface rock. Angular clasts of basalt and samples of other rocks that lie far beneath the desert floor are displayed in the walls of Fort Rock for all to see. The spongy-looking walls are composed of a rock called palagonite, a yellowish ash formed when basalt lava interacts with water and steam.

The desert basins here had begun to accumulate large amounts of groundwater by the early Pleistocene. As small pulses of basalt, probably related to nearby Newberry Crater, tried to rise through this saturated ground, the water flashed to steam and mixed with the hot lava. The result was an explosive eruption, rich in ash, that transformed the basaltic liquid into froth. This froth chilled and solidified rapidly, forming a tuff ring or tuff cone. Where the ground was relatively dry or the basalt voluminous, the tuff ring often filled with basalt as the eruptive violence waned. South of Christmas Valley, Table Rock represents this sort of filled tuff ring.

Rhyolite at the summit of Newberry Crater, southeast of Bend, probably dates to the earliest of several caldera-forming eruptions about 510,000 years ago.

Left: Crack in the Ground is a 2-mile-long fissure that cuts through basalt flows of the Four Craters lava field northeast of Christmas Valley. It represents a fault or cooling crack that allowed the east part of the lava field to drop downward, forming a small graben.

Above: Fort Rock is a Pleistocene tuff ring that stood as an island in Pleistocene Fort Rock Lake. Wind-driven waves breached its southern side and carved a wave-cut bench that still measures the lake's prehistoric level.

Where the basalt was limited, or the ground extremely wet, there often was simply an enormous explosion when hot ascending lava encountered cold groundwater. This type of eruption produces only steam. It leaves behind a round depression in the ground, called a maar. Several maars dot the Fort Rock Basin. Hole in the Ground, northwest of Fort Rock, is one of the best documented. Hole in the Ground is a circular, 500-foot-deep crater about a mile in circumference. Its rim rises 200 feet above the original ground level. The area around Hole in the Ground is covered with rocks and ash blasted out of the Earth in a huge steam explosion. Most is ash or cinder-sized rock, though rare larger blocks scattered through the pine and juniper reach 26 feet in diameter. Explosions tossed large, angular rocks as far as 2⅓ miles from the center of the maar at speeds up to 650 feet per second.

At the other end of the spectrum, some basalts on higher ground north of Fort Rock erupted without the interference of groundwater. These lavas created Devils Garden and other nearby lava flows, a malpais landscape of ragged basalt.

Lakes Fill the Desert

The Pleistocene landscape of southeastern Oregon looked very different from today's High Desert. It was a lake—several lakes, to be more precise. As Basin and Range faulting lifted rimrock and down-dropped the basin floors, the resulting basins had no drainage outlet. In the more humid late Pliocene and Pleistocene climate, water began to collect in these enclosed basins. Lakes overshadowed by dark rimrock took the place of grassland. In the Basin and Range of Utah, Lake Bonneville covered almost 20,000 square miles to depths of as much as 1,100 feet. We know its shrunken rem-

The lakes and summer-dry playas of the southeastern Oregon, including Warner Lakes near Plush, are tiny remnants of the huge Pleistocene lakes that covered more than 3,000 square miles of Oregon's desert basins.

nant today as Great Salt Lake. In northwestern Nevada and northeastern California, Lake Lahontan covered about 8,500 square miles to a depth of 700 feet. And in Oregon, nine large lakes stretched across today's desert floor.

The largest of these was Fort Rock Lake. Covering almost 1,000 square miles, it reached a maximum depth of about 200 feet. Lake waters inundated Fort Rock Valley and Christmas Valley. Wind-driven waves sliced terraces into the surrounding landscape and carved away the southern side of Fort Rock, one of many small volcanoes that erupted through the wet lake-bed sediments during the Pleistocene. Other pluvial (rain-filled) lakes occupied Warner Valley west of Steens Mountain and Hart Mountain, Alvord Valley east of Steens Mountain, Harney Basin south of Burns, and the basin of Alkali Lake south of Wagontire. At the western margin of the Basin and Range, Lake Modoc filled 1,100 square miles of the southern Oregon and northern California landscape, including today's Upper Klamath Lake in Oregon, and Lower Klamath Lake and Tule Lake in California. At their maximum extent, lake water occupied almost half the land area in the Basin and Range.

Probably the best documented of Oregon's pluvial lakes is Lake Chewaucan. At its largest extent it covered at least 480 square miles to a maximum depth of 375 feet. This lake encompassed the Summer Lake valley, the Chewaucan River, Chewaucan Marsh, and swung north beneath Abert Rim where Lake Abert is today. Incoming streams deposited their sediment as they entered the lake, building up deltas. And like other lakes around the Basin and Range, Lake Chewaucan etched its shorelines into the geography. Today, these ancient beaches appear as lines or terraces on slopes far above arid valley floors. They record the periodic fluctuation of lake levels throughout the late Pleistocene. Lake waters rose as glaciers shrank. And lake waters receded as the climate cooled and glaciers expanded. The shorelines of Lake Chewaucan record at least six major changes in level. The highest stand of waters was about 33,000 years ago. One of the lowest was 22,000 years ago, the time when glaciers reached their maximum size and power.

Diamond Craters, Jordan Craters, and Late Pleistocene Eruptions in Southeastern Oregon

Very late in the Pleistocene, small basalt volcanoes erupted in southeastern Oregon. These are Basin and Range lavas, the products of a thin, expanding, rifting crust, and the mantle underneath. The two most remarkable vent areas are Diamond Craters and Jordan Craters. Today, the ropy, glassy flows of both these sites look remarkably fresh and provide textbook examples of pahoehoe basalt.

Diamond Craters, between Steens Mountain and Burns, erupted less than 25,000 years ago, perhaps as recently as 17,000. Basalt lavas here cover about 40 square miles. As the initial flows cooled, more basalt was injected beneath the original ones, inflating the area into six fluid-filled domes. Ultimately, the domes cooled and collapsed. Ensuing eruptions spewed ropy, fluid basalt from vents around the edges of the collapsed domes. Diamond Craters present one of the best places in Oregon to explore the dynamics of a basalt flow.

Jordan Craters, on the southern edge of the Owyhee Mountains and a very long 35 miles west of the town of Jordan Valley, are similar to Diamond Craters though more extensive as an eruptive center. The lavas cover about 300 square miles of desert floor. The oldest vent of the complex is Three Mile Hill. This low shield volcano dates to about 1.9 million years, the very late Pliocene or early Pleistocene. Lavas to the south of the Jordan Craters complex are 440,000 years old. They erupted at a time when many High Cascade volcanoes we see today were beginning their first major eruptive cycles. Rocky Butte, a small and barren hillock, repre-

Fluid, ropy-textured pahoehoe basaltic lavas erupted at Diamond Craters, south of Burns, about 20,000 years ago.

Above: Fresh in appearance, the basalt from Coffeepot Crater, the youngest vent at Jordan Craters, is 150,000 years old and covers about 50 square miles of desert grassland north of Jordan Valley.

Right: At Diamond Craters, hot, fluid lava jetted from the tops of solidifying lava flows, forming spatter cones.

sents the youngest lavas at Jordan Craters. Dated at 30,000–90,000 years, Rocky Butte erupted a little earlier than Diamond Craters. So the whole of the Jordan Craters complex had completed its eruptions before those at Diamond Craters began.

The lavas we most often associate with the name Jordan Craters are those erupted from Coffeepot Crater. These lavas are a middle-aged feature of the eruptive complex, dated at 150,000 years by William Hart of Miami University, Ohio, and Stan Mertzman of Franklin & Marshall College. But the fresh-appearing, dark basalts make for spectacular, if bleak, malpais scenery. Like Diamond Craters, these basalts display the glassy surface and flow features typical of pahoehoe basalt flows, including lava tubes, pressure ridges, lava gutters, and a ropy surface. And like Diamond Craters, there is a cinder cone that caps the main lava vent. The basalt at Jordan Craters erupted in at least two stages: eruptions that built the cinder cone, followed by lava flows that covered about 50 square miles.

Middle and Late Pleistocene Flora and Fauna

The pluvial lakes of the Great Basin provided a refuge from the severe conditions that beset higher elevations. During the middle and late Pleistocene, from 700,000 to 10,000 years ago, the lakes of southeastern Oregon lay in grassy, forested basins ringed with pine, spruce, and aspen. The now barren landscape was, as local cowboys might say, pretty well haired over. A remnant of these trees can be found in the remote northeastern corner of Lake County, where ponderosa pines (the Lost Forest) persist near the shores of Fossil Lake. Other relicts of eastern Oregon's wetter Pleistocene climate include a stand of cedars on the northern slope of the Aldrich Mountains west of the town of John Day.

Although Pleistocene vegetation might seem familiar but misplaced, Pleistocene animals, the Pleistocene megafauna, were uniquely adapted to a cold and variable climate. In southeastern Oregon, the remnants of

two types of camels, three species of zebralike horses, as well as tapir are preserved at Fossil Lake, a smaller remnant of Fort Rock Lake. A large bighorn sheep, with horns that put modern Boone and Crockett records to shame, was recovered near Adel in southern Lake County. The sheep likely grazed along the shores of a Pleistocene lake 65 miles long and 7 miles wide, where it may have encountered a Pleistocene bear, *Arctotherium*, whose 10-inch-long paw prints were preserved in mud at Drews Gap in eastern Lake County.

Found in a variety of locations both east and west of the Cascades, Oregon's more ubiquitous Ice Age inhabitants included woolly mammoths, found at Fossil Lake, in Bridge Creek near Mitchell, in downtown Lakeview, in the Grande Ronde Valley near La Grande (beneath home plate of the college baseball field, in fact), and at several locations in the Willamette Valley.

The mostly complete skeleton of an elderly female mastodon named Tu Tu Tuala occupies a hallway of the library in the City Offices building in Tualatin. With smaller bodies and narrower tusks than woolly mammoths, mastodons were well suited to browse on grasses and navigate thick groves of alder, oak, and cottonwood in the Willamette Valley's late Pleistocene lowland environments. When she died, Tu Tu Tuala was 27 or 28 years old, stood 8 feet tall at the shoulder, and weighed about 3 tons. The remains were excavated from the organically rich wetland soils of a strawberry field—now the Tualatin Fred Meyer's parking lot—by John George in 1962.

The nearly complete skeleton of a female mastodon was found in Tualatin. This is now mounted in life position in a quiet hallway in the Tualatin Public Library, near the site of the Pleistocene swamps and quicksand where she met her death 11,300 years ago.

True elephants also roamed Oregon's wet landscape. The remains of three species have been found, including the extinct *Elephas columbi*, 11 feet tall at the shoulder and a consummate grazer of grasses. This elephant has been found at Newberg, McMinnville, Dayton, St. Paul, Silverton, Harrisburg, and Eugene west of the Cascades as well as at The Dalles and near Baker City and Umatilla to the east. Where shopping malls loom today near Medford, a giant bison with a horn spread of 3 feet grazed on lush grasses. Similar animals lived in the northern Willamette Valley near Oregon City and in eastern Oregon; there are fossil bison from Lick Creek in Wallowa County. Horses ranged throughout the Wallowa Valley. Ground sloths, vegetarian bearlike animals that stood 12 feet tall, lived near La Grande in northeastern Oregon, with an address on Foothill Road. Other ground sloth remnants have been unearthed from the peat deposits at Woodburn south of Portland along with a variety of beaver, muskrat, and rodent remains.

Where there were oversized herbivores, there were large predators. At the Woodburn peat site (Oregon's drippy, marshy equivalent of the La Brea tar pits) the remains of a dire wolf were recovered in 1998. This animal was similar in appearance and size to the modern gray wolf, probably averaging 110 pounds as an adult. But it had a more massive (yet smaller-brained) head, bigger teeth, and stronger jaws. Its legs were somewhat stockier. Unlike its swifter cousins, the gray wolf and coyote, who employ chase-and-catch methods of hunting, the dire wolf ambushed its prey, then crushed the bones.

One of the Willamette Valley's more interesting residents, found in excavations for Woodburn High School, was a bird—a very big bird. Known as a teratorn (*Teratornis merriami*), it sported a wingspan of 12 feet and likely weighed about 170 pounds. In contrast, the largest California condors achieve a puny 9-foot wingspan. A relative of both storks and vultures, equipped with hawklike hooked beaks and effective

talons, the teratorn may have hunted live prey on the ground, gliding above and then grasping its victim. Or teratorns may have simply been mammoth-sized vultures, because they scavenged the carcasses of mammoths and other large Pleistocene mammals. Or they may have been both predators and scavengers. Teratorns also hung out around what would become downtown Los Angeles, where their remains are also found in the La Brea tar pits. Similar oversized vultures lived in Argentina, where they reached truly respectable wingspans of 24 feet.

End of the Ice Age
Floods scour the landscape

The Pleistocene was a bizarre age of oversized glaciers and oversized fauna. And at its end, there were oversized floods. Some of the most stupendous floods in Earth's 4.6-billion-year history scoured the Pacific Northwest landscape as the epoch closed.

In northernmost Idaho, the Clark Fork River empties into Lake Pend Oreille. Just upstream, the river moves through a deep canyon more than 2,500 feet from its top to the riverbed. In the Pleistocene, glaciers periodically dammed this canyon. Robbed of its outlet, the Clark Fork River backed up into an enormous lake—glacial Lake Missoula. This enormous body of water drowned the region under as much as 900 feet of water. Successive lakeshores line the slopes around Missoula now like giant bathtub rings. Water backed up all the way to Anaconda, near the Clark Fork's headwaters in southwestern Montana. It transformed the hills on today's National Buffalo Refuge, north of Missoula, into stair-stepped hill slopes. It inundated 3,000 square miles of Montana. It bided its time.

Ice, of course, is less dense than water. And ice melts. Ultimately, the glacial dam was no match for the lake. Water may have lifted the ice; it may have melted it. But, importantly, the waters of glacial Lake Missoula, all 500 cubic miles, poured through the dam in a sudden catastrophic outburst, flowing at about 17 million gallons (64 million liters) per second, according to U.S.

Geological Survey hydrologist Victor Baker. Water washed across the Rathdrum Prairie in Idaho, leaving ripple marks as high as houses. It scoured the soils from the clay-laden loess hills of the Idaho and Washington's Palouse Hills. It transformed fertile prairie into a wasteland of barren basalt channels and oversized waterfalls. A day after it fled Montana, the water surged through the Columbia River Gorge. At Wallula Gap, Washington, water completely filled the 1,000-foot-deep river canyon, creating a hydraulic dam, backing up floodwaters into the drainage of the Snake River all the way to Lewiston, Idaho. Once past Wallula Gap, flowing at the rate of about 10 million cubic yards (or cubic meters) per second, according to U.S. Geological Survey hydrologist Jim O'Connor, the floods eroded the southern side of the Columbia's canyon. Water rushed over the top of Crown Point, again filling the entire Columbia River Gorge to overflowing. Water ripped the northern face off of Portland's Rocky Butte. Slowing as it entered the Portland Basin, the turbulent water deposited a gravel bar that extended from Rocky Butte west more than 5 miles, almost to the Willamette River. Today, we know this gravel bar as Alameda Ridge, one of northeast Portland's higher and longer topographic features.

Floodwaters transformed the Willamette Valley into a lake 100 miles long, 60 miles wide, and 300 feet deep. The sediments from the largest flood and subsequent smaller inundations coated the valley floor with 15 feet or more of mucky sediment. Today, Willamette Valley farmers plow fields of fertile Montana soil and clays from Washington's Palouse.

As the Willamette Valley slowly drained, the floodwaters continued down the Columbia River to the sea. In the valley and in other lakes created along their route, the floodwaters left evidence of their passing: ice-rafted rocks from Montana and Washington. These granites and metamorphic rocks are thoroughly exotic to the Willamette Valley, foreigners among the native basalts. One of these, a huge clast of metamorphosed mudstone called argillite, from Montana, is enshrined at Erratic Rock State Natural Site near Sheridan. Others are cemented into stone walls in Laurelhurst in Portland, where the floods left a hill of rounded Montana stones.

In eastern Oregon, enterprising locals in Boardman harvested the biggest granite boulders and made tombstones out of them. In Portland, granite-laden flood gravels were partly responsible for closing Whitaker Middle School in 2001 when elevated levels of radon—a radioactive gas generated by the decay of uranium in the granite—were detected in classrooms.

It is hard enough to imagine one such flood, but there may have been hundreds. Not all were as big as the largest events; some may have been a mere trickle in

Relict of a Pleistocene flood, an iceberg-rafted boulder of Montana gneiss rests in grasslands south of Boardman.

comparison. Richard Waite of the U.S. Geological Survey has documented at least 40; Brian Atwater, also of the Survey, counts at least 89. At least 25 of these floods had discharges exceeding 1 million cubic yards (or cubic meters) per second as they scoured through the Columbia River Gorge. In some, water from glacial Lake Missoula was joined by icy meltwater from glacial Lake Columbia, north of Washington's Grand Coulee. The earliest floods occurred about 19,000 years ago, the latest less than 13,000, says Jim O'Connor. The largest of the Ice Age Missoula floods has not been precisely dated, but O'Connor's work suggests it occurred sometime between 19,000 and 15,500 years ago.

There is another noteworthy Pleistocene flood. Known as the Bonneville flood, it roared through Hells Canyon about 14,500 years ago. This was a one-time event, but it was as incredible as the Missoula floods (sometimes called the Bretz floods). One of the largest Pleistocene lakes in western North America was Lake

Bonneville; its shrunken remnant today forms Great Salt Lake. But above Salt Lake City and Provo, Utah, there are terraces, evidence of Lake Bonneville's former glory. Late in the Pleistocene, glacial meltwaters, largely from the Wasatch Range in Utah and Idaho, swelled Lake Bonneville's size. The lake level rose sufficiently to spill over a ridge of soft sedimentary rock at Red Rock Pass, Idaho, at the lake's northern end, far above Pocatello. As water moved over the pass, it rapidly eroded a gully more than 300 feet deep, accelerating the outpouring of water. Jim O'Connor calculated that almost 1,220 cubic *miles* of water spilled over the divide and into the drainage of the Snake River, flowing at a rate of 1 *million* cubic yards per second. This water ponded briefly onto the

In the Willamette Valley, an 8-foot-long boulder rafted from Montana on an iceberg is the focal point at Erratic Rock State Natural Site near Sheridan.

flat-bottomed Snake River Plain. But as it entered Hells Canyon, where the Snake River's gradient steepens, it gathered momentum. Through the narrowest parts of the canyon, the floodwater was 615 feet deep and flowed at a rate of 600,000 cubic yards per second (16.2 million cubic feet or 460,000 cubic meters per second). This water, says O'Connor, moved at a peak speed of almost 40 miles per hour.

These late Pleistocene floods significantly altered river channels and, indeed, entire landscapes. Today, more than 300 feet of sediment from the Missoula and Bonneville floods lie in the floor of the Willamette Valley. Portland's Rocky Butte still bares its wounded northern and eastern sides to freeway travelers. Across eastern Washington's scablands, desolate basalt and scoured channels take the place of soft and fertile rolling hills. In Portland, homeowners whose houses are perched on flood-borne granite gravels check radon detectors in their basements and eat local vegetables organically grown on refurbished Montana soils.

The Pleistocene rearranged things, and it is still with us. It is likely, in fact, that we are still living in the Pleistocene even though the glaciers seem long gone. In the normal order of climate change, ours may only be an interglacial epoch, a time to catch breath before the next glacial advance. It has been about 12,000 years since the glaciers last retreated, but warm interglacial periods have lasted much longer. And in the Pacific Northwest, some interglacial periods have been even warmer than today's climate. During the last interglacial period, called Interglacial Substage 5e, the interval between 125,000 and 115,000 years ago, what is now the California coastal redwood forest became a forest of oak,

notes Mitchell Lyle of Boise State University. The climate in Oregon, he says, was warmer by as much as 4°F (2°C) on average, and much drier than today, based on plant communities and on the kinds of radiolarians found in deep-sea cores. Even warmer conditions developed during Interglacial Stage 11, about 400,000 years ago.

What caused these warm interglacials? In part, the Earth's orbit was slightly less eccentric than before, bringing the planet very slightly closer to the sun and assuring that the planet received a somewhat greater amount of solar radiation year-round—an orbit similar to today's. But there is more. Tiny amounts of ancient atmosphere archived deep in Antarctic ice confirm that during warm interglacial intervals like 5e and 11, the levels of carbon dioxide and other greenhouse gases were elevated above today's. While the source of that carbon dioxide is unknown, the effect is clear. Antarctic ice melted. Sea level rose by more than 60 feet. Then, as atmospheric carbon dioxide declined, the ice advanced, sea level dropped, and another Ice Age began.

Ice-core data also reveal a lag time of as long as 1,000 years between the rise of greenhouse gas and the ultimate elevation of temperature. Today's carbon dioxide levels are even higher than those of the warmest interglacial 400,000 years ago. Then, during Interglacial Stage 11, average annual temperatures in the Pacific Northwest were warmer by about 5°F (3°C) than today, and pine and Sitka spruce again grew where redwoods are today. Sea level was also higher; Portland might have been a deepwater port.

And we are, evidently, poised for this to happen again.

CHAPTER 13

Holocene

Humans, earthquakes, and eruptions

By 10,000 years ago, the Pleistocene's glacial grip had loosened. The ice retreated, melting back to its mountain strongholds. Deserts became lakes. Valleys once choked with glaciers blossomed into gravel-bottomed alpine meadows. Pines ventured into higher elevations. Sea level rose. And humans began to disperse more widely across the landscape. This time is known as the Holocene—it is the geologic epoch in which we live today. During the Holocene's hundred centuries or so, humans have had an especially close-up view of geologic processes, of eruptions and earthquakes. We have flourished in a mild climate. While some consider today's climates and landscapes to be permanent fixtures, geologists know better. Landscapes are made to change. Climates vary from year to year and eon to eon. Many geologists and climatologists consider the Holocene to be only another interglacial period, a time-out while the Pleistocene, with its ice, regroups though human influence on global climate is altering even geologic scenarios.

Crater Lake, 1,943 feet deep—deepest in the United States and seventh deepest in the world—was formed as rain and snow filled the caldera after the explosive eruption of Mount Mazama 6,850 years ago. Wizard Island is an andesite cone built after the explosive eruption but before the caldera filled with water.

During the next 50,000 years, glaciers would carve away at these two peaks, a twin-spired version of Mount Mazama. They left U-shaped valleys and glacial grooves that would be filled and preserved in the next episode of eruption about 200,000 years ago. These eruptions built the layered rocks of Dutton Cliff on the southern slopes of Crater Lake above the Phantom Ship. Rising to an elevation of 8,106 feet, these rocks have an imposing presence. They formed a low-slung eruptive center of pasty lavas and reddish cinders. The final eruptions of this first phase of volcano building extruded dark andesite flows about 100,000 years ago, building a small shield volcano on Mount Mazama's southern flank.

The mountain lay dormant about 25,000 years before shifting into gear for its second phase of eruptions. About 75,000 years ago, Mazama began producing andesites. The eruptions became more explosive. The viscous andesite lavas built Hillman Peak and the rocks now found above Cloudcap Bay. These andesites were followed by sporadic ash-rich eruptions. Finally, about 60,000 years ago, Mazama quieted.

When it awoke again, it was sheathed in ice. During the last glacial maximum, from 22,000 to 12,000 years ago, andesites erupted and were promptly attacked by glaciers. The Watchman, a high promontory capped by a lookout tower on the western side of Crater Lake, is one such flow.

By the end of the Pleistocene, Mount Mazama was a cluster of overlapping and eroded volcanic cones that formed an east–west asymmetric ridge from Hillman Peak to Mount Scott, according to Charles Bacon. This was no single-spired peak; it was a geologic hydra with

Llao Rock, on the northern rim of Crater Lake, is composed of rhyodacite, a slow-flowing volcanic rock with a granite-like composition. It was formed by an eruption about 7,020 years ago, one of the last lava flows from Mount Mazama before the cataclysmic eruption 6,850 years ago.

many threatening vents, a grizzled victor in its battles with Pleistocene glaciers. But it was about to die from self-inflicted wounds.

In the few hundred years before Crater Lake was born, four areas of Mount Mazama erupted significant amounts of a viscous, silica-rich lava called rhyodacite. Redcloud Cliff and the upper portions of Cloudcap oozed into place about 8,000 years ago. Eruptions continued, blasting out a crater on Crater Lake's northern side, then filling it with a single huge andesite flow, ½ cubic mile of viscous, glowing lava. Today, the cooled and solid stone forms the towering cliffs of Llao Rock above Crater Lake's northwestern shore. Pumice from this vent fell as far away as Steens Mountain, western Nevada, and eastern Washington. Similar rhyodacites erupted and cooled as Grouse Hill on the northern side of the caldera. The last batch of this extremely viscous lava elbowed its way to the surface just days before the climactic eruption. Today, its gray fissile stone forms outcrops above Cleetwood Cove. The top of this flow may have still been soft when rock fragments from Mount Mazama's final paroxysm hit.

Were it not for the oozing rhyodacites, Mount Mazama might have been a more sedate volcano. But the eruption of more than 3 cubic miles of pasty lava, flowing ponderously upward and sealing the cracks that had allowed the large magma chamber to exhale, provided room for gases to fill the chamber below—but allowed no escape. Pressure built up until, finally, not even the rocks of a volcano could contain it.

The climactic eruption of Mount Mazama occurred about 6,850 years ago. This multistage eruption developed in three stages from two different types of vents. The first eruption probably resembled that of Mount St. Helens. It came as a blast from a single central vent. This eruption propelled an ash column tens of thousands of feet into the atmosphere, laden with rocks 3 feet in diameter. It left deposits 70 feet thick on the slopes of the mountain, 20 inches thick at Newberry Crater, about 70 miles northeast, and ½ inch thick as far away as southwestern Saskatchewan.

This relatively cool, high-rising ash column was soon replaced with hotter stuff. Ash flows, moving at perhaps 100 miles per hour with temperatures as high as 1,800°F (980°C), swept out of the central vent and blew northward toward Mount Thielsen. Eruption of these dense rhyodacite ignimbrites removed the last vestige of support from the mountain's frayed summit. The result was, simply, collapse.

The magma below, with more and more pressure removed, continued to effervesce. As the summit collapsed along huge concentric cracks, more ash flows erupted. They carried fragments of the mountain's interior, big angular clasts, more than 3 miles. Blasts transported 10-inch-diameter stones more than 5 miles. As the bottom of the magma chamber was tapped, basaltic andesites were encountered—and erupted—dark lavas that now cap the spires at The Pinnacles southeast of Crater Lake.

By the end of this Holocene eruption, 12–13 cubic miles of rock had vanished. In its place was a hole, a classical stratovolcano caldera 4,000 feet deep. Shortly after this cataclysmic eruption, the last lavas—andesites—erupted more conventionally to form what we see as Wizard Island. Wizard Island was erupted long before the caldera filled with water to create Crater Lake. This dark andesitic volcano-within-a-volcano accounts for about ¼ cubic mile of lava erupted along the western margin of the caldera. Its foundation extends almost halfway across the lake and represents substantial postcaldera activity. A second small volcano, Merriam Cone, forms a second, smaller, postcaldera vent in the northeastern portion of the caldera. Several other smaller eruptive structures, mostly rhyodacite domes, have been identified on the caldera floor by submarine mapping. These, according to Charles Bacon, may represent the uppermost climactic magma, which escaped eruption prior to formation of the caldera, or the first leak from a new batch of silicic magma following the climactic eruption.

Like many other volcanoes of the Cascades, Mount Mazama is far from dead. Two areas of very high heat flow and hot-water springs were found during detailed surveys of the crater floor in 1992. The lake's waters, reputedly the purest lake water in the world, contain elevated amounts of sodium, chlorine, and other compounds that may come from volcanic springs.

Activity at Other Cascade Volcanoes and at Newberry Crater

Mount Mazama has provided the most bombastic Holocene eruptions of any Cascade volcano to date, but it was not alone in its activity. Mount Hood and multiple vents in the Three Sisters area produced a variety of lavas and ash-rich eruptions. The U.S. Geological Survey still considers Mount Hood an active volcano. And an uplifted area of high heat flow on the western flank of South Sister may be the site of a future eruption.

At the northern base of Mount Hood, just beyond the peaceful pear and apple orchards of Parkdale, a dark, barren jumble of basalt rises above the even rows of trees and marks the limit of cultivation. It seems an anomaly here, a jagged, abrupt feature impinging on an orderly world. This is the Parkdale Flow, a gaggle of basaltic andesite that leaked from the northern flanks of Mount Hood about 7,700 years ago, a century prior to Mount Mazama's cataclysm. The basalt's rough surface makes it look as though it was deposited here by herculean dump trucks. It does not look like a lava flow at all. In fact, much of it is aa, a silica-rich basaltic lava similar in form and composition to more recent eruptions from the Cascades (McKenzie Pass) and Newberry Crater (Lava Butte). Aa is a slightly more viscous basalt than the ropy, fluid pahoehoe. The surface of aa cools, solidifies, and breaks into irregular, sharp-edged pieces as the flow moves, carrying a crust that looks like a crumb cake borne above a fluid base. As the aa cools, the top retains the crumb-cake appearance, but the bottom turns into more solid stuff. Aa rests on a solid base. It just takes a while to find it.

The Parkdale Flow appears to have been an isolated eruption that began and ended in a week or two. Although its age coincides with the beginning of Mount Mazama's cataclysmic eruptions, radiometric dating is precise within a few years. There is no telling whether the Parkdale Flow erupted at exactly the same time, somewhat earlier, or somewhat later than Mazama. A few other Cascade volcanic vents were active at this time

as well, including Sims Butte near Three Sisters. A large cinder cone on the eastern slope on South Sister (Le Conte Crater) and Cayuse Crater may have erupted at this time or slightly earlier. Lavas also poured from vents near Mount Bachelor. Known as the Egan Flows, they fringe the southern shore of Sparks Lake. Slightly more fluid than most aa, these lavas left many open pressure ridges and other features that can be scrutinized along the Ray Atkeson Trail at the lake's southern end.

Poised at the western end of the Brothers fault zone, Newberry Crater, like the High Cascade volcanoes, began erupting in the middle Pleistocene. Newberry's oldest rocks are the Tepee Draw tuff, dated at 510,000 years. Its younger rocks, dating to about 7,000 years ago, include the line of cinder cones and basalt flows that extend northwest toward Bend: Lava Butte and Lava Cast Forest among others. Its youngest rocks include the Big Obsidian Flow, about 1,200 years in age and one of Oregon's youngest lavas. It is interesting to note that human occupation at Newberry dates to at least 9,000 years ago and may extend back to 11,000. At Fort Rock, just east of Newberry, sandal manufacturing was in full swing 9,200 years ago. So it is highly likely that humans witnessed the drama of Newberry as well as the eruptions of Mount Mazama and the central Cascades.

Anyone who has traveled U.S. Route 97 south from Bend to Sunriver has seen Lava Butte. It juts naked from the basalt-strewn landscape west of the thoroughfare. A single-lane road spirals up its sloping, crumbly, red-brown sides, offering a view of the Cascade Range and Newberry Crater, and of the lava-flow wasteland that stretches west from the butte to Benham Falls on the Deschutes River. At the top of Lava Butte,

Top right: Lava around Sparks Lake, south of South Sister (background, left) and Broken Top (right), erupted about the same time as Mount Mazama's cataclysm 6,850 years ago.

Right: Basalt flows erupted from the base of Lava Butte, the westernmost vent along Newberry Crater's Northwest Rift Zone, about 7,000 years ago.

a small crater indents the summit like a giant thumb-print. Back on level ground, near the entrance to the Lava Butte site, the U.S. Forest Service has placed a visitor's center with paved trails to help navigate the brittle and broken aa lava field to Lava Butte's broad base. Along the way, there are interpretive signs explaining lava gutters, lava balls, and lava breaches, where lava leaked out at the cone's base.

Lava Butte is a stunning, 7,000-year-old (7,020 plus or minus 120 to be more precise) example of a breached cinder cone. It is not a Cascade volcano. Instead, it marks the northwesternmost frontier of Newberry's eruptions. From Newberry's northern flank, seven basaltic vents form a 14-mile-long segment known as the Northwest Rift Zone, that extends through basalt flows of similar age and composition. Among these are the Mokst Butte Flow and the Lava Cast Forest Flow, where the vacant forms of trees that were overrun, engulfed, and incinerated are still visible as cavities in the basalt. The Lava Cast Forest is a place where form is defined by emptiness, a place where a Buddhist would feel at ease. Eruptions of silica-rich lavas were active at Newberry's summit area about the same time; these include the Intralake Obsidian Flow, Gamehut Obsidian Flow, and the pumice eruption that built the central Pumice Cone.

Middle Holocene

Mount Hood and Three Sisters volcanic activity

Between 3,000 and about 1,000 years ago, a profusion of small eruptions peppered central Oregon and Mount Hood. For Mount Hood, this is the Timberline eruptive period. This relatively recent phase of Mount Hood's eruptions began about 1,800 years ago. Most material came from vents on Mount Hood's south-western side and consisted mostly of ash with very little lava. The ash and ignimbrites choked the Sandy, Salmon, and Zigzag Rivers. Ignimbrites dated at 1,440 years raced down the Zigzag River about 6 miles. The amphitheater where Crater Rock sits today, high on the

mountain's southwestern slope, was created when a huge debris flow of mud, ash, and boulders swept down the Sandy River drainage. Other lahars followed the Sandy all the way to the Columbia. The scene might have been similar to the Toutle River's plight when Mount St. Helens erupted in 1980.

A pulse of volcanic activity began somewhat earlier, about 3,000 years ago, around Three Sisters. Lavas from the Sand Mountain chain of vents and cinder cones, an elongate cluster of forty-one vents and twenty-two cinder cones about 8 miles south of the junction of U.S. Route 20 and Oregon Highway 22 (Santiam Junction), diverted the channel of the McKenzie River. Sahalie Falls and Koosah Falls were left where the McKenzie crosses these lavas. Basaltic andesites of similar age erupted from Nash Crater and are responsible for the ragged lava beds at the junction of Route 20 and Oregon Highway 126 west of Santiam Junction. Contemporary flows dammed the McKenzie River, creating Clear Lake, where a forest of drowned fir and hemlock has been carbon-dated at about 3,000 years by Oregon State University geologist Ed Taylor. Belknap Crater, between Mount Washington and North Sister, began to erupt basaltic cinders, ash, and aa lava about 3,000 years ago. The lava built a small flat cone, a shield volcano, that extended about 6 miles east of the vent. New eruptions about 2,880 years ago added more lava, expanding the volcano's size and activating a new vent: Little Belknap. After these eruptions, the Belknap Crater eruptions quieted. They would not reawaken for more than a millennium. But 1,000 years is a short time if you are a volcano.

Other small basaltic vents and cones between Belknap Crater and North Sister were active about the same time as the eruptions of Little Belknap. The aa basalts that cover McKenzie Pass came from Yapoah Crater, about 3 miles south of the highway. Yapoah is a breached

---

Top right: Most of the lava at McKenzie Pass came from Yapoah Crater, a 2,900-year-old cinder cone about a mile to the south. These are aa flows.

Right: Collier Cone, at the base of North Sister, is a young basaltic cinder cone.

cinder cone that shot ash and cinders into the air about 2,900 years ago, and then, its volatile gases released, erupted two extensive lava flows. The first surged from the base of the cone about 2,700 years ago. The second followed from the same vent area on the western base of the cone about 2,600 years ago. Other nearby cinder cones, notably Four in One Cone and Fourmile Butte, erupted at about the same time. Collier Cone, at the base of North Sister, may have erupted about the same time or slightly later.

The Youngest Eruptions

The three youngest eruptive centers in Oregon apart from Mount Hood are Belknap Crater near McKenzie Pass, Devils Chain on the southwestern flank of South Sister, and Big Obsidian Flow near the summit of Newberry Crater. They produced the youngest lava flows known in Oregon—so far. All are relatively minor vents that erupted in a short span of time, most likely less than a month. But they mark vent systems that remain on the U.S. Geologic Survey's active volcano list.

The oldest is South Belknap cone, a mile south of Belknap Crater, where basalt lavas erupted about 1,775 years ago. Lavas from this multistage eruption flowed 8 miles westward toward the McKenzie River. Then the central vent (Belknap Crater) erupted 1,500 years ago, producing similar lavas.

The title of youngest lava flow probably belongs either to South Sister or Newberry Crater. Both exuded pasty flows of silica-rich lava at about the same time, 1,200–1,300 years ago. Given the range of possible errors in radiogenic dating, it is impossible to award the title unequivocally. The gold medal must be shared.

Near the northern end of Sparks Lake, the Cascade Lakes Highway skirts a brazen, lumpy outcrop of gray and rosy rock. This mass of stone spills unabashedly from the base of South Sister. It erupted from several vents along a single rift. This line of contorted and broken lava is called Devils Chain. Similar rocks appear on the western slope of South Sister. There, they form a

Top left: Collier Cone last erupted about 2,600 years ago.

Above: Light gray ash from eruptions along the Devils Chain about 1,200 years ago still blankets the landscape between Three Sisters and Broken Top.

Right: Glassy, brittle dacite of the Devils Chain forms rubble-strewn domes on the southeastern flank of South Sister.

steep-sided, flat-topped glassy promontory about ½ mile in diameter: Rock Mesa. Although it is now protected in the Three Sisters Wilderness, it was once mined for kitty litter.

The rocks of both outcrops are rhyodacite, a silica-rich, pasty lava, the same sort of stuff that was erupting when Mount Mazama blew its top. Rhyodacites are common in the final stages of stratovolcano eruptions, and they are part of the reason that mature stratovolcanoes, especially those of the Cascades, are so dangerous. Their gooey consistency often plugs the volcanic vent, leading to a high-pressure buildup of volatile volcanic gases, leading to an explosive eruption. This factor makes the more recently discovered and growing bulge, 3 miles west of South Sister's summit, a very ominous development.

Bands record the looping direction of flow in Newberry Crater's 1,200-year-old Big Obsidian Flow. This black, glassy rock is one of the youngest volcanic features in Oregon.

Newberry Crater's obsidian flows

The odds-on but unproven favorite for the title of youngest rock in Oregon is Newberry Crater's Big Obsidian Flow. Readily accessible, tamed by metal stairs and with interpretive signs, it is visitor-friendly. Not only is this mass of striped black glass the youngest rock in Oregon, Big Obsidian Flow ranks as the fifth largest obsidian flow in North America. The shiny dark rocks are attractive. Flecked with a few tiny gas pockets and banded with reddish oxidized iron and the gray of undigested water, this is the sort of stuff that might look good in the living room. The obsidian is true volcanic glass, a rhyodacite lava that was supercooled before it erupted and then chilled so fast that no crystals could form, save microscopic iron oxides. The broad and uniform dispersion of this iron gives obsidian its black color. Where the rock is reddish brown, the iron was oxidized by interaction with minuscule amounts of water that were also trapped in the rapidly chilling lava. The gray colors are bands of microscopic water bubbles or trails of other volatiles carried along in the moving lava. These bands reveal the direction of flow. Not surprisingly, this textural feature is called flow banding, named no doubt by a geologist who had never studied Latin or Greek.

Mount Hood's most recent eruptions

Newberry Crater and South Sister sport the youngest lava flows. But the honor of youngest known eruption belongs to Mount Hood. Two decades before Lewis and Clark explored the Sandy River delta, Mount Hood produced a significant eruption of ash and gas from a vent high on its southwestern slope. The eruption included a small nuée ardente and slow, sticky dacite lava that built a dome known as Crater Rock. By using tree rings of a western red cedar stump buried by a lahar in the Sandy River, and a Douglas fir buried along a tributary of the Zigzag River, Patrick Pringle of the state of Washington's Department of Natural Resources determined that the eruption occurred in the fall of 1781 or winter of 1781–1782.

This most recent spasm of volcanism is known as the Old Maid episode. It is named for Old Maid Flat, a cobble-strewn terrace of stunted lodgepole pine and mossy undergrowth where the Sandy River descends from its steep mountain headwaters. The puny vegetation here seems odd in a forest of Douglas fir and mountain hemlock. Lodgepoles are natives of eastern Oregon's gravel slopes and the coast's oceanfront well-drained dunes; they are trees that thrive on disturbance. These trees are here in the wettest part of the Cascades for a reason—lodgepoles are the only trees that can survive in the gravel-laden, ash-rich soils along Sandy River.

Somewhat more than 200 years ago, these gravels were debris flows. This is a valley that, suddenly and catastrophically, filled with coarse lahars from Mount Hood. The Sandy River debris flow, Patrick Pringle notes, was triggered by an explosive eruption originating at Crater Rock near the summit of the mountain. The lahar buried forests in sticky ash and boulder-laden mud as deep as 30 feet along the Zigzag and Sandy

Rivers for at least 22 miles downstream from their sources on the mountain. Mud choked the Sandy River all the way to its confluence with the Columbia. A decade later, when the Corps of Discovery ventured up the Sandy's delta, they found a treacherous landscape of quicksand and swamps. On November 3, 1805, William Clark wrote,

> The Fog So thick this morning that we could not See a man 50 Steps off, this fog detained us untill 10 oClock at which time we Set out, ... The under groth rushes, vines &c. in the bottoms too thick to pass through, at 3 miles [from the camp-

The victim of Mount Hood's most recent significant eruptive blast in 1781 or early 1782, a bleached and sandblasted whitebark pine stump rests on a ridge above Mount Hood Meadows Ski Area.

site on the northern side of the Coumbia River] I arrived at the enterance of a river [the Sandy River] which appeared to Scatter over a Sand bar, the bottom of which I could See quite across and did not appear to be 4 Inches deep in any part; I attempted to wade this Stream and to my astonishment found the bottom a quick Sand, and impassable—I called to the Canoes to put to Shore, I got into the Canoe and landed below the mouth, & Capt Lewis and my Self walked up this river about 1½ miles to examine this river which we found to be a verry Considerable Stream Dischargeing its waters through 2 Chanels which forms an Island of about 3 miles in length on the river and 1½ miles wide, composed of Corse Sand which is thrown out of this quick Sand river Compressing the waters of the Columbia and throwing the whole Current of its waters against its Northern banks, within a Chanel of ½ a mile wide, ... [from Moulton 1990]

This delta, encompassing the area from the present mouth of the Sandy River to about 1½ miles upstream along the Columbia, has since been washed away as the Columbia reclaimed its channel. But Clark's description of the mudflow-engorged delta is strikingly similar to the Toutle River delta's appearance a few years after the 1980 Mount St. Helens eruption.

Today, a small part of the old-growth cedar forest on Mount Hood's flanks, buried by these mudflows, has been exhumed by running water. Lost Creek and Cast Creek, on the western side of the mountain, each flow among giant stumps—the relics of the ancient forest. The Lost Creek Nature Trail, on U.S. Forest Service Roads 18 and 1825 en route to Ramona Falls, provides an easy, interpreted, ½-mile stroll among the remnants of this forest. And at higher elevations, a trail from Timberline Lodge to the White River (part of the Pacific Crest Trail) provides a view of giant stumps deep in the canyon of the White River—another forest buried by the Old Maid mudflows and exhumed by an active stream.

But debris flows were not the only feature of this recent Mount Hood eruption. A small amount of intrusive lava fortified the dome at Crater Rock. There were lateral blasts and nuées ardentes, too. Above Mount Hood Meadows Ski Area there is a ridge of shattered stumps. These trees were once whitebark pines. Today, most are ashen gray trunks and overturned root wads. The trunks all point away from the mountain, like the forest leveled by the blast from Mount St. Helens. Some wood is charred; all is sandblasted. This is a scene of death in which ridge-dwelling groves of high-elevation trees were leveled in a moment by a single, searing, volcanic blast.

Even more recently, in 1859, 1865, and 1903, activity has been observed at Mount Hood. To date, this has been only steam and ash accompanied by red glows or "flames" from the Crater Rock area. In 1934 a climber suffocated in volcanic gas (most likely carbon dioxide) while exploring an ice cave on Coalman Glacier. Mount Hood and the Cascades are not finished yet, as the eruption of Mount St. Helens clearly demonstrates.

Mount Hood may not be the site of the next eruption. U.S. Geological Survey scientists have detected a slight swelling of the ground surface over an area about 10 miles in diameter on the western flanks of South Sister. The uplift began in 1996. Without highly accurate remote-sensing instruments, we would not have detected it. When measured in 2001, the maximum amount of uplift at the center of this 10-mile circle was about 4 inches. However subtle the bulge seems, it troubles volcanologists. New intrusions of magma, new vents, new eruptions begin this way. Ongoing measurements of helium and carbon isotopes from nearby springs indicate that magma is accumulating slowly about 4 miles beneath this growing uplift. The South Sister bulge may never amount to a thing. Or it could herald a new contender for the title of youngest rock in Oregon. With their instruments tuned for increased heat flow and earthquake activity, geologists are waiting to find out.

Exhumed by the diligent erosion of Lost Creek, a tree buried by mudflows from Mount Hood's eruption in 1781 or early 1782 emerges into daylight again, but in the middle of the stream.

Earthquakes

Until a few years ago, Californians moved to Oregon to escape earthquakes. But since the 1980s, we have found that Oregon is no slouch when it comes to temblors. Between 1993 and 2002, about twenty "felt" earthquakes of magnitudes greater than 3 rattled areas across the state. Three quakes, magnitudes 5–6, have caused more than $35 million in damage. And a great quake, magnitude 8–9, is waiting in the wings.

Five major areas of faulting are active in Oregon: the Olympic–Wallowa lineament (OWL) in northeastern Oregon; Basin and Range faults in southeastern Oregon; the Brothers fault zone in central Oregon; the Portland Hills fault, East Bank fault, and others that allow the Portland and Tualatin Basins to shift; and the Mount Angel fault system. Faults in all these systems are capable of at least magnitude 5 earthquakes. Some geologists estimate that magnitude 7 quakes are possible. But all these faults combined are not as scary as the great, magnitude 8–9, subduction zone earthquake that may strike the Oregon coast during the twenty-first century. Conclusive evidence shows that such quakes have occurred every 300–600 years, the last one in 1700.

In northeastern Oregon, the complex OWL set of faults has spawned quakes with magnitudes as high as 5.6. This diffuse zone of faults angles from Brownlee Dam on the Snake River, separating and following both the northern and southern sides of the Wallowa Mountains. These faults continue to uplift the Wallowas and down-drop the adjacent Pine Valley and Wallowa River Valley. OWL-related faults continue through Baker Valley and the Grande Ronde Valley, and across the Blue Mountains to Milton-Freewater. The faults trend across Washington to the Seattle area and the Olympic Peninsula, running through Hanford Reservation on the way.

Many geologists believe that biscuit scabland, or pimple mounds, like this topography south of Maupin and elsewhere in eastern Oregon, may be generated by severe earthquake shaking (rather than rapid cycles of freezing and thawing at the end of the Pleistocene, or soil movement by gophers).

Movement on OWL faults is probably related to the continuing clockwise rotation of the Cascades, Klamaths, and Coast Range. This zone of faults allows the rocks to its south to move westward, continuing the clockwise rotation of the Pacific Northwest.

An earthquake recorded by seismographs on this system shook Milton-Freewater at a magnitude estimated between 5.6 and 6.1 at 11 P.M. on July 15, 1936. But on March 6, 1893, a much larger OWL quake, estimated as magnitude 6 or 7, flattened a large stone building in Umatilla. Quakes of magnitude 2 or 3 rattle Baker City and the Grande Ronde Valley. Gary Mann of the U.S. Geological Survey has calculated that the faults along the OWL system, including those beneath Brownlee Dam, are capable of a magnitude 7 quake.

Large, active, earthquake-capable faults in the Basin and Range include the Alvord fault at the base of Steens Mountain and faults along the base of other rimrocks. In June 1968, more than 100 small earthquakes shook Warner Valley on the western side of Hart Mountain. Although Basin and Range quakes are less likely to cause damage to human communities than temblors in more populated areas, their frequent occurrence reminds us that Nevada and southeastern Oregon are still moving, expanding the crust.

Not all Basin and Range quakes are benign. On September 20, 1993, two earthquakes measuring 6.0 and 5.9 occurred just north of Klamath Falls. These were Basin and Range quakes, from rocks moving as the Klamath Basin stretched. They were the largest earthquakes ever measured in Oregon. They occurred along a fault at the westernmost boundary of the Basin and Range. Following the two largest events, there were so many aftershocks, says Bob Norris of the U.S. Geological Survey, that the ground shook like Jell-O. Portable seismographs hastily set up by the Survey and other agencies often could not resolve the thousands of individual seismic events. The Klamath quakes destroyed the structural integrity of the Klamath County courthouse (a new, seismically savvy courthouse stands today in place of the historic rock and brick building), knocked down chimneys and masonry walls, and altogether caused an estimated $7 million in damage. Two deaths were attributed to the Klamath quakes.

In a similar fashion, faults of the Brothers fault zone that accommodate Basin and Range expansion also provide frequent small-magnitude quakes in isolated areas. The earthquakes that get our attention are those that wield the greatest threat to human lives and structures. In Oregon, that means quakes west of the Cascades. There are two areas, two generalized zones of faulting, where earthquakes have struck and will strike again. Both are on fault systems that facilitate the widening of western Oregon basins, including the Portland Basin and the Willamette Valley.

The more remote of these is the Mount Angel fault zone. It extends about 40 miles from near the community of Mount Angel, through Scotts Mills, and northwest to Newberg on the western side of the Willamette River. For years, geologists mapped the zone of faults and recorded small earthquakes but were slow to recognize and warn about the seismic risk. Then, on March 25, 1993, the Mount Angel fault zone unleashed a magnitude 5.6 earthquake. Its epicenter was about 3 miles west of the town of Scotts Mills; hence, the event

Seismologist Bob Norris of the U.S. Geological Survey with the data drum of a field seismograph that recorded aftershocks of the 1993 Klamath Falls earthquakes. So many small quakes occurred that their records often overlapped.

is known as the Scotts Mills earthquake officially, though many call it the "Spring Break quake." The major shock rattled surrounding communities, including Salem, cracking the dome of the state capitol and damaging Molalla High School. Almost 200 aftershocks were recorded. Damage was estimated at $28 million. More than any other previous earthquake, it shook Oregon awake to the reality of seismic risk. Because the northern portion of the Willamette Valley appears to be an extensional basin, earthquakes are a thing of the future as well as the past here.

The place that stands to lose the most from the earthquakes that accompany crustal stretching is Portland. One major fault runs through downtown, slipping beneath some of Portland's tallest buildings before slicing northwest along the base of Forest Park. Known as the Portland Hills fault, this strike-slip structure is more than 40 miles long. It has been active for most of the Pleistocene and all of the Holocene. Evidence found in an excavation at Rowe Middle School in Portland by geologist Ian Madin of the Oregon Department of Ge-

New construction, including the addition to the Oregon Convention Center in Portland, must include structural reinforcements for earthquake safety. The addition, completed in 2003, includes thick concrete shear walls to provide stability, braces to hold the building together during shaking, and (as shown) a space between the old and new parts of the building to allow them to move independently.

ology and Mineral Industries indicates that a large quake, perhaps greater than magnitude 7, occurred on this fault less than 12,000 years ago.

Two other, parallel faults bound the Portland Basin. The Oatfield fault cuts through the length of the West Hills. The East Bank fault lies hidden under Portland east of the Willamette River. Discovered only through remote-sensing techniques, this fault runs beneath the Oregon Convention Center, Lloyd Center, and the University of Portland. Studies by Tom Yelin of the U.S. Geological Survey suggest that the East Bank fault extends southeast to the Clackamas River and may have experienced as much as ½ mile of offset since the Miocene, 5 million years ago.

Not surprisingly, small earthquakes are fairly common in the Portland Basin. More than 1,000, many too small to be felt, have been recorded since 1841. On November 5, 1962, a temblor estimated between 4.9 and 5.2 occurred, centered about 7 miles north of downtown Portland. Windows broke. Chimneys fell. A few light fixtures fell from store ceilings. In December 1941 a magnitude 4 earthquake hit. In 1892 a severe earthquake, estimated magnitude 5, shook downtown Portland's brick buildings and lasted as long as 30 seconds. In 1841 a quake estimated as magnitude 3 or 4 shook Fort Vancouver, Washington. Frequent small earthquakes, like the 1991 cluster of three (magnitude 3) on the Oatfield fault (centered about 12 miles northwest of the Oregon Zoo), release stress on Portland's multiple faults. But all these faults appear capable of larger and more destructive activity.

Subduction zone earthquakes

For most earthquakes it is difficult to reconstruct their history beyond seismic records and anecdotal human descriptions. In Oregon, that means our vision of Holocene quakes is generally limited to the nineteenth century through the present. But there is a fortunate exception—the great subduction zone earthquakes, measuring magnitude 8 or 9, that have devastated the coast every 300–600 years. Geologists like Curt Peterson, Mark Darienzo, and Brian Atwater have traced the tracks of a dozen such quakes dating back at least 7,500 years through the sediments of tsunamis, drowned coastal wetlands and cedar groves, and layers of peat suddenly covered by beach sand. The record is clearest for quakes of the past 3,000 years, when the dating is more precise and the evidence less likely to be obscured.

In the last 5,000 years, notes Portland State University's Peterson, there have been ten earthquakes of magnitude 8 or greater along the Oregon coast and in the subduction zone beneath it. These quakes are an inevitable consequence of plate tectonics. The seafloor that slips under Oregon does not glide unimpeded into the mantle. It stops. It sticks. And then, when sufficient stress builds up, it lurches into motion again. Those lurches are the mechanism of big earthquakes, magnitude 8 or 9. For comparison, the Good Friday, 1964, Alaska earthquake is now considered to be about magnitude 9; the 1906 San Francisco earthquake was a piddling 7.9. (For each 1.0-increase in magnitude, the amount of energy released increases tenfold. Earthquake magnitude is usually measured by the amplitude of waves produced by the quake's energy. In the old Richter scale, this was determined by physically measuring the record on seismographs. Today, a variety of waves can be used to determine intensity.)

Based on evidence from buried peat layers, Peterson established a history of quakes along the central Oregon coast. Coastal swampland usually subsides when there is strong shaking because the highly organic sediment is rather fluffy and unconsolidated. The shaking of a major quake compresses it, submerging it below the waves and allowing a layer of sand to build over it until more peat begins to collect at the site again. Peterson's work is corroborated by evidence from drowned coastal forests and the dates of tsunami deposits as well as a thick stack of offshore sediments shaken form the continental shelf.

Peterson's work suggests that major subduction zone earthquakes occurred about 2,700, 2,200, 1,700, 1,270, 660, and 300 years ago. These dates are imprecise because they are based on the peat, material that includes plant debris that died at varying times. But all these large quakes, he notes, would be magnitude 8 or higher, based on the amount of subsidence and the likely length of the rupture along coastal faults above the subduction zone.

We do, however, have a precise date, and a fairly good estimate of the time that the last great subduction zone quake occurred: January 26, 1700, at 9 P.M. In the late 1980s, Brian Atwater of the U.S. Geological Survey was exploring the coast of Washington for evidence of large earthquakes. Along the Copalis River and in Willapa Bay, he found entire groves of dead-but-still-standing cedar trees. These coastal cedars and spruces had drowned when the earthquake's sudden and violent shaking compacted the soils the trees grew in, dropping their roots permanently below high tide. After a period of submersion, the trees died. Radiocarbon tests showed they died some time between 1680 and 1720. Narrowing the date to 40 years was an exciting development. But then, Japanese researchers took it one step further.

Big earthquakes produce big tsunamis. The tidal wave generated by this coastal Oregon-Washington earthquake would have hit not only Alaska but also the literate and inhabited communities of the Pacific Far East, especially in Japan. Might there be a record of the tsunami destruction, complete with date and other observations? There was.

Four Japanese researchers—Kenji Satake, Kunihiko Shimazaki, Yoshinobu Tsuji, and Kazue Ueda—dug through tsunami records, searching for a tsunami during that period that seemed to have no accompanying earthquake. They found records from four coastal villages of 5- to 10-foot-high tsunamis that struck a wide area of the eastern coast of the island of Honshū, causing damage to houses and businesses. The date was

Some of the most compelling evidence for great subduction zone earthquakes is found in partly submerged coastal woodlands. Here, in marshes and wetlands along the banks of the Copalis River in western Washington, the stumps, root wads, and trunks of ancient cedars are stark reminders of the powerful quake that struck on January 26, 1700, at about 9 P.M. Sudden violent shaking collapsed the peat-rich boggy soils, toppling some trees and sinking roots below the water, drowning others. By dating tree rings in drowned woodlands along the coast, geologists have established a record of major subduction zone quakes that occur every 300–800 years.

January 27, 1700; the time, close to midnight at the end of the day. Based on computer models of tsunami energy and travel times, Satake and colleagues calculated that the waves were generated by a magnitude 9 quake off the Oregon-Washington coast about 10 hours earlier, at 9 P.M., January 26. A close examination of the annual growth rings in the dead trees discovered by Atwater showed that they had died in the early spring of 1701, several months after the quake submerged their roots.

Such major earthquakes may engender other events, including huge landslides. Unpublished carbon-14 dates, based on the trees buried or drowned by the slide, suggest that the Bridge of the Gods landslide, just above Bonneville Dam, occurred in the fifteenth century or earlier. It may have coincided with a great earthquake in the 1400s, or it may have been triggered by a cause unrelated to subduction zones and shaking ground. Although the fifteenth-century dates seem reliable, some geologists harbor suspicions that this massive slide was more recent, triggered by the great quake of 1700. Whatever its date or cause, this slide dammed the Co-

The Bridge of the Gods landslide, a huge slide that dammed the Columbia River at Cascade Locks, allowing native Americans to walk across the river for a short time until the dam's collapse. Cliffs and rugged landscape on the Washington side of the Columbia above Bonneville Dam mark the head of the slide.

lumbia River for weeks or months, allowing people to walk across the river and giving rise to Chinookan legends of volcanic eruptions and shaking ground. Though inundated now by the water behind Bonneville Dam, landslide debris and the natural Bridge of the Gods dam were still evident when the Corps of Discovery reached the area on October 30, 1805. William Clark wrote, noting that they

> Passed several places where the rocks projected into the river & have the appearance of having Seperated from the mountains and fallen promiscuisly into the river, Small nitches are formed in the banks below those projecting rocks which is comon in this part of the river, . . . a remarkable circumstance in this part of the river is, the Stumps of pine trees are in maney places are at Some distance in the river, and gives every appearance of the rivers being damed up below from Some cause which I am not at this time acquainted with, ... [from Moulton 1988]

There is a long-standing geologic maxim established by James Hutton (1726–1797): The present is the key to the past. The reverse is also true: The past is the key to the present, and also to the future. If subduction zone earthquakes have struck on average every 300–600 years in the past, the process is likely to continue. In fact, there is substantial evidence that the subduction zone below us is not moving and that the Oregon coast is ac-

cumulating stress, shoved up by a locked plate beneath it, at the rate of 5 millimeters per year, about 2 inches per decade. When—not if—this plate breaks free, the recoil of Oregon's stressed coast will wreak havoc from Newport to Astoria, Newport to Coos Bay. But there is no way of knowing when this will happen, or where the quake will be centered.

Mark Murray of the University of California, Berkeley, says that strain is accumulating uniformly along the entire coastline of Cascadia, from Cape Blanco, Oregon, to the Olympic Peninsula, Washington. However, some locations seem to be rising or moving more than others. The University of Washington Geophysics Laboratory has measured coastal and Puget Sound strain rates between 1/10 inch (Seattle) and 1/3 inch per year along the Washington coast. Motion at Astoria is about 1/4 inch of strain per year and slightly more at Newport. And at Corvallis, an inland site that might be considered unaffected by a locked subduction zone 30 miles below, Oregon State University researcher Chris Goldfinger has found that strain, or ground motion, is accumulating at almost 1/2 inch per year.

Like a bronc rider in the chute, we know the bucking will come. Oregon has invested millions of dollars in retrofitting and remodeling, building to newly stringent seismic codes, and establishing tsunami evacuation routes. They may save us. Or they may save future generations. Whatever fate awaits us, we can only be sure we are in for a ride.

Epilogue

For most of us, a century seems a long time, and a million years stretches forever. But geology, with timescales that calibrate years by the million, provides another perspective, a longer gauge. In the next 100 years, Oregon is likely to experience a severe earthquake and may see an eruption sprout from South Sister or Mount Hood. These are events within sight of a few generations, well within our mental grasp.

These same generations will experience global climate changes and extinctions that are truly geologic in scope. We are witnesses to, and in large part the cause of, Earth's sixth great extinction. Biologist E. O. Wilson calculates that by the year 2050, 20 percent of all species present at the beginning of the Holocene will be extinct. Conservation efforts have staved off the certainty of extinction for condors, whooping cranes, peregrine falcons, bald eagles, and other charismatic animals, and reintroduction holds promise for others, including big horn sheep, mountain goats, and wolves. But for many less-appealing species whose functions are foundational to natural ecosystems, there is no second chance. Like Oregon's woolly mammoths and sockeye salmon, many other animals and plants are already gone.

As the climate changes, glaciers are disappearing. As recently as 1980, Collier Glacier extended almost to Collier Cone, at the base of North Sister. Now the glacier has virtually disappeared, leaving lateral moraines as a legacy.

The record of the past 400 million years in Oregon and elsewhere around the globe unequivocally documents that as atmospheric carbon dioxide increases, global temperature rises and climate changes. The record also reassures us that ecosystems adapt and change. Faunas disappear and are replaced by better-adapted animals. Forests shuffle their species composition or give way entirely to grass or shrubs. As climate shifts continue, our descendants may again see pines or oaks instead of redwoods; the whitebark pine of Oregon's mountaintops will be a thing of the past as disease and global warming take their toll. Unfortunately, trees cannot pick up their roots and migrate—they die where the climate is no longer suitable. And seedlings survive only in locations where conditions are more salubrious. The rate that a forest can migrate by this process of die-off and dispersal is no more than a few miles per decade—global climate change moves much faster.

What makes the current extinction event different from all the previous ones is that humans have changed the playing field. Ecosystems no longer adapt merely to climate change. They must attempt to adapt to us as well, for we have disrupted or modified every natural system on the planet. Instead of a single meteoritic impact that resets the system, we are a source of constant and increasing disturbance. We may in fact be witnessing, as author Bill McKibben suggests, the end of nature, for there is no place on the face of the Earth that human presence or industry does not affect. From the depths of the most remote wilderness we can look skyward to find contrails instead of clouds (a constant challenge when shooting photographs for this book). The chemistry of rain falling on New England's Mount Washington Wilderness is affected by Midwestern coal-fired power plants. Dust from the overgrazed steppe of China settles onto eastern Utah.

In the Holocene's *Homo*-centric world, whatever thrives must be adapted to live in the human habitat. Plants such as knapweed, star thistle, and cheatgrass evolved along with human agricultural disturbance in

We can anticipate future eruptions from the Cascades, including Mount Rainier and Mount St. Helens as well as Mount Hood and South Sister.

Asia and Europe over thousands of years. They are better suited to human-inflicted disturbance than North America's bunchgrasses and are rapidly supplanting many of Oregon's native species. The invasion has already begun, and since the beginning of the twentieth century, a mere geologic instant, many of the invaders have become well established. Eastern Oregon cattle graze and, in fact, rely upon invasive non-native cheatgrass across much of their range. The landscape is changing before our eyes.

We modify habitat, introduce exotic species, and now threaten to reconstruct the genetic playing field. In his book *Future Evolution,* University of Washington paleontologist Peter Ward calls these actions by humans "the functional reuniting of Gondwanaland." And the ancient supercontinent, he notes, had record low biodiversity. There is imminent danger, according not only to Ward but other paleontologists, including Norman Myers of Oxford University, that as we simplify ecosystems, decimate planetary biodiversity, and exterminate most larger wild animal species, we may effectively eliminate the ability of whatever ecosystem is left to produce and evolve new types of species to fill the niches. And, both Ward and Myers warn, we may never see new species of wild animals that are larger than a house cat or perhaps a raccoon or beaver. It is now up to human whim, Myers notes, whether we maintain two species of elephants on the planet or one, or any elephants at all. Ward's view of the next million years or so, derived from the fossil record and what he views as the human penchant for control, seems dismal and even draconian. Evolution, Ward assures us, will not stop. But based on the inability of larger animals to flourish in a human-dominated world, he expects that we will halt the natural evolution of larger animals. It will be the smaller animals, better adapted to survive on their own in human-determined circumstances, that will continue to evolve: rats, crows, opossum, raccoon. Insects should do well, facilely evolving new strategies to cope with us.

But this is not to say that we should assume all is lost. We can and must work to maintain and enhance biodiversity, for biological systems, along with tectonics, are part of the engine that has kept the Earth running for the last 3 billion years. Alone, we cannot manufacture the world's supply of oxygen or clean its water. With or without us, over thousands or millions of years, things will change.

And what of Oregon's landscapes, its rocks and mountains, its folds and faults and volcanic outbursts? What will Oregon's geology be like 10 million or 100 million years in the future? North America should overrun the Juan de Fuca Ridge (rising from the seafloor of the Pacific Ocean about 300 miles west of Newport and extending north-northeast toward Vancouver Island) in about 10 million years, accreting it as yet another exotic terrane and moving the coast westward once again. Subduction will cease on the western coast of North America perhaps 20 million years from now. The Basin and Range may continue its expansion, rotating the coast farther northwest, possibly opening a new inland sea. There are likely some surprises in store.

Some models of future plate movements predict that within 50–100 million years, subduction will begin along North America's eastern seaboard. The Atlantic Ocean floor will slide beneath New York and Washington, D.C., generating a new line of volcanoes atop the nearly vanished Appalachians.

And who will be here to witness there events? Humans, predicts Peter Ward—humans and other life that we can hardly imagine, along with life-forms like seagulls and starlings, and the horsetail rush whose fossils are found in the 350-million-year-old rocks of the Blue Mountain island arc's Coffee Creek Formation. For, despite human tinkering with the rest of the world, geologic change will persist. Plates will shift, mountains will rise, and sediment will be washed to the sea. In a world where change is constant, geologic change is perhaps the most constant of all. Geology will continue. Some things are destined to endure.

Above: Geologic processes, including eruption and erosion, will continue (Ecola State Park).

Right: Fossils of horsetail rush, *Equisetum,* occur in 350-million-year-old rocks in Oregon's Blue Mountain island arc terranes. Today, it still grows along stream banks across the state.

Map of Oregon

Conversion Tables

INCHES	CM		FEET	METERS		MILES	KM		SQUARE MILES	SQUARE KM		CUBIC MILES	CUBIC KM		POUNDS	TONS	KG
$1/10$	0.3		1	0.3		$1/4$	0.4		100	260		$1/10$	0.4		100		45
$1/6$	0.4		2	0.6		$1/2$	0.8		200	520		$1/4$	1.0		200		91
$1/4$	0.6		3	0.9		1	1.6		300	780		$1/2$	2.1		300		140
$1/3$	0.8		4	1.2		2	3.2		400	1,000		$3/4$	3.1		400		180
$1/2$	1.3		5	1.5		3	4.8		500	1,300		1	4		500		230
$3/4$	1.9		6	1.8		4	6.4		600	1,600		2	8		600		270
1	2.5		7	2.1		5	8.0		700	1,800		3	13		700		320
2	5.1		8	2.4		6	9.7		800	2,100		4	17		800		360
3	7.6		9	2.7		7	11		900	2,300		5	21		900		400
4	10		10	3		8	13		1,000	2,600		6	25		1,000		460
5	13		20	6		9	14		2,000	5,200		7	29		2,000	1	910
6	15		30	9		10	16		3,000	7,800		8	33			$1\frac{1}{2}$	1,400
7	18		40	12		20	32		4,000	10,400		9	38			2	1,800
8	20		50	15		30	48		5,000	13,000		10	42			$2\frac{1}{2}$	2,300
9	23		60	18		40	64		6,000	16,000		20	83			3	2,700
10	25		70	21		50	80		7,000	18,000		30	120			$3\frac{1}{2}$	3,200
20	51		80	24		60	97		8,000	21,000		40	170			4	3,600
30	76		90	27		70	110		9,000	23,000		50	210			$4\frac{1}{5}$	4,100
40	100		100	30		80	130		10,000	26,000		60	250			5	4,500
50	130		200	60		90	140		20,000	52,000		70	290			$7\frac{1}{5}$	6,800
60	150		300	90		100	160		30,000	78,000		80	330			10	9,100
70	180		400	120		200	320		40,000	100,000		90	380			100	91,000
80	200		500	150		300	480		50,000	130,000		100	420			1,000	910,000
90	230		600	180		400	640		60,000	160,000		200	830			10,000	9,100,000
100	250		700	210		500	800		70,000	180,000		300	1,200				
			800	240		600	960		80,000	210,000		400	1,700				
			900	270		700	1,100		90,000	230,000		500	2,100				
			1,000	300		800	1,300		100,000	260,000		600	2,500				
			2,000	610		900	1,400		200,000	520,000		700	2,900				
			3,000	910		1,000	1,600		300,000	780,000		800	3,300				
			4,000	1,200		1,500	2,400		400,000	1,000,000		900	3,800				
			5,000	1,500		2,000	3,200		500,000	1,300,000		1,000	4,200				
			6,000	1,800		2,500	4,000					1,100	4,600				
			7,000	2,100								1,200	5,000				
			8,000	2,400								1,300	5,400				
			9,000	2,700								1,400	5,800				
			10,000	3,000								1,500	6,300				
			15,000	4,600													

Glossary

The simplest stuff of geology is often obscured by professional jargon. Though this book tries to avoid esoteric terms whenever possible, some words, like diktytaxitic, ignimbrite, or pahoehoe, simply have no equivalent in everyday English. To some degree, to understand rocks, you must know their language.

aa Type of basalt flow characterized by rough, jagged blocks of basalt on the surface, aa appears to be a pile of unconsolidated blocks or rubble. However, the bottom of the flow is quite solid. This type of lava is found at McKenzie Pass and is typical of basalts with more silica. Aa is a Hawaiian word.

accretion Process of adding new land or new material to another body. In Oregon's geology, the term applies to the addition of a series of islands and small volcanoes to North America. Accretion of the volcanic islands that constitute most of the Blue Mountains and Klamaths was complete by about 100 million years ago. The rocks of Oregon's Coast Range were accreted during the late Eocene to early Oligocene, about 35 million years ago.

alteration Rock that has experienced change by exposure to atmospheric processes or, more often, to hot fluids far below the surface is called altered. Altered rock is often associated with ore deposits and the process of ore deposition, or with seafloor processes that modify the minerals and composition of seafloor basalts.

amphibole Iron-rich mineral with a strong, chainlike crystal structure common in andesites, diorites, and many metamorphic rocks. The most common amphiboles are black (hornblende) but some found in metamorphic rocks are green (actinolite) or blue (glaucophane).

amphibolite Dark metamorphic rock composed mostly of the mineral amphibole, especially hornblende.

andesite Volcanic rock, generally gray, usually associated with stratovolcanoes like the Cascades. Andesites are diagnostic of volcanoes, like the Cascades, that are fed by subduction zones. They contain about 60 percent silica, with abundant feldspar and either pyroxene (a dark, iron-, magnesium-, and calcium-rich mineral common in basalt and gabbro) or hornblende. Andesites are intermediate in composition between basalt (50 percent silica) and rhyolite (70 percent silica). The name andesite comes from the abundance of this kind of rock in the volcanoes of the Andes in South America.

anticline Fold that bows upward. Anticlines (and folding in general) result from compression of the Earth's crust. Size is irrelevant. An anticline be a tiny fold, only a few inches or less in amplitude, or large, regional structures many tens of miles across. The Blue Mountains represent a very large scale anticline. A syncline is a fold of any size that bows downward, such as that in Columbia River basalts centered at Mosier along the Columbia River.

argillite Dense, thinly layered, sedimentary rock consisting of clay and silica. Argillite is often considered to be a deep-sea deposit. In Oregon, the Elkhorn Ridge Argillite is found in the southern half of the Elkhorn Mountains and through much of the Baker terrane.

ash Very fine, solid particles erupted from a volcano, usually associated with explosive eruptions. Ash is less than 2 millimeters ($\frac{1}{10}$ inch) in diameter. An ash flow is a highly heated mixture of ash and volcanic gases that travels down the flanks of a volcano, sometimes at high speed. Ash is often produced by the explosive disintegration of fluid lava or the explosive eruption of boiling lava and a lava-gas mixture. Also known as a pyroclastic flow or nuée ardente, which see. See also tuff.

basalt Dark igneous rock that usually originates as a lava flow. Basalt contains a high percentage of iron and magnesium, and relatively low amounts of silica, potassium, and sodium. Basalt is the most abundant and common rock in Oregon. It forms the cliffs in the Columbia River Gorge, the rimrock of Steens Mountain and Hells Canyon, many coastal headlands, and many cinder cones and lava flows associated with Newberry Crater in central Oregon.

Basin and Range Geologic and physiographic province of southeastern Oregon (extending east to central Utah and south through Nevada to southern Arizona and New Mexico, west Texas, and into Sonora, Mexico) characterized by crustal extension. The result is abrupt mountain ranges separated by broad, flat valleys.

batholith Large body of granite or granitic rocks, generally exposed over an area greater than 40 square miles. Batholiths are generated at depths of 2–20 miles by melting of the lower crust. The coarse-grained rocks cool and solidify over millions of years and are folded or faulted to the surface. In Oregon, batholiths generated during accretion of exotic terranes form portions of the Wallowa, Elkhorn, and Klamath Mountains.

beds, bedding Bedding is the common arrangement of sedimentary rocks in layers; each layer is called a bed. Sedimentary rocks commonly provide a record of floods, storms, and other events that transport and deposit sands, clays, silts, and gravels. In Oregon, sedimentary rocks that display well-developed bedding include the Tyee and Flournoy and Lookingglass Formations in the Coast Range, the Cretaceous rocks of the Mitchell Basin, and some formations in the Izee terrane of the Blue Mountains.

biotite Common and dark-colored, biotite is a type of mica. It cleaves into very fine layers. Its high iron content imparts a dark color, though when weathered, biotite may appear golden. It is abundant in many granitic rocks and may look like flecks of gold on the bottom of a stream.

blueschist Metamorphic rock formed at very high pressure and low temperature, diagnostic of subduction zones, the only environment where such a combination is known to occur. The blue color comes from the mineral glaucophane, an amphibole. In Oregon, blueschist is found near Mitchell and represents the Triassic subduction zone of the Blue Mountain island arc.

breccia Coarse, angular fragments cemented together to form a rock. Breccias are commonly produced by explosive volcanic processes (volcanic breccia) or high-pressure fluids that may deposit ores. Breccias are also produced along faults as rock moves and fractures (fault breccia; fault gouge).

caldera Flat volcano characterized by explosive eruptions of ash and gas. Calderas are dangerous volcanoes because they are often not perceived as "real" volcanoes. Modern examples include Yellowstone and the Long Valley Caldera in eastern California, both of which threaten devastating eruptions. In Oregon, past caldera eruptions include the Mahogany Mountain and Three Fingers calderas in the Owyhees (14–15 million years old) and eruptions of the Rattlesnake and Devine Canyon ash-flow tuffs 6 and 8 million years ago from vents west of Burns. Eruptions of stratovolcanoes and shield volcanoes may also produce a summit caldera or collapse caldera. Crater Lake is an example of a collapse caldera, created by explosive eruption of the magma beneath Mount Mazama.

caprock Resistant rock formation that protect softer underlying layers.

Carboniferous Geologic period from 360 million to 286 million years ago. Subdivided into Mississippian (before 323 million years ago) and Pennsylvanian (after 323 million years ago) periods, and characterized by warm climates and dense, forests of fernlike plants that produced major coal deposits.

Cenozoic Most recent geologic era of Earth's history, beginning 65 million years ago and extending to the present; mammals and flowering plants dominate the Earth's fauna and flora.

chert Hard, dense, silica-rich sedimentary rock, usually composed of evenly spaced, 1- to 2-inch-thick layers. Chert generally represents a deep-sea deposit. Many cherts contain microfossils of radiolarians: single-celled animals with silica-rich shells that compose much of the rock but that are also mostly dissolved as chert forms, leaving few identifiable representatives. Cherts are found in both the Blue Mountains and Klamaths.

cinder cone Small conical volcano constructed mostly of volcanic cinders, solidified particles of lava. Most cinder cones erupt iron-rich basaltic cinders; many also produce basalt lava flows. Lava Butte near Bend is a good example of a cinder cone.

clast A fragment of rock or mineral created by mechanical breaking, weathering, or abrasion. The particles or rock found on beaches, in river gravels and sediments, on talus slopes, and even in human excavations such as quarries or road excavations are clasts. A clast may be rounded, like a river cobble, or angular, like a rock found in talus. Clasts also may be any size, though the term is most commonly applied to sand- through cobble-sized fragments, 62 micrometers (2.5 thousandths of an inch) to 10 inches or so in diameter. A sedimentary rock composed of clasts is called a clastic rock. Shale, sandstone, and conglomerate are examples of clastic sedimentary rocks. Ash-rich volcanic rocks that include fragments of pumice or solid chunks of lava are called volcaniclastic rocks.

clay Rock or mineral fragment with a diameter of less

than 4 micrometers (1.5 ten-thousandths of an inch). Also, a mineral with a specific layered structure that often comprises clay-sized fragments.

claystone Soft, often dark to medium brown rock composed of clay but lacking the fissility and well-defined bedding of the harder and more common shale. Claystone is one rock type included in the Astoria Formation's Miocene sedimentary rocks exposed on the northern Oregon coast.

cobble A rock fragment 2½–10 inches in diameter, larger than a pebble but smaller than a boulder. Cobbles are generally rounded and most commonly associated with high-energy river or beach environments. In Oregon, sedimentary formations that include cobbles are a major constituent in the Goose Rock conglomerate in the John Day Fossil Beds National Monument near Dayville, and much of the Troutdale Formation in the Portland area.

conglomerate Sedimentary rock composed of gravel, especially rounded pebbles and cobbles and/or boulders more than 2 millimeters (1/10 inch) in diameter. Conglomerates are often stream or stormy beach-related deposits. Their presence indicates a high-energy environment of fast-moving water or strong currents. Good examples in Oregon are the Cretaceous Hornbrook Formation near Ashland, and Gable Creek conglomerate near Mitchell.

cordierite trondhjemite Light-colored, granite-like rock (trondhjemite) containing the aluminum-rich mineral cordierite. Usually associated with continents, or granitic magmas that melted and incorporated a large proportion of aluminum-rich sedimentary rocks.

Cretaceous Geologic period from 144 million to 65 million years ago. Rocks in the Mitchell area and east of Medford are the sole examples of Cretaceous rocks in Oregon.

dacite Silica-rich volcanic rock, intermediate between rhyolite and andesite. Common in the last stages of stratovolcano eruptions, dacites are formed by slow, sluggish lavas that seldom move far and often build into domes directly above the vent. Crater Rock on Mount Hood is a dacite dome that capped the mountain's last significant eruption, about 1781.

debris flow Flowing mass of unconsolidated earth, clay, sand, rocks, uprooted vegetation, and other material; often associated with volcanic eruptions (compare with mudflow).

Devonian Geologic period from 408 million to 360 million years ago, characterized by early amphibians and armored fish. Devonian rocks in the Blue Mountains are the oldest rocks in Oregon.

dike Narrow, elongate igneous body that cuts across bedding and other structures. Dikes often served as conduits for volcanic eruptions. Many dikes that fed Columbia River basalt eruptions are exposed in the Wallowa Mountains.

diktytaxitic Texture found most commonly in basalts, in which small crystals protrude into very small vesicles (holes) left by gases. Such rocks often are gray and have a rough, sandpaper-like feel. Many of the flows of the Boring volcanic field, especially on Mount Sylvan, are diktytaxitic.

diorite Coarse-grained, black-and-white, salt-and-pepper-appearing igneous rock with the same composition as andesite. Diorite cools slowly under the surface. It sometimes represents the magma chambers of volcanoes that erupted andesite lavas. Diorite contains the minerals hornblende and feldspar (see under andesite), and is found in most batholiths in Oregon.

dome Lava that mounds over a vent without flowing. Domes are usually composed of rhyolite or dacite and are commonly the last stage of eruption in Cascade volcanoes.

dunite Rock composed chiefly of olivine; a type of peridotite, commonly originating in the Earth's mantle and faulted to the surface. Named for the Dun Mountains, New Zealand, dunite weathers to a tawny brown color, hence the name dun.

Eocene Geologic epoch from 56 million to 34 million years ago. In Oregon, the principal rocks of Eocene age are the Clarno Formation, which extends from Prineville east to Mitchell and the Greenhorn Mountains.

epicenter Point on the ground surface directly above the location of earthquake's subsurface location (point of rock fracture); usually the location of maximum intensity of shaking.

erratic Rock transported by a glacier or by glacially related processes, including major floods that occur when ice dams break. Many granitic rocks and other stones transported by water or on glacial icebergs during the Missoula (or Bretz) floods are erratics.

fault Plane of breakage in rocks along which movement occurs. In Oregon, significant faults include the West Hills fault and East Bank fault in Portland. A normal fault, typical of the Basin and Range, is created by tension or crustal extension, in which one side slips down relative to the other. A thrust fault is a low-angle fault that allows large blocks of the crust to slide up and over adjacent rocks, and may transport the top block many miles. Thrust faults are a response to crustal compression. See also strike-slip.

fault scarp An abrupt rise or cliff produced by faulting (fault scarp), not erosion (scarp). An escarpment is a large, regionally and topographically significant expression of a major fault.

fault zone A series of short faults that together allow crustal movement over a long distance. In Oregon, the Brothers fault zone extends from Burns to the Cascades west of Bend. Movement on individual faults is minor, but collectively, the Brothers fault zone allows the Basin and Range to continue its extension.

feldspar Most common and abundant mineral on the Earth's surface (with the possible exception of clay minerals). Feldspar is a white to pink mineral composed of silica, aluminum, and varying proportions of calcium, sodium, and potassium. It is very abundant in granitic rocks and in most light-colored volcanic rocks. It also forms 20–60 percent of most basalts. Because feldspar is relatively hard, it resists weathering and is a common constituent of Oregon beach sands.

fiamme Wispy, elongate, glassy clasts common in welded tuff. While the tuff (or ignimbrite) is still a cloud of gas and molten particles, a nuée ardente or or pyroclastic flow, the clasts that will become fiamme travel as molten blobs of pumice. When the tuff comes to rest, the weight of overlying tuff squashes the pumice balls into pancakes. Seen in cross section, fiamme appear as elongate bits of glass. The name fiamme is from the Italian word for flame.

fissure Elongate crack in the ground, usually associated with volcanic, or fissure, eruptions. Fissures may extend for miles. Most large Columbia River basalt flows emanated from fissures and fissure eruptions.

fluvial Pertaining to rivers; fluvial sediments are deposited in or by a river.

formation (1) A distinctive body of rock that was horizontally continuous at the time it was deposited or formed by relatively uniform or related processes and is now locally and often regionally extensive. A formation is usually considered an easily recognizable rock unit that can be mapped over a substantial area. Formations may be relatively heterogeneous, but all the rocks are related. For example, the John Day Formation consists of Oligocene tuffs, volcanic lava flows, and sedimentary rocks that were deposited in the John Day Valley and adjacent areas from about 34 million to 20 million years ago. Formations are usually named after a place where they are well exposed. Once given a formal name such as John Day Formation, Clarno Formation, or Tyee Formation, the word Formation is capitalized. (2) A topographically dis-tinctive-appearing group of rocks; a rock formation such as a cliff or spire, for example, Monkey Face at Smith Rock State Park.

gabbro Dark, coarse-grained iron- and magnesium-rich igneous rock with the same composition as basalt. Gabbro is found in Oregon's Canyon Mountain Complex in the western Strawberry Range, and in the Klamath Mountains.

glacier Mass of ice formed by the accumulation and compaction of snow, moving slowly by the process of downslope creep, from the stress of its own weight, and surviving without melting from year to year. In Oregon, the only surviving Holocene glaciers are found in the High Cascades on Mount Hood, Mount Jefferson, and Three Sisters.

glaucophane Blue mineral, member of the amphibole family, that forms at very high pressures and low temperatures; characteristic of metamorphism in subduction zones.

Gondwana (or Gondwanaland) Paleozoic and Mesozoic supercontinent in the Southern Hemisphere; included modern India, Australia, Antarctica, Africa, and South America. It joined with Gondwana in the Permian to create the supercontinent Pangaea.

graben Valley that is down-dropped and bounded by faults, usually diagnostic of crustal extension. In Oregon, the Grande Ronde Valley is an example of a graben.

granite Light-colored, coarse-grained, salt-and-pepper-appearing intrusive igneous rock that contains abundant quartz and potassium-rich feldspar. Biotite (in the mica group) is usually the most abundant dark mineral. True granite is characteristic of the continental interior (Wyoming, Wisconsin). Most Oregon rocks that look like granite contain less potassium and are granodiorites.

granitic (or granitoid) Generic, catch-all term for coarse-grained, light-colored, salt-and pepper-appearing igneous rocks that are similar in composition and appearance to granite. Granitic rocks include granite, granodiorite, and other varieties of similar-appearing intrusive rocks.

granodiorite Light-colored, coarse-grained, intrusive igneous rock that contains more sodium-rich feldspar and less quartz than a true granite; common in Oregon's batholiths.

gravel Unconsolidated, coarse-grained sediment consisting of rounded pebbles (mostly greater than 2 millimeters, 1/10 inch, in diameter), cobbles, and/or boulders. Commonly associated with stream deposits, the presence of gravel indicates a high-energy environment of fast-moving water. Gravel may also be deposited by glaciers or on stormy beaches where high-energy waves are common.

greenstone Igneous rock, usually olive to gray-green and usually basalt or andesite, metamorphosed at temperatures of about 660°F (350°C) with abundant water and under low to moderate pressure, typical of ocean-floor metamorphism at mid-oceanic ridges; also, the name given to these metamorphic conditions.

Holocene Geologic epoch from 10,000 (or by some newer estimates, 8,000) years ago to the present.

hornblende Black mineral with abundant iron and aluminum, often with a long or rectangular shape, hornblende is found in andesites and diorites.

hot spot Volcanic result of a plume of magma that rises from the mantle. Hot spots may persist for millions of years. The rising mantle plume remains in a fixed position while that crustal plates above it move; the result is a chain of volcanoes. Hawaii is the best example, Yellowstone is another.

Ice Age Time during the Pleistocene when glaciers dominated the landscape of North America and Europe, generally considered to be from 700,000 to 12,000 years ago. Also, loosely used as a synonym for the Pleistocene.

igneous Rock that cools from a hot fluid lava or magma.

ignimbrite Igneous rock formed from a hot, glowing, fast-moving cloud of ash and gas (nuée ardente or pyroclastic flow) that erupted explosively from a volcano. Some ignimbrites, like the Rattlesnake ignimbrite (6.1 million years old), were formed from enormous eruptions of tens of cubic miles of ash and searing gas from calderas. Ignimbrites vary from glassy rocks with elongate, compressed shards of pumice that were deposited at very high temperatures to crumbly and almost unconsolidated ash that came to rest at cooler temperatures.

intrusion An igneous body of fluid magma that forces its way or flows into place between rocks below the surface. Intrusive bodies come in all sizes, from batholiths to veins. Intrusive rock is igneous rock, part of an intrusion, that cooled and solidified.

island arc Curving chain of volcanic islands that develop above a subduction zone. The Aleutians and Marianas are good modern examples. In Oregon, the Wallowa and Applegate terranes are examples of accreted island arcs.

isotopes Forms of the same chemical element (same number of protons) but with different numbers of neutrons; hence, of the same atomic number but different atomic weights. For example, carbon (six protons) has three isotopes: carbon-12 (six neutrons) is the common variety; carbon-13 (seven neutrons) is rare; carbon-14 (eight neutrons) is relatively abundant and decays to carbon-12 at a known rate by losing two neutrons. Hence, their ratios can be used to date materials.

jade Gemstone composed of highly metamorphosed peridotite.

joint Fracture in a rock created by stress but not permitting movement. Joints usually occur in sets or patterns; they may also develop in response to the cooling and shrinking of a lava flow or intrusion. Columnar joints define the columns in a basalt flow. Large granitic bodies usually display many sets of joints that show their cooling history.

Jurassic Geologic period from 208 million to 144 million years ago. Dinosaurs were the dominant life-form. Oregon was still only islands somewhere off the Idaho coast.

keratophyre Type of greenstone, usually metamorphosed andesite or dacite, found in the southern portion of Hells Canyon as part of the Wallowa terrane of the Blue Mountain island arc.

lahar Volcanic mudflow, usually hot, originating on a volcano and including ash, volcanic rocks, and melted snow as well as rainwater. Lahars commonly are associated with stratovolcano eruptions but may occur with eruptions of only steam or hot gas and without any production of lava or ash. Lahars are among the greatest threats from Mount Hood and Mount Rainier.

Laurasia Paleozoic and Mesozoic supercontinent in the Northern Hemisphere; included North America, Greenland, and Eurasia. It joined with Gondwana in the Permian to create the supercontinent Pangaea.

lava Hot (1,100–2,600°F, 590–1,400°C), fluid rock that flows on the surface and cools to form an extrusive volcanic rock.

lignite Very soft brown coal with low heat-producing potential, only slightly more compressed and solidified than peat; found bedded between some Columbia River basalt flows.

limestone Sedimentary rock composed mostly of calcium carbonate (calcite). Usually fossil-rich, it may include coral reefs, mollusks, crinoids, and bryozoans as well as sponges and fish remains. Limestone also is readily soluble in slightly acid water and hosts most of the world's caverns. In Oregon, limestones are found in the Wallowa Mountains and near Cave Junction and Oregon Caves National Monument.

loess Layers or masses of fine silt, deposited by wind. Common near glacial fronts, and in desert regions, most of the soils of Washington's Palouse and Oregon's wheat fields near Pendleton are deep loess.

maar Low-relief, shallow volcano that erupts only steam. Maars are created when hot magma intrudes into a very wet substrate. The hot magma boils the groundwater instantly, producing an explosive eruption of steam. The magma is generally chilled by the water and does not reach the surface. In Oregon, Hole in the Ground is an excellent example of a maar volcano.

magma Hot, fluid rock that remains beneath the surface. The cavity full of magma is called a magma chamber. Magma chambers may feed volcanic eruptions, or they may solidify entirely beneath the surface as a pluton or intrusion.

malpais Term used in the southwestern United States for an area of rough and barren lava flows; from the Spanish for badland.

mélange Chaotic zone or body of rock that includes a wide variety of large and small fragments and blocks. Mélanges lack stratigraphic order and are associated with subduction zones, where mixing occurs. Mélange is the French word for mixture. The Baker terrane includes a variety of mélanges, especially in the Greenhorn Mountains.

Mesozoic Geologic era from 248 million to 65 million years ago, comprising the Triassic, Jurassic, and Cretaceous periods. During the Mesozoic, dinosaurs originated, developed, and finally, died.

metamorphic Adjective describing rock changed from its original form and composition by the application of heat and/or pressure.

mica Soft, silicate mineral characterized by excellent cleavage that creates thin layers or flakes; common in granitic rocks.

Miocene Geologic epoch from 24 million to 5 million years ago; in Oregon, characterized by eruption of voluminous basalts and ignimbrites (ash-flow tuffs).

moraine Mound, ridge, or other accumulation of unsorted gravel and sand carried and deposited by a glacier. A lateral moraine is deposited along the sides of a glacier, a terminal moraine at the farthest advance of the glacier, and a recessional moraine marks the location where the glacier held its ground during a retreat. Excellent examples may be seen at Wallowa Lake.

mudflow Flowing mass of unconsolidated earth, clay, and rocks; often associated with volcanic eruptions (compare with debris flow).

mudstone Fine-grained sedimentary rock composed primarily of clay and silt particles. Mudstone indicates quiet depositional environments. It is similar to shale but generally lacks the well-defined layering and fissility of shale. Mudstones are more blocky and less fragile than shales. In Oregon, mudstone is relatively common and is recognized in the Miocene Astoria Formation and in the Cretaceous Hudspeth Formation near Mitchell.

nuée ardente Fast-moving, hot, often incandescent cloud of ash and gas erupted explosively from a volcano. The expression nuée ardente is French for glowing cloud. The resulting rock is an ignimbrite.

obsidian Silica-rich volcanic glass, obsidian has the same composition as rhyolite and other light-colored igneous rocks. Its dark color is from the presence of very fine, uniformly dispersed iron and iron oxide particles that constitute 1–2 percent of the rock. Obsidian occurrences in Oregon include Newberry Crater and Glass Buttes.

Oligocene Geologic epoch from 34 million to 24 million years ago. Eruptions of the early Cascades and the appearance of abundant grass are among the accomplishments of the time.

olivine Dense, olive green, rock-forming mineral composed of silicon, oxygen, magnesium, and iron. Olivine crystallizes at high temperatures and is present in many basalts. It is a fundamental constituent of the rocks in the Earth's mantle and is present in most peridotite.

ophiolite A specific, stratigraphic sequence of igneous rock that represents oceanic crust. A complete ophiolite includes, from bottom to top: mantle peridotite, gabbro, and pillow basalt. In addition, some sedimentary rock, usually chert, may be present. This package of oceanic crust may represent a mid-oceanic ridge or the floor of a small oceanic basin that has been thrust over other rocks during the collision of tectonic plates or during the process of subduction. The Josephine ophiolite in the southeastern Klamath Mountains is a noteworthy example.

ore Any naturally occurring deposit of minerals that can be mined economically.

outcrop Bedrock that is exposed on the Earth's surface. The term usually implies a naturally occurring exposure rather than a road cut, mine shaft, etc.

oxbow Closely looping stream meander or bend in the shape of a U, or the bow that fits around an ox's neck in a yoke.

pahoehoe Basalt lava that flows rapidly and cools with a characteristic ropy surface. Most pahoehoe has a relatively low silica content, even for basalt. In Oregon, noteworthy examples of pahoehoe textures are present at Diamond Craters and Jordan Craters. The word pahoehoe is a Hawaiian term.

palagonite Clay-rich, yellow to orange rock composed of glassy basalt that has interacted with water at high temperatures and thus been transformed to a soft clay. Palagonite is commonly associated with pillow basalts, where it forms the matrix surrounding the pillows. It is named after Palagonia in Sicily, one of its localities. In Oregon, palagonite is visible in road cuts that expose pillow basalts on Interstate 84 near Hood River and along U.S. Route 97 in The Dalles.

Paleocene Geologic epoch immediately following the dinosaur extinction 65 million years ago, lasting to 56 million years ago; a time of many experimental mammals, and warm temperatures.

paleontology Study of fossils and ancient life.

Paleozoic Geologic era from 544 million to 248 million years ago, comprising the Cambrian, Ordovician, Silurian, Devonian, Carboniferous, and Permian periods. Oregon's oldest rocks date to the Devonian. The Paleozoic and succeeding eras, the Mesozoic and Cenozoic, constitute the Phanerozoic eon. Before the Phanerozoic, there were the Proterozoic (from 2.5 billion to 544 million years ago), the Archean (from 3.8 billion to 2.5 billion), and the Hadean (from 4.5 billion to 3.8 billion), dating back to the formation of the Earth.

Pangaea Single supercontinent that stretched from pole to pole. It modified oceanic circulation and global climate, and was partly to blame for the vast Permian extinction. Pangaea developed as Laurasia and Gondwana, the northern and southern supercontinents, joined together about 300 million years ago. It ended with the opening of the Atlantic Ocean and development of an east–west seaway that would become the Mediterranean Sea about 200 million years ago, in the early Jurassic.

peat Unconsolidated deposit of semicarbonized plant remains that develops in wetlands or bogs.

pebble Usually water-worn and rounded stone ⅙–2½ inches in diameter.

peridotite Dense, iron- and magnesium-rich rock (in the Klamath Mountains, for example) of the upper mantle.

Permian Geologic period from 286 million to 248 million years ago. Volcanoes of the Blue Mountain island arc were active.

phyllite Thinly laminated metamorphic rock that contains small but recognizable micas. Usually representing a metamorphosed shale or mudstone, phyllite is often highly deformed.

pillow lava Extrusive igneous rock (usually basalt) that flows into water as a lava or erupts underwater, especially on a seamount or mid-oceanic ridge, and cools in irregular, lumpy, generally pillow-shaped forms. Pillows have a specific structure: a round form with radial joints or cracks, vesicles (holes) around the rim, and a glassy exterior.

Pleistocene Geologic epoch from 1.8 million to 10,000 (or by some newer estimates, 8,000) years ago; includes the Ice Age.

Pliocene Geologic epoch from 5 million to 1.8 million years ago, when global climates fluctuated from hot to cool, finally accelerating a cooling trend that would culminate in the Pleistocene Ice Age.

pluton Subsurface body of magma, or the rock that results when the magma cools and solidifies. The resulting rocks, including granite, granodiorite, diorite, and gabbro, are called plutonic rocks.

pumice Frothy, light-colored, low-density volcanic rock with the composition of rhyolite to andesite, produced usually during explosive eruptions. Some pumice will float on water. After the eruption of Krakatoa in 1883, pumice blocks were found floating in the Pacific Ocean hundreds of miles from shore.

pyroclastic Adjective used for hot rocks and ash erupted from a volcano; broadly, includes ash-flow tuffs and ignimbrites, and also refers to volcanic bombs and another material erupted as a solid or semisolid hot particles.

quartz A common mineral, silicon dioxide. Quartz is hard and among the last minerals to crystallize in a magma. It is abundant in granite but absent in basalt and gabbro.

rhyodacite Silica-rich, usually light-colored volcanic rock, intermediate in composition between rhyolite and dacite. Llao Rock and other pasty, slow-moving lavas of the cataclysmic eruptions at Crater Lake are rhyodacite.

rhyolite Silica-rich, usually-light colored volcanic rock with the same composition as granite. Rhyolite lava is extremely pasty and moves very slowly, creating thin flow laminations that are often preserved as bands or layers when the rock solidifies. Thus rhyolites may appear to be bedded or folded. The layering, however, is an artifact of flow direction, not folding in the usual geologic sense.

rift Long, narrow valley or zone where the Earth's crust is pulling apart.

rimrock Outcrop of resistant rock that forms the upper portions of a cliff, or a relatively vertical face of rock along a canyon or near the top of a large butte.

riverine Pertaining to, deposited by, or formed by a river.

sand Rock or mineral fragment (usually quartz or feldspar) between 62 micrometers to 2 millimeters (2.5 thousandths to 1/10 inch) in diameter.

sandstone Common sedimentary rock composed mostly of rounded or angular, sand-sized particles. Sandstones may represent deposits of beaches, lake beds, streams, or wind deposits as well as deltas and submarine fans. In Oregon, the Tyee Formation in the Coast Range is an extensive deposit of mostly sandstone that represents an Eocene delta and submarine fan.

savanna Open, grassy, mostly treeless plain in subtropical or tropical regions.

schist Metamorphic rock with thin and usually fragile, mica-rich layers produced by deep burial, long-term pressure, and folding, at temperatures of about 660°F (350°C). In Oregon, the Galice Formation in the Klamath Mountains includes some schist or schistose (schistlike) rocks.

sea stack Pinnacle of rock just offshore but close to the beach.

serpentine Clay-like mineral formed by the interaction of the minerals olivine and/or pyroxene with water at temperatures of about 660°F (350°C).

serpentinite Metamorphic rock composed mostly of the mineral serpentine, commonly green to black, that bears shiny, polished surfaces. Serpentinites are metamorphosed peridotite and represent part of the Earth's upper mantle that has been thrust or faulted to the surface. They are commonly associated with subduction zones, mélanges, and ophiolites.

shale Sedimentary rock composed of clay; usually fragile, fissile, thinly bedded, and easily broken.

shield volcano Volcano that erupts mostly fluid basaltic lavas and, hence, maintains a low profile, in contrast to the more dramatic, high-rising stratovolcano. Shield volcanoes in Oregon include Newberry Crater southeast of Bend and the Pliocene Green Ridge vents near the Metolius River.

siltstone Sedimentary rock composed mostly of silt (particles 4–62 micrometers in diameter, 2 ten-thousandths to 2.5 thousandths of an inch, smaller than sand but larger than clay). Siltstone is an abundant type of sedimentary rock in the Miocene Astoria Formation exposed along the northern Oregon coast.

Silurian Geologic period from 438 million to 408 million years ago. Rocks of this age are unknown Oregon but are present in the Klamath Mountains of California, including gabbro and other rocks in the Trinity Alps.

stratigraphy The vertical order of geologic strata, or layers. The stratigraphy, or stratigraphic order, of rocks helps determine how the environment or conditions of their deposition changed through time. For example, if a layered sequence of rocks progresses from conglomerate at the bottom (the oldest rocks) upward to sandstone and finally to shale (the youngest rocks), then through time the environment changed from fast water, to slower, calmer, less energetic depositional conditions, possibly a lake or floodplain.

stratovolcano Volcano built of varying eruptive products, usually alternating eruptions of ash and lava; also known as a composite volcano. Mount Hood and Mount Jefferson are outstanding examples. The eroded remnants of Mount Thielsen and Three Fingered Jack display the characteristic alternating layers. Most stratovolcanoes, including the High Cascades and the Andes, develop above subduction zones.

striation Parallel groves or scratches on a rock surface; commonly etched by glaciers.

strike-slip Fault along which movement is in a horizontal plane. Most faults in the Brothers fault zone are strike-slip faults, with very little vertical offset.

subduction Process of one crustal plate's descending beneath another. Not far offshore from Oregon, the eastern margin of the Juan de Fuca plate is descending beneath the North American plate, giving rise to the Cascades as well a major earthquake every 300–600 years. A subduction zone is the belt extending from the crust into the mantle, through which the descending plate moves as it pushes its way into the mantle.

sulfide mineral Mineral composed of sulfur and a metal; galena (PbS, lead sulfide) and pyrite, or fool's gold (FeS_2), are examples. Sulfides are usually associated with mineral deposits or metamorphosed rocks.

tectonics Movement of the Earth's plates, and consequent deformation of the crust.

terrane Group or package of rocks produced at one locality by a variety of geologic processes. When these rocks are transported via plate tectonics to another locality, they become exotic terranes. Today, the Hawaiian Islands might be considered a terrane. As the Hawaiian chain is carried north and accreted to Alaska, it will become an exotic terrane. In Oregon, the Blue Mountains contain exotic terranes developed in the Blue Mountain island arc, with rocks that formed as volcanic islands from 400 million to 160 million years ago and were accreted to North America about 100 million years ago. The Klamaths contain similar exotic terranes.

Tertiary Geologic period comprising the first 63 million years of the Cenozoic era and including the Paleocene, Eocene, Oligocene, Miocene, and Pliocene epochs. The Tertiary was named before the Paleocene and Pliocene were recognized and subdivided from, respectively, the Eocene and Miocene. The most recent epochs of the Cenozoic, the Pleistocene and Holocene, constitute the Quaternary period.

Triassic Geologic period from 248 million to 208 million years ago. Triassic rocks are found in the Blue Mountains and Klamaths.

tsunami Ocean wave or series of waves generated by an earthquake. Tsunamis have washed over the Oregon coast at least eleven times in the past 7,000 years, according to sedimentary records in coastal wetlands from Willapa Bay, Washington, south to the Sixes River.

tuff Compacted deposit of volcanic ash and debris. An ash-flow tuff is rock deposited by an ash flow and is composed of ash, pumice, and other volcanic particles. It may be quite solid and even glassy if deposited while still warm, or crumbly and fragile if deposited after the ash and gases have cooled. A welded tuff is rock formed when a hot nuée ardente or ash flow comes to rest while some ash particles are still molten. The central portions of a welded tuff are glassy; the top and bottom are porous, but welded into solid rock.

turbidite Dense cloud of submarine sediment, often generated by an earthquake, that moves rapidly into deeper water and deposits sands far from shore.

vein Thin body of rock that is an offshoot of a larger intrusion. Veins often carry the last fluids to crystallize in a granitic pluton; hence, they also carry gold and ores that, along with quartz, are the last minerals to solidify.

vent Site of a volcanic eruption.

vesicle Small cavity in a volcanic rock caused by the presence of a gas bubble in the cooling, fluid lava.

volcanic Adjective signifying generated by a volcano. Volcanic rocks are those that erupted from a vent and/or cooled on the surface from a lava flow.

volcano A vent in the surface of the Earth through which molten lava as well as ash, hot gas, and steam erupt. There are many types of volcano, including low-lying shield volcanoes that erupt mostly basalt, stratovolcanoes that erupt lavas, ash, and pyroclastic flows, and flat-lying calderas that erupt explosive ash flows and nuées ardentes.

vug Small cavity in a rock, usually lined with crystals differing in composition from the rock.

xenolith Foreign inclusion in an igneous rock, from the Greek *xeno*, foreign, and *lithos*, stone. For example, the Columbia River basalt feeder dikes carry xenoliths of granitic rock, and rocks of the crust beneath the Wallowa Mountains.

References, Recommended Reading & Web Sites

The following works are the most important reference material for *In Search of Ancient Oregon*. It is not a comprehensive bibliography but rather the most significant, seminal, or controversial works used in compiling and writing this book. Most of theses works are suitable, in whole or in part, for non-geologists as well as students and professionals. Some are related specifically to Oregon, some to North America, and some take a global perspective. Books marked with an asterisk are relatively nontechnical and written for the general reader. Some comprehensive, classical, summary, or very current journal articles are also cited. They provide far greater detail than most general readers would wish to tackle. With patience and a geological dictionary close at hand, however, these papers can be understood by non-geologists.

GENERAL REFERENCES

*David Alt and Donald Hyndman, 1995. Northwest Exposures: a Geologic Story of the Northwest. Mountain Press.

*Ellen Morris Bishop, 2004. Field Guide to Pacific Northwest Geology. Timber Press.

*Ellen Morris Bishop and John Eliot Allen, 2004. Hiking Oregon's Geology, second edition. Mountaineers.

Howard C. Brooks and Len Ramp, 1968. Gold and Silver in Oregon. Oregon Department of Geology and Mineral Industries Bulletin 61.

Thomas Condon, 1902. The Two Islands and What Came of Them. Gill.

*Wade Davis, 2002. The Light at the Edge of the World. National Geographic Society.

*Tim Flannery, 2001. The Eternal Frontier: an Ecological History of North America and Its Peoples. Atlantic Monthly Press.

*Richard Fortey, 1998. Life: a Natural History of the First Four Billion Years of Life on Earth. Knopf.

*Stephen Jay Gould, editor, 1993. The Book of Life: an Illustrated History of the Evolution of Life on Earth. Norton.

Mason L. Hill, 1987. Centennial Field Guide: Cordilleran Section of the Geological Society of America. Geological Society of America.

David G. Howell, 1985. Tectonostratigraphic Terranes of the Circum-Pacific Region. Circum-Pacific Council for Energy and Mineral Resources.

David A. Johnston and Julia Donnelly-Nolan, editors, 1982. Guides to Some Volcanic Terranes in Washington, Idaho, Oregon, and Northern California. U.S. Geological Survey Circular 838.

*John McPhee, 1998. Annals of the Former World. Farrar, Straus, Giroux.

Gary E. Moulton, editor, 1988–1990. The Journals of the Lewis and Clark Expedition, Volume 5, July 28–November 1, 1805; and Volume 6, November 2, 1805–March 22, 1806. University of Nebraska Press.

Keith Oles, J. Granville Johnson, Alan R. Neim, and Wendy A. Neim, editors, 1980. Geologic Field Trips in Western Oregon and Southwestern Washington. Oregon Department of Geology and Mineral Industries Bulletin 101.

*Elizabeth Orr and William Orr, 1999. Oregon Fossils. Kendall/Hunt.

Elizabeth Orr, William Orr, and Ewart Baldwin, 1999. Geology of Oregon, fifth edition. Kendall/Hunt.

*Miles F. Potter, 1976. Oregon's Golden Years. Caxton.

*Peter Ward, 2001. Future Evolution. Freeman.

THE PALEOZOIC & MESOZOIC

*Walter Alvarez, 1997. *T. rex* and the Crater of Doom. Princeton University Press.

*Derek E. Briggs, Douglas H. Erwin, Frederick J. Collier, and Chip Clark, 1995. The Fossils of the Burgess Shale. Smithsonian Institution Press.

Douglas H. Erwin, 1993. The Great Paleozoic Crisis: Life and Death in the Permian. Columbia University Press.

*Stephen Jay Gould, 1990. Wonderful Life: the Burgess Shale and the Nature of History. Norton.

David S. Harwood and M. Megan Miller, 1990. Paleozoic and Early Mesozoic Paleogeographic Relations: Sierra Nevada, Klamath Mountains, and Related Terranes. Geological Society of America Special Paper 255.

*James Lawrence Powell, 1999. Night Comes to the Cretaceous: Comets, Craters, and Controversy, and the Last Days of the Dinosaurs. Harvest.

*Pat Shipman, 1998. Taking Wing: *Archaeopteryx* and the Evolution of Bird Flight. Simon and Schuster.

Tracy L. Vallier, 1998. Islands and Rapids: a Geologic Story of Hells Canyon. Confluence Press.

Tracy L. Vallier and Howard C. Brooks, 1986. Geology of the Blue Mountains Region of Oregon, Idaho, and Washington: Geologic Implications of Paleozoic and Mesozoic Paleontology and Biostratigraphy, Blue Mountains Province, Oregon and Idaho. U.S. Geological Survey Professional Paper 1435.

Tracy L. Vallier and Howard C. Brooks, 1995. Geology of the Blue Mountains Region of Oregon, Idaho, and Washington: Petrology and Tectonic Evolution of Pre-Tertiary Rocks of the Blue Mountains Region. U.S. Geological Survey Professional Paper 1438.

TECHNICAL PAPERS

Luann Becker, R. J. Poreda, A. G. Hunt, T. E. Bunch, and M. Rampino, 2001. Impact event at the Permian–Triassic boundary: evidence from extraterrestrial noble gases in fullerenes. Science 291: 1,530–1,533.

Bradley R. Hacker, Mary M. Donato, Calvin G. Barnes, M. O. McWilliams, and W. G. Ernst, 1995. Timescales of orogeny: Jurassic construction of the Klamath Mountains. Tectonics 14: 677–703.

Kunio Kaiho et al., 2001. End-Permian catastrophe by a bolide impact: evidence of a gigantic release of sulfur from the mantle. Geology 29: 815–818.

Kevin Pope, 2002. Impact dust not the cause of the Cretaceous–Tertiary mass extinction. Geology 30: 99–102.

William N. Orr and Kurt Katsura, 1985. Oregon's oldest vertebrates [*Ichthyosaurus* (Reptilia)]. Oregon Geology 47: 75–77.

THE CENOZOIC

*John Eliot Allen, 1979. The Magnificent Gateway: a Layman's Guide to the Geology of the Columbia River Gorge. Timber Press.

*John Eliot Allen, 1986. Cataclysms on the Columbia: a Layman's Guide to the Features Produced by the Catastrophic Bretz Floods in the Pacific Northwest. Timber Press.

*David Alt, 2001. Glacial Lake Missoula and Its Humongous Floods. Mountain Press.

Erick A. Bestland, Gregory J. Retallack, and Theodore J. Fremd, 2000. Eocene and Oligocene Paleosols of Central Oregon. Geological Society of America Special Paper 344.

*Edmund Blair Bolles, 1999. The Ice Finders: How a Poet, a Professor, and a Politician Discovered the Ice Age. Counterpoint.

*Roger Downey, 2000. Riddle of the Bones: Politics, Science, Race, and the Story of Kennewick Man. Copernicus.

Alan Graham, 1999. Late Cretaceous and Cenozoic History of North American Vegetation North of Mexico. Oxford University Press.

*Stephen L. Harris, 1988. Fire Mountains of the West. Mountain Press.

Robert A. Jensen, 1995. Roadside Guide to the Geology of Newberry Volcano. CenOreGeoPub.

Stephen Reidel and Peter R. Hooper, 1989. Volcanism and Tectonism in the Columbia River Flood Basalt Province. Geological Society of America Special Paper 239.

*David Rains Wallace, 1999. The Bonehunter's Revenge. Houghton Mifflin.

TECHNICAL PAPERS

Chris Beard, 2002. East of Eden at the Paleocene–Eocene boundary. Science 295: 2,028–2,029.

Erick Bestland, 1987. Volcanic stratigraphy of the Oligocene Colestin Formation in the Siskiyou Pass area of southern Oregon. Oregon Geology 49: 79–88.

Gabriel J. Bowen, William C. Clyde, Paul L. Koch, Suyin Ting, John Alroy, Takehisa Tsubamoto, Yuanqing Wang, and Yuan Wang, 2002. Mammalian dispersal at the Paleocene–Eocene boundary. Science 295: 2,062–2,068.

Mark E. Darienzo and Curt Peterson, 1995. Magnitude and frequency of subduction-zone earthquakes along the northern Oregon coast in the past 3,000 years. Oregon Geology 57: 3–11.

Peter Hooper, G. B. Binger, and K. R. Lees, 2002. Ages of the Steens and Columbia River flood basalts and their relationship to extension-related calc-alkaline volcanism in eastern Oregon. Geological Society of America Bulletin 114: 43–50.

Steven R. Manchester, 1995. Yes, we had bananas. Oregon Geology 57: 41–43.

Steven R. Manchester and Herbert W. Meyer, 1987. Oligocene fossil plants of the John Day Formation, Fossil, Oregon. Oregon Geology 49: 115–126.

Patrick T. Pringle, Thomas Pierson, and Kenneth Cameron, 2002. The circa 1781 eruption and lahars at Mt. Hood—evidence from tree-ring dating and Lewis and Clark in 1805–06. Geological Society of America Abstracts, Annual Meeting.

Gregory J. Retallack, 2001. Cenozoic expansion of grasslands and climatic cooling. Journal of Geology 109: 407–426.

Gregory J. Retallack, Erick Bestland, and Theodore Fremd, 1996. Reconstructions of Eocene and Oligocene plants and animals of central Oregon. Oregon Geology 58: 51–67.

Gregory Retallack, Erick Bestland, and Theodore J. Fremd, 2000. Eocene and Oligocene paleosols of central Oregon. Geological Society of America Special Paper 344.

Kenji Satake, Kunihiko Shimazaki, Yoshinobu Tsuji, and Kazue Ueda, 1996. Time and size of a giant earthquake in Cascadia inferred from Japanese tsunami records of January, 1700. Nature 379: 246–249.

Martin J. Streck and Anita Grunder, 1999. Field guide to the Rattlesnake tuff and high lava plains near Burns, Oregon. Oregon Geology 61: 64–76.

Ralph E. Taggart and A. Cross. 1980. Vegetation change in the Miocene Succor Creek flora of Oregon and Idaho: a case study in paleosuccession. Pages 185–210 in David L. Dilcher and Thomas N. Taylor, editors, Biostratigraphy of Fossil Plants. Dowden, Hutchinson & Ross.

Terry L. Tolan, Marvin H. Beeson, and Beverly F. Vogt, 1984. Exploring the Neogene history of the Columbia River: discussion and geologic field guide to the Columbia River Gorge. Part 1: Discussion. Part 2: Field Trip Guide. Oregon Geology 46: 87–96, 102–112.

Jay Van Tassell, Mark Ferns, Vicki McConnell, and Gerald R. Smith, 2001. The mid-Pliocene Imbler fish fossils, Grande Ronde Valley, Union County, Oregon, and the connection between Lake Idaho and the Columbia River. Oregon Geology 63: 77–96.

Ivan A. Wong, Mark A. Hemphill-Hailey, Lee M. Liberty, and Ian P. Madin, 2001. The Portland Hills fault: An earthquake generator, or just another old fault? Oregon Geology 63: 39–50.

WEB SITES

The Internet is a rich source of excellent and timely information. Web sites are more ephemeral than printed publications. However, they also convey new, updated, and real-time information, especially about volcanoes and earthquakes. The following Web sites should be available for many years and as of this writing are extraordinary sources of geologic information. This list barely scratches the surface of available information.

OREGON'S GEOLOGIC HISTORY

http://geopubs.wr.usgs.gov/open-file/of99-374/
Plutons and accretionary episodes of the Klamath Mountains, with geologic and terrane map

http://www.mnh.si.edu/arctic/html/kennewick_man.html
Kennewick Man; James C. Chatters

http://www.kennewick-man.com/
Kennewick Man virtual interpretive center; Tri-City Herald

http://www.uoregon.edu/~anthro/fieldresearch.html
University of Oregon Department of Anthropology, human life in the Fort Rock Basin and adjacent regions

GEOLOGIC TIMESCALE

http://geology.er.usgs.gov/paleo/geotime.shtml
Geologic timescale, U.S. Geological Survey, with links to more detailed information about each time period

http://www.ucmp.berkeley.edu/help/timeform.html
University of California, Berkeley, Museum of Paleontology Web time machine, with links to each time period

http://www.auburn.edu/academic/science_math/geology/docs/wetumpka/timescal.htm
Geological timescale from the Geological Society of America, very detailed

http://www.es.ucsc.edu/~bmartini/RelTimeScale.html
Simple timescale with major events

http://wrgis.wr.usgs.gov/docs/parks/gtime/gtime2.html
Proportional geologic timescales, U.S. Geological Survey, showing each time period in correct proportion; with discussions

PLATE TECTONICS

http://www.scotese.com/
Paleomap Project, Christopher R. Scotese, showing positions and animated demonstrations of continental movement; an exceptional site

http://www.geol.ucsb.edu/~atwater/Animations/Pacificmovie-preview.html
Movement of North America during the last 50 million years; Tanya Atwater

VOLCANOES

http://vulcan.wr.usgs.gov/
> *U.S. Geological Survey Cascades Volcano Observatory, including Long Valley Caldera and Yellowstone*

http://volcanoes.usgs.gov/Products/Pglossary/pglossary.html
> *U.S. Geological Survey Volcano Hazards Program photoglossary of volcanic terms*

PALEONTOLOGY, EXTINCTIONS, IMPACTS, & CLIMATE CHANGE

http://tabla.geo.ucalgary.ca/~macrae/Burgess_Shale/
> *Burgess Shale fossils; the Cambrian explosion; Andrew MacRae*

http://woodshole.er.usgs.gov/epubs/bolide/ancient_cataclysm.html
> *U.S. Geological Survey, Chesapeake Bay impact 35 million years ago*

http://www.nmnh.si.edu/paleo/blast/index.html
> *Smithsonian Institution Department of Paleobiology, Cretaceous–Tertiary (dinosaur) extinction*

http://hannover.park.org/Canada/Museum/extinction/permass.html
> *Permian mass extinction and other extinction events*

http://www2.opb.org/ofg/1001/missoula/
> *Missoula floods; Oregon Public Broadcasting synopsis of the Missoula (Bretz) Ice Age floods*

PAST & PRESENT EARTHQUAKES

http://spike.geophys.washington.edu/recenteqs/
> *Recent earthquakes in the Pacific Northwest, with map showing magnitudes and locations*

http://www.geophys.washington.edu/SEIS/PNSN/WEBICORDER/welcome.html
> *Pacific Northwest Seismograph Network; actual, working, digital seismograph records*

http://wwwneic.cr.usgs.gov/current_seismicity.html
> *U.S. Geological Survey Volcano Hazards Program National Earthquake Information Center, current earthquake information*

http://aslwww.cr.usgs.gov/Seismic_Data/telemetry_data/map_sta_eq.shtml
> *Earthquakes from the past 24 hours, updated every 30 minutes; world map showing locations, with table of detailed data*

http://quake.geo.berkeley.edu/bdsn/quicklook.html
> *Current seismograms from the Berkeley Digital Seismic Network, University of California; explanation of seismograms, seismographs, and seismic data*

http://nwdata.geol.pdx.edu/DOGAMI/IMS-15/
> *Oregon's Department of Geology and Mineral Industries earthquake scenario and probabilistic ground shaking maps for the Portland metropolitan area; Portland Hills fault magnitude 6.8 earthquake*

Acknowledgments

The concepts and facts in this book have all been determined by the work of hundreds of dedicated geologists who deciphered Oregon's geologic past. Any errors in the presentation of the facts or interpretation of their work are mine. Those scientists upon whose work I have relied most heavily include Brian Atwater, Hans Avé-Lallemant, Charles Bacon, Calvin Barnes, Marvin Beeson, Howard Brooks, Kathy Cashman, Richard Conrey, Michael Cummings, Mary Donato, Mark Ferns, Michael Follo, Theodore Fremd, Anita Grunder, Bradley Hacker, Peter Hooper, William Porter Irwin, M. Allan Kays, Robert Lawrence, Steven Manchester, Gary Mann, Ellen Moore, Merland Nestell, William Orr, Curt Peterson, George Priest, Stephen Reidel, Gregory Retallack, George Stanley, Martin Streck, William Taubeneck, Edward Taylor, Terry Tolan, Tracy Vallier, Beverly Vogt, and Nick Walker.

My own research has focused on the exotic terranes of the Blue Mountains, including the Baker terrane (subduction zone) and the Canyon Mountain Complex, as well as the Clarno Formation volcanics—work funded by the National Science Foundation. The book's tilt toward eastern Oregon geology reflects my own experience of its landscapes and geology.

Ted Fremd provided access to the collections of the John Day Fossil Beds National Monument for photographs, and for discussion; paleontological technician Matt Smith aided in photographing fossils. A number of property owners provided access to their land, including the Cherry Creek Ranch and GI Ranch, for field trips and photographs. The manuscript benefited from the reviews of Ted Fremd, Martin Streck, Mike Cummings, Greg Retallack, Bev Vogt, and Scott Burns. Others who contributed substantially include Pam Minster and the staff of Timber Press.

The quiet, placid environment that elicits my best writing has been supported by others. The manuscript for this book was begun during a Fishtrap writers' retreat at Dr. Mike and Kathleen Driver's home along the Imnaha River, for which I thank Rich Wandschneider for scheduling the time. Special thanks go to my husband, David, who encouraged and supported me throughout my long absences in the backcountry, and stints of writing at home.

Notes on the Photography

Photographing the geological landscape differs subtly from the normal practice of landscape photography. Composition alone is not enough. In addition to a meaningful and thought-provoking balance of color and form, geological images should evoke time that exceeds our experience, and scales that dwarf our imagination. Revealing the landscape's elusive temporal and geologic underpinning adds a significant challenge to a photographer's mission. I am still learning the practice.

Photographic convention and experience decree that the best time to photograph landscapes is early in the morning and late in the evening. At these times the sun seems to move at its fastest, and photography is much like police work—hours of waiting and a few minutes of frantic activity. The more subtle the topography, the more critical the light. Images of Oregon's biscuit scabland on the Deschutes Plateau or the Brothers fault zone west of Burns allowed a 15- to 20-minute window of perfect angle to reveal the landscape's low-slung but significant character. I would sometimes hike to locations before dawn, set up the camera, and wait for the light to come, as in the image of granitic rocks in the Wallowas, and the close-up of chert. Other times, I would scout for images during the day and shoot in the last moments of light. There were a few times that I hauled the tripod and camera upslope to afford not only a different perspective but also a few more seconds of good light. There were also the serendipitous times, familiar to us all, when the perfect light existed just long enough to exhume the camera from the backpack and set up the tripod.

There are places and times that defy the dawn or dusk convention. Shooting the face of vertical features such as cliffs is one of them. The reason we seldom take landscape photographs at midday is that the sun shines directly onto the surface of the ground like a flashlight used to read a road sign. This direct light leaves few shadows; the landscape looks bland. But cliffs are not horizontal like most of the ground. They are vertical, and the slanting, nearly flat rays of the evening (or early morning) midsummer sun shines directly on them, obscuring details. In the late afternoon, Owyhee cliffs can look just as bland as the Brothers fault zone might at midday. So instead of shooting vertical surfaces at dawn or dusk, their textural details are more evident when the sun is almost vertical—and hence at a low angle to the cliff—between 10 A.M. and 2 P.M. Images of cliffs at Smith Rock were shot about 1 P.M.; images of Owyhee cliffs are also mostly midday images. Images of vertical features are also perhaps more dependent on season than landscape images in general. By late October, for example, most cliffs on the Oregon side of the Columbia River Gorge are seldom lit by sunlight because the sun is too low in the southern sky. The photographs of columnar joints in the eastern portion of the gorge, for instance, were taken in mid-June at about 9:30 A.M. during an hour-long time when diffused sunlight highlighted the cliffs.

In photographing Oregon's diverse geology, I have begun to appreciate, both as a geologist and an image maker, how similar and yet unique rock formations can be. Towering outcrops of Miocene tuff appear in the Owyhees, near Ashwood, and at Smith Rock. Each is tawny; each bears subtle layering and cavities where once there was choking, steamy gas. But each is different in color, in the shapes and sizes of the gas-crafted vugs, and in the forms revealed by time and weather. The columns of basalt in the gorge bear semblance to columns of much younger rocks along the Hood River or more ancient andesite at Pilot Rock. Yet, even if I discard my expertise, they are distinct to a careful eye. This is one function of photography: to reveal differences in form while acknowledging the greater resemblance to the family of basalts or tuffs, sandstones, or chert. In this, portraits of the Earth's face and family are little different from portraits of our own.

Images in this book were shot during two field seasons of traveling throughout Oregon. Scale is indicated by use of natural objects usually present at the location, though a few images purposely lack scale in the hope of engendering thought. The photographs include large-, medium-, and 35-mm-format photographs. Large-format photographs were taken with a 4×5 field camera, using 65-, 90-, 135-, and occasionally, 245-mm lenses. Medium-format images were shot with a 6×7 single-lens reflex camera with 45-, 55-, 65-, 90-, and 300-mm lenses during the first year of work, and a lighter 6 × 7 range-finder camera with 43- and 65-mm lenses during the second year. I also employed a 6 × 17 panoramic camera for appropriate images, especially the open landscapes of eastern Oregon, and a 35-mm camera with a 17- to 35-mm lens. Most exposures were made on an ISO 50 transparency film at $f/22$ at speeds varying from several seconds to about 1/60 second; cameras were tripod-mounted. Polarizing filters were applied in most photographs of whole landscapes, but bare lens or skylight filters were used in most close-ups. All close-ups were photographed with natural daylight as the principal light source. Choosing from among the more than 3,000 images shot for this book was perhaps the most difficult task, one that was aided by the staff at Timber Press.

Index

For plant names, the common name used in the text is given with the scientific name in parentheses, usually only the genus. Because fossil plants are not necessarily the same as those living now, the scientific name should be interpreted only as indicating a close relative.

279

DATE DUE

PRINTED IN U.S.A.